Praise for *W*

'Andrew North has a deep empathy and understanding for Afghanistan and has seen sides of it – both good and horrifying – that very few international observers have encountered'

Rory Stewart, author of *Politics On the Edge*

'Weaves in his own reporting with sharp insights'

The Economist

'For anyone seeking an account that allows them to re-examine the most bewildering of the "Wars on Terror," North's book is an excellent choice. In his careful hands, we see Afghanistan – that chronically misunderstood warscape – as a place of uncommon humanity. We are all better for it'

Jon Lee Anderson, author of *The Fall of Baghdad*

'By weaving personal stories into a modern history of Afghanistan, Andrew North provides a touching and intimate portrait of the country he grew to love. His beautiful illustrations add a unique perspective on how war has destroyed or transformed generations of Afghans'

Lindsey Hilsum

'A profoundly moving account of Afghanistan's hopes and agonies. Crammed with vivid characters, North brings the country's tortured history to life with nuance and hard-won understanding. A thrilling read'

Andrew Harding, author of *A Small, Stubborn Town*

'A powerful, compassionate and clear-eyed account of the tragedies and occasional triumphs of Afghans over the last 20 years by one of the best-informed reporters covering the conflicts there. Readable, perceptive and engaging, North's writing and drawings together vividly portray Afghanistan as it was, is now and, perhaps, how it might one day be'

Jason Burke, author of *On the Road to Kandahar*

'Anyone who wants to learn about Afghanistan, its people and its turbulent history, must read *War & Peace & War*. Andrew North tells the story of my generation, the one before me and the new generation beautifully. While the title of the book breaks my heart as an Afghan, it also reminds me of the popular prayer our grandmothers say: "My child, may you taste peace in our homeland in your lifetime"'

Zarghuna Kargar, author of *Dear Zari: The Secret Lives of Women in Afghanistan*

'North's experience as a reporter is combined with his unmistakable affection for Afghanistan, making this a work of empathy and insight. This is an important book for anyone seeking to understand the country beyond the ephemeral news cycle'

Taran Khan, author of *Shadow City: A Woman Walks Kabul*

WAR & PEACE & WAR

Twenty years in Afghanistan

ANDREW NORTH

ITHAKA

First published by Ithaka Press
An imprint of Bonnier Books UK

5th Floor, HYLO
103–105 Bunhill Row
London, EC1Y 8LZ

Owned by Bonnier Books
Sveavägen 56, Stockholm, Sweden

Hardback – 978-1-80418-235-2
Trade Paperback – 978-1-80418-489-9
Ebook – 978-1-80418-484-4
Paperback – 978-1-80418-689-3

A CIP catalogue of this book is available from the British Library.

Typeset by IDSUK (Data Connection) Ltd
Printed and bound by Clays Ltd, Elcograf S.p.A.

1 3 5 7 9 10 8 6 4 2

www.bonnierbooks.co.uk

For my family, always; and the women of Afghanistan,
who never picked their fight

Charahi Qamber
IDP camp, Kabul

A settlement on the edge of Kabul for people displaced by the fighting, 2019.

Contents

Television Hill, Kabul

Preface

At the time of writing, it is more than three years since the Taliban regained power in Afghanistan in the wake of America's withdrawal. The Western powers involved in the conflict have reacted with a mixture of injured pride and recrimination, but above all, with a desire to forget. One of my reasons for writing this book is to do the opposite – to remember and record why Afghanistan's story turned full circle, as well as to understand the lessons that holds.

With its troops no longer there, the West's interest in Afghanistan has largely faded. In the United States, the country's plight has been reduced to a partisan political talking point, with the focus on the chaotic 2021 exit overseen by President Joe Biden. Donald Trump's denunciations of America's "endless wars" in Afghanistan and elsewhere helped pave the way for his return to the White House. But so far, there has been no substantive analysis or reflection.

In Britain, both main political parties have preferred to draw a curtain over the country's involvement in Afghanistan over the past two decades. It is, in fact, the fourth conflict Britain has fought there in its history. But there is currently no prospect of a full Iraq war-style inquiry into British operations in Afghanistan, particularly its disastrous deployment to Helmand.

Injured pride, in both America and Britain, has encouraged amnesia rather than self-reflection. But the war's legacy lives on outside Afghanistan among thousands of maimed and traumatised veterans, and hundreds of thousands of new Afghan refugees scattered around the world. Some are building new lives in Britain, among them three of the Afghans whose stories I tell in the book.

In Afghanistan itself, the Taliban have used their triumph to re-impose draconian restrictions, particularly targeting girls and women. Though not always fully enforced, their edicts have served to deny and dilute the sweeping social changes Afghanistan underwent during the US occupation.

As I write, the Taliban have all but crushed opposition to their rule. The dissident movement that has emerged in exile is divided, both along ethnic lines and over strategy and goals. Many of its figureheads have been discredited due to their association with the failures of the recent Western-backed government, or because of their ties to some of the darkest periods of the last four decades of war. And there is no significant support, either inside or outside Afghanistan, for those dissidents calling for a renewed effort to oust the Taliban regime. While many Afghans resent its repressive rule, they also appreciate the relative peace since the West withdrew.

But the Taliban is far from a monolithic movement and ideological divisions still persist. Some key figures want to give girls and women more rights, including the right to education. These internal fissures could grow and undermine the Taliban's grip. And, as with all authoritarian regimes, the more repressive they are, the more brittle they become.

Though the West's humiliation in Afghanistan followed a well-thumbed-script, it was not inevitable. Unlike the Soviets before them, the Americans and their allies were welcomed when they overthrew the Taliban in 2001. Many Afghans hoped that the Western powers' arrival would mark the end of the civil war which had raged since the late 1970s. That is what brought people like Farzana – who features in the book – and her family back to the country from exile.

Instead, the Americans ended up starting a new cycle of conflict, because of the mindset with which they invaded – prioritising revenge for the September 11 attacks rather than Afghan peace. It is often forgotten that Taliban leaders initially offered to accept the new American-sponsored order. When this offer was rejected, they returned to the battlefield, and the US military's tactics played into their hands. There were many other factors, but the roots of America's defeat in Afghanistan can be traced back to 2001.

From that quest for vengeance was born the "War on Terror", leading to America's unprovoked invasion of Iraq. It unleashed a calamitous legacy which is still playing out, not only in the region, but in the United States itself and the rest of the world.

If the US and its allies had paid more heed to Afghanistan's history and the hopes of its citizens, there was a chance that things could have turned out differently. Through the voices and experiences of Afghans, this book tells the story of why the West's initial victory in Afghanistan turned instead into slow-motion defeat, and explains what we can learn from it.

Andrew North
November 2024

Prologue

'You Are Our Guest'

A Taliban guard I could only sense steered me into a room I couldn't see. I'd been wearing a hat against the winter cold, and he had turned it into a blindfold, pulling it down hard over my eyes. After manoeuvring me inside, he pushed me into a seat.

From my left, the way I had come in, I heard the sound of the guard leaving and closing the door. The room smelt stale and airless. For a moment, I thought I was alone. But then, from my right, came the unmistakable metallic clicks of a gun being loaded and charged. I froze, too scared even to breathe.

It was early February 2022, three days since a Taliban patrol had stopped my driver and me in the Afghan capital, Kabul. At first, we had thought it was a routine security check, but it had turned into an abduction. They chained me up in their base overnight and, next day, drove us blindfolded to a prison complex somewhere in Kabul, where we were locked into basement cells. It was 20 years since I had first set foot in Afghanistan and everything had turned full circle.

When I first arrived, the Taliban had just been overthrown by the United States and its allies. I had been sent there to report on the country's early efforts to form a new government and rebuild. Over the ensuing decades I returned again and again, living there

1

for several years and getting to know Afghans from many different walks of life.

In that early period, Afghanistan was a place electric with promise, where many people believed that their fortunes were finally turning after nearly a quarter of a century of war. Much of their history has been defined by conflict and determined resistance to invaders. But, like so many previous visitors, I was struck by the hospitality and warmth I encountered almost everywhere. Aside from the Taliban, most people seemed to want to give the latest foreign force on their soil a chance, offering a welcome rather than a new war. In early 2002, it was impossible to imagine that two decades later, this US-led army would be reeling from defeat, and that the Taliban would have been replaced by the Taliban.

* * *

There was silence for several seconds after I'd heard the gun being loaded. Then I heard a voice tell me to take off my hat, in English.

Sitting behind a desk was a powerfully built man wearing a black skullcap and a bulky camouflage jacket which made him look even larger. He had a white patch on one shoulder bearing the Arabic words 'Allahu Akbar'.[1] 'Don't worry,' the Talib chuckled. 'There are no bullets.' I forced a smile as he ejected the magazine and put the weapon on the desk.

'Tell me, what kind of gun this is,' he continued.

'I know it's a handgun,' I said. 'But I don't know what kind.'

'You're lying,' he said, shaking his head.

---

[1] Allahu Akbar means 'God is most great' and is an Arabic phrase known as the 'takbir', used by all Muslims in prayers and other situations. The Taliban have long used the 'takbir' in their official insignia.

I felt utterly helpless, and very aware of the precious liberty I had lost. By then, I knew that the man interrogating and taunting me worked for the Taliban's intelligence department. My Afghan cellmates had informed me that we were being held in the basement prison at their headquarters. But why?

It was my third trip back since the Taliban's takeover. I had been all over the country on those previous visits without trouble, writing about the early stages of their return to power. On this trip, I was due to travel with three colleagues to one of the areas most affected by the recent conflict, to cover the worsening humanitarian situation there. But just before I arrived in Kabul, my colleagues were detained. One of them was my driver's brother. We were trying to find out what had happened to them when we were taken as well.

Was it a sign of the Taliban resorting to one of their old tactics: kidnapping people to use them as bargaining material? Westerners had been a frequent target in the past, and I was deeply conscious of my nationality. My country, Britain, had been America's closest ally in Afghanistan from the start. There were certainly things the Taliban wanted. Their leaders were infuriated that the West had frozen billions of dollars of Afghan reserves, and was refusing to recognise them as the country's legitimate rulers.

I had no idea why they were holding us. But it was just one of many signs that the Taliban's old, authoritarian instincts were returning to the fore, as their secretive supreme leader tightened his control.

Hopes that the Taliban would moderate their policies second time around had faded as they throttled the rights of Afghan women and girls. Employees of the former government had been abducted and killed, despite promises of an amnesty. Afghanistan's once-vibrant media had been cowed and dissenting voices silenced, with many local journalists arrested and beaten. The treatment they received was far worse than that meted out to foreign reporters. But now it appeared that we had also been caught up in a widening crackdown.

Once we were moved to the basement prison complex, I started to prepare myself mentally for the possibility of being held for a long time. I recalled the advice of a former BBC colleague, Alan Johnston, who had been taken hostage in the Gaza Strip: 'Keep negative thoughts at bay.' But in detention only negative thoughts came to mind.

The tally marks and graffiti left by past inmates, dating back years, were a reminder that this place had performed the same function under the previous government. Back then, the operatives based here had worked closely with the CIA and other Western intelligence services, dedicated to the Taliban's destruction.

My interrogator was now determined to prove I was working with them too. Through his efforts, he also offered me a selective tour of his own worldview.

'I'm an agent,' he declared at our first session, staring hard at me. 'And an agent always knows another agent.' Leaning over the desk, he said: 'What do you think about 007?'

'You mean James Bond?' He rolled his eyes. 'I've seen a few of the Bond films.'

'Which ones?'

My mind went blank. I couldn't remember the last Bond film I had seen. Eventually, I said, 'The Spy Who Loved Me and GoldenEye.' I was showing my age.

'I've never heard of them,' he scowled. 'What about Quantum of Solace?'

'I've heard of it, but I haven't seen it.'

'How have you not seen it?' he shot back. 'Hasn't everyone in your country seen it?'

He paused for a moment: 'And what do you think about MI6?'

'Well, I know it exists.'

'Of course you do,' he sneered. 'Or is it MI5 that you work for?'

I told him what I had said to the Taliban unit who had first detained me: that I was a journalist, and that their own press office had all the details of my past trips to Afghanistan.

'Why are you holding me?'

'First, we have to find out what you are really doing,' he replied.

A long silence followed as he wrote on some papers on his desk. He had a full beard, which blurred his age. But I could still see a younger face underneath, and I reckoned he was in his late twenties at most.

'It's good to have a chance to practise my English,' he said, looking up again, with a thin smile. 'All I had were films and YouTube until now.' He didn't seem to need much practice. I wondered if he had been a 'sleeper' operative, one of the many people the Taliban recruited to operate undercover in Kabul during the US occupation, to collect intelligence and facilitate their attacks.

'Have you seen *Prison Break*?' he asked suddenly. 'It's very good. I learned a lot about America.'

When I said I hadn't, he looked annoyed. 'How is it that you haven't seen Bond films or programmes like this?'

After panning my film and TV viewing, he channel-hopped for his next set of questions, flipping between international and regional politics, existential philosophy and comparative religion. And why, he asked proudly, did I think the Emirate[2] had defeated America? I answered by putting my words in the mouths of others, saying that people said it was because the Taliban had been patient and determined. He cut me off and said, 'It was because Allah was with us.'

Next, the illuminati got a mention, so too did President Vladimir Putin. Not because of the war he was about to start in Ukraine, but because my interrogator wanted to know what I thought about his policies towards the Taliban. Had I been to Iran? How many times?

---

[2] As in the 'Islamic Emirate of Afghanistan', the Taliban's official title for their regime.

What did I think of the anti-Taliban resistance leader Ahmad Shah Massoud?[3] And how many times had I been to his home base in the Panjshir Valley?

He returned to his espionage theme, bringing up Edward Snowden and asking me to name the classified US surveillance programmes that he had leaked, back in 2013. When I answered that it was so long ago I couldn't remember, he glared and said: 'You're lying again.'

The topics kept coming. 'What is life for?' he asked. I had barely started speaking when he cut me off again: 'Life is for serving our Creator.' Next on his list was Yvonne Ridley, a British journalist captured by the Taliban in 2001 who later converted to Islam. 'Maybe you will follow her and become a Muslim too,' he added. 'We would be happy about that.'

There was another long pause while he wrote on his papers, before he leaned forward again.

'Why do Christians always defend the Jews? Look what they did to your prophet.' I let him go on without responding. 'So, explain to me something. In your religion you have the Son, the Father and the Holy Spirit? What is it you call it?'

He put his hand to his beard. I was about to respond, but he answered his own question first: 'Ah yes, the Trinity. And all three of them are God?'

'That's right,' I nodded.

'But how is that possible? Where's the logic? I think Christianity is a very strange religion.'

'You're hiding something, I can tell,' he said, switching his focus back to me.

---

[3] Ahmad Shah Massoud was a veteran mujahideen commander from the Panjshir Valley, north of Kabul, and leader of the anti-Taliban Northern Alliance until his assassination by Al Qaeda followers two days before the 9/11 attacks on the United States.

'I'm not hiding anything,' I said, feeling another wave of anxiety welling up inside me but trying to stay calm. 'I told you. I'm a journalist.'

He added another note to his papers and then said: 'You're going to be hanged.'

I barely noticed the guard appear before he blindfolded me again. Back in my cell, I slumped against the wall. *They're just trying to scare me,* I told myself. *They are not going to hang me.* But as I tried to control my panicked thoughts, I had never felt so powerless. I couldn't stop thinking about my family, working out what they would be doing at that moment, worrying about them worrying about me.

One of my cellmates interrupted my ruminations with a tap on my arm. Pointing to an unoccupied mat, he told me to take it. There were 13 of us in the cell, and not enough mats and blankets to go round. But I was the only foreigner, and so they had agreed between themselves that I should have a mat and blanket to myself.

When I protested, saying I was happy to share, he wouldn't hear of it. My other cellmates nodded their agreement.

Putting his hand to his chest in a gesture of respect, he smiled and said: 'You are our guest.'

Friday Prayers:
Taliban guard.
Herat Great
mosque
Nov 2021

Introduction
War and Peace and War

By the time Abdul Tayib was in his teens, he had already lived through three violent changes of power in his country. On 27 September 1996, when he was 22 years old, he woke to the early signs of a fourth.

The evening before, the Afghan government – such as it was – had imploded and an upstart movement of Islamic warriors called the Taliban had started moving into Kabul. They had persuaded some of their opponents to switch sides or lay down their arms without a fight. Those who had held out were fleeing to the mountains.

When Abdul went out to fetch bread, he saw a convoy of dust-glazed pickups rolling past, filled with turbaned Taliban fighters, exultant in victory. It felt like a watershed moment. Just two years old at the time, the Taliban had seemingly brought an end to the forever war that had consumed Afghanistan for most of the past two decades.

A coup by Afghan communists in 1978 had led first to civil war, then Soviet invasion and occupation. More than 1 million Afghans died in the ensuing fighting and millions more became refugees as their country turned into a Cold War battleground. With the help of weapons sent in by the United States, 'mujahideen' rebels[1] forced the Soviets to pull out and eventually seized power. But then they turned on each other, igniting a new civil war which destroyed Kabul and split the country. From the midst of this turmoil, one group of mujahideen in southern Afghanistan banded together to try to restore order: the Taliban.

So, Abdul was feeling hopeful, jubilant even, when he joined some friends on an exploratory bicycle tour to test the water. 'We thought that there would be peace, because now just one group was in charge.' On that late September morning in 1996, he even dared to hope he could fulfil his long-held dream of becoming a doctor. Just before the latest civil war had erupted, he'd been offered a scholarship to study medicine in India. At last, he thought, he would be able to go.

One of his friends suggested they head towards the presidential palace. He had heard that the Taliban had opened it up, allowing anyone to go inside. Known to Afghans as the 'Arg', it was there that the war had begun in 1978, when communist revolutionaries assassinated the president and his family. Eighteen years later, there was an air of revolution in Kabul once again, this time with a religious rather than socialist flavour.

The city's latest conquerors flung open the gates of the old centre of power and Abdul and his friends entered, full of excitement. Inside, they roamed around freely, going wherever they wanted, Abdul recalled. 'We felt very happy.' After their tour of the palace, they followed the crowd out of the main palace gate and turned back towards home.

But when they reached a crossroads known as Ariana Square, they were met by a gruesome sight. Hanging from a police traffic control platform were the bodies of two men, one of them heavily mutilated. Bystanders told Abdul that this was 'Dr Najib', the name

---

[1] The word 'mujahideen', or 'holy warriors', is derived from 'jihad' or holy war. The singular is 'mujahid'.

Afghans used for Mohammad Najibullah, the last leader of the Soviet-backed regime, who had been living under United Nations protection. The other man was his brother.

A Taliban hit squad had abducted the two men, castrated Dr Najib, and then dragged them both around the streets before stringing them up with banknotes stuffed into their noses. Abdul could see the blood on their bodies was still fresh. Taliban fighters stood grinning along-side, reaching out to give Dr Najib's corpse a spin. And while their leaders would soon ban music, they celebrated the moment with their own Islamic chants, or 'taranas', playing from a speaker set up on one of their vehicles.

Abdul moved closer to the former president's mangled body to check it was really Dr Najib. 'And then I became really upset and I thought to myself: "This group, the Taliban, is also bad."'

His reaction said so much about his country's plight. Najibullah was a hate figure for many Afghans, despised as Moscow's puppet and for his murderous record while serving as the communist regime's secret police chief. But his stature had grown towards the end of his rule as he rebranded himself as a nationalist strongman, emphasising Afghanistan's Islamic traditions. Some had even dared hope the Taliban would work with Dr Najib – and one of them was Abdul. The idea sounded naive later on, he admitted, but it was testament to how much he and other Afghans wanted an end to division and war.

Of course, the war didn't end. It mutated into a new one when the Taliban's guest, the Saudi millionaire Osama bin Laden, used Afghanistan as a base from which to plan his attack on the United States on 11 September 2001. But America's vengeance for what became known as 9/11 also turned into a new inflection point for Afghanistan. After US-led forces ousted the Taliban in a matter of months, millions of Afghans dared to hope that their war could finally end, with the world's most powerful nation now deeply involved on the ground.

The United States had a different perspective and priority. It had just started a war, against terror, with Afghanistan only the first front. That mismatch in viewpoints is one reason why a lasting peace stayed out of reach.

This book tells the story of these repeating cycles of war and glimmers of peace, through the lives and experiences of Abdul Tayib and four other Afghans whom I got to know during my 20 years of reporting from their country – Bilal, Jahan, Farzana and Naqibullah.[2]

It sets their stories against the backdrop of Afghanistan's past as a battleground for outside powers, including the legacy of Britain's 19th-century colonial invasions, the Soviet occupation during the Cold War and America's role in backing the anti-Soviet mujahideen. And it interweaves their journeys with my own, as an outsider who spent two decades working and living in Afghanistan. In my work as a reporter, I was focused on the war. But in my day-to-day life, I was witness to a country changing and growing in spite of it. So this is also my perspective on that other side to Afghanistan's story.

The five people I focus on are from very different backgrounds. When the 9/11 attacks happened, Abdul was fitting in his medical studies between running a cafe to support his family. Though barely a teenager then, Jahan was also providing for his family, as a shoeshine boy. Bilal was an 18-year-old refugee in Pakistan with a job selling carpets in a hotel lobby. Farzana was 10, and also a refugee, living with her family in a two-room shack on the edge of Tehran. Naqibullah was the son of a rural cleric in a remote corner of southeastern Afghanistan. He knew nothing about 9/11 or America until US planes and helicopters appeared in the sky in 2002 and started

---

[2] Farzana, Abdul Tayib and Jahan are pseudonyms.

attacking his district when he was 11 years old. Soon after, he was scooped up in one of their raids and taken to the US military prison camp in Guantanamo, Cuba.

I was a BBC reporter based in London at the time of the 9/11 attacks and I was sent to the United States to cover the initial response and the countdown to the invasion 26 days later. I then went to Afghanistan and witnessed the early efforts to build a new order after the Taliban's demise. As America's focus shifted to Iraq, I went there to cover the invasion and early occupation, before returning to Afghanistan in 2004.

For the next two years, I was based in Kabul as the BBC's resident correspondent, travelling all over the country. Later, I moved on to new postings in Baghdad, Washington and Delhi and eventually left the BBC, but I kept returning to report from Afghanistan, keeping in touch with friends and contacts while I was away. The country had a hold on me. But my fascination with it had started long before I actually set foot there.

During my late teens, in the 1980s, I saw TV news reports of the David and Goliath struggle between the mujahideen and the far-better-armed Soviets. The news footage inevitably focused on fighting, but behind the violence I could sense a landscape unlike anywhere I'd seen before.

I read about Britain's attempts to control Afghanistan in the 19th century and pored over books of photos of the country, compiled both when it was at war and at peace. I imagined a day when I could follow in the footsteps of the French–Moroccan photographer couple Roland and Sabrina Michaud, who recorded their journeys through Asia in the 1960s.

I went to boarding schools in rural Britain from an early age, and by the time I left that strange and closeted world, I craved difference and challenge. I decided that I wanted to be a foreign correspondent, and part of me felt that I could only really be one if I reported from Afghanistan.

Trying to kick-start my plan to become a journalist, the year before I left university, I travelled through Pakistan with a sketchy plan to do some stories on Afghan refugees along the border. I planned to cross over if I got the chance.

It was 1990. Soviet troops had departed the year before and Saddam Hussein had invaded Kuwait that summer. Afghanistan was becoming a forgotten war for the West. Looking back, it was no surprise that I only managed to get my reports published in a small specialist magazine, not the national titles I had naively hoped for. But I never forgot the sight of the vast refugee settlements I encountered when I reached the north-western frontier city of Peshawar.

As the gateway to the storied Khyber Pass, the main eastern entrance to Afghanistan, Peshawar was still a hub for most of the mujahideen factions. At that time, in the summer of 1990, they were fighting the Moscow-backed government of President Najibullah – the man Abdul would see suspended from a traffic control post six years later. The mujahideen regularly came back and forth to Pakistan to resupply, rest and see their families, just as the Taliban would do in years to come. Osama bin Laden had co-founded Al Qaeda in Peshawar a couple of years before. He was back in Saudi Arabia at the time, but I heard talk of Arab-Afghan war veterans who had settled in the area with their families.

I knew that there was no chance I could cross the frontier officially. The Pakistani authorities had banned foreigners from entering the Khyber Pass. But a group of burly Afghan fighters I met in one refugee camp were heading back the next day, and they offered to smuggle me over with them.

It was a terrible idea. I had no idea where my new mujahideen acquaintances intended to take me. I was just 21, travelling alone with almost no money at a time when it was difficult even to make local phone calls. I spoke no Pashto or Urdu, the main languages in Peshawar. And I stood out like a sore thumb. On the long bus ride there, I had learned that I was attracting dangerous attention.

My neighbour explained that because of my white, European complexion, some passengers suspected me of being a Russian spy. 'Be careful,' he warned.

Luckily, the story ended not long afterwards. When the mujahideen introduced me to their commander, he took one look at the wannabe war reporter his men had found, and instantly decided there was no way I was coming with him to Afghanistan. But I knew I'd be back.

* * *

When I landed in Afghanistan for the first time in early 2002, I was shocked at the destruction I encountered. Much of Kabul was in ruins. It was not the result of the US bombing the Taliban, but of the civil war during the decade before. Mounds of uncleared rubble, worn smooth by years of rain, sun and wind, made some areas look like a moonscape. There was barely a building without at least a shrapnel or bullet scar. What I saw then became a benchmark against which I gauged how things changed in the years that followed.

Over the next two decades, I watched the country change decisively. And during my later visits, I also brought along a sketchbook, to draw some of these changes. On a trip there in 2019 to cover the country's fourth presidential election since the overthrow of the Taliban, Afghanistan was a very different place. It was more urbanised and more connected to the outside world, through travel and trade, digital links and culture. Life expectancy had risen by more than 50 per cent.

Since the overthrow of the first Taliban regime, a whole new generation had come of age, with different aspirations and values. At least two-thirds of the estimated 40 million Afghans alive were under 25, and more than half had been born since the 9/11 attacks, making Afghanistan's one of the youngest populations in the world.

Among them were millions of young women who had been the first in their families to go to school, many moving on to higher education both inside the country and abroad. A new media and entertainment scene had grown up to serve the new Afghanistan, making the country freer in many respects than any of its neighbours.

The new Afghan generation which prospered as a result included Farzana, Bilal, Jahan and Abdul. But the big changes in Afghan society were mainly in the cities, the evidence most obvious in Kabul, which grew into a metropolis of some 5 million people. Living in a rural area, Naqibullah was left behind. Afghanistan remained in many ways two separate countries, and the Taliban would exploit this division as the West's interest in Afghanistan waned.

Back in the United States, most Americans had had enough of the war – if they were paying attention at all. 'Is there still war in Afghanistan?' was often the first question Google offered when you typed in the country's name. President Donald Trump crystallised those sentiments into a deal with the Taliban in 2020, agreeing to a full US withdrawal in return for Taliban commitments to constrain Al Qaeda. But it was his successor, Joe Biden, who took the crucial decision in April 2021 to pull out unconditionally, channelling his own, long-held scepticism about the US mission in Afghanistan.

By then, the US troop count was down to 2,500. But as America pulled out the last of its soldiers and its logistical support for the Afghan army it had created, the Taliban advance sped up and increasing numbers of people switched sides.

As their fighters converged on Kabul, my phone was pinging with messages and calls. Many long-time friends and contacts were calling me and others with connections to Afghanistan, asking for help and advice. The ground was disappearing beneath their feet, and their association with the Western-backed order made them vulnerable. Among those I heard from were Abdul, Jahan and Farzana.

When the Taliban finally overran the capital on 15 August, it sparked a panicked dash for Kabul airport, with tens of thousands of Afghans trying to get on to Western evacuation flights. I was trying to get back into the country at the time, to report on the fall of Kabul. Instead, I became part of an ad hoc, remote rescue effort, helping people through the deadly crush around the airport and on to flights. Twenty years earlier, many Afghans had put their faith in the West to change their lives. Now they were forced to fight their way through a sewage canal leading to one of the airport gates to save themselves from Taliban reprisals.

I returned to Afghanistan to cover the early stages of the Taliban's takeover, looking for answers to the questions so many were asking. How did an insular religious movement reviled by so many Afghans manage to recover from total defeat in 2001 and reclaim power 20 years later? How did the United States and Britain spend two decades replacing the Taliban with the Taliban? And what is Afghanistan's future now?

My efforts to find more answers to these questions inside Afghanistan itself were brought to a halt when I and my colleagues were imprisoned in early 2022. We were fortunate to be released unharmed. Many Afghan journalists have been detained for much longer and treated more harshly. The experience did not alter my affection for the country and its people; some aspects of my captivity even made me appreciate it more. But after my release I knew I would not be returning to Afghanistan for a long time.

In the meantime, so many people I had first got to know there were now scattered around the world, building new lives as exiles – in some cases for the second time. After living through six violent changes of power in Afghanistan, Abdul finally made it out of the country with his family and reached Britain. Jahan and Farzana are also in Britain with their families, and Bilal made it to Canada. It was time, I decided, to tell their stories.

The 9/11 Wars: Reporting Afghanistan and Iraq.

People
Principal and Other Characters

Principal Characters

Abdul Tayib was born near Kabul in 1974 when Afghanistan was at peace. He wanted to follow in his father's footsteps and become a doctor.

Farzana was born a refugee in Tehran in the early 1990s. She moved to Afghanistan with her family after the Taliban were overthrown in 2001, and became a successful lawyer.

Bilal Sarwary was born in Kabul around 1983, but was forced into exile in Pakistan. After the September 11 attacks, he returned to Afghanistan as a translator and became a journalist.

Jahan was born in Kabul in the late 1980s and grew up in extreme hardship, shining shoes to support his family. But shining shoes created a connection that led to a career as a journalist.

Naqibullah was born a refugee in Pakistan in the early 1990s and grew up in south-eastern Afghanistan. When he was 11, he was incarcerated in the US prison camp at Guantanamo Bay and held there for nearly two years.

Other Names and Characters

AFGHANS

Shah Shuja Durrani: British-installed Amir, or ruler, of Afghanistan, 1839–42.

Dost Mohammad Khan: Amir unseated by the British in 1839, whose son **Wazir Akbar Khan** orchestrated the revolt that led to the massacre of the British garrison in 1842.

Abdul Rahman Khan: British-installed Amir, 1880–1901.

Amanullah Khan: Amir and then King, 1919–29, who secured Afghan independence.

Zahir Shah: King, 1933–73; named 'Father of the Nation' in 2002.

Mohammad Najibullah: last president of the Soviet-backed Afghan government.

Mullah Mohammad Omar: co-founder and first leader of the Taliban.

Ahmad Shah Massoud: veteran mujahideen commander from the Panjshir Valley and leader of the anti-Taliban Northern Alliance, 1996–2001.

Hazrat Ali, Haji Zaman Ghamsharik, Haji Zahir: Northern Alliance commanders hired by US forces to hunt Osama bin Laden at Tora Bora in 2001.

Hamid Karzai: President of Afghanistan, 2001–14.

Mohammad Qasim Fahim: succeeded Ahmad Shah Massoud as leader of the Northern Alliance and became defence minister in the first Karzai administration.

Ismail Khan: veteran mujahideen commander and later Governor of Herat.

Mirmen Parveen: the first woman to sing on Afghan radio in the 1950s.

Saad Mohseni: Afghan-Australian businessman who co-founded Tolo TV.

Kamal Sadat: journalist and later Afghan government official.

Jalaluddin Haqqani: anti-Soviet mujahideen commander.

Gulbuddin Hekmatyar: mujahideen commander with close ties to Pakistan.

Sher Mohammad Akhundzada: governor of Helmand province, 2001–05.

Abdullah Abdullah: Afghan foreign minister, 2001–09; chief executive, 2014–20.

Ashraf Ghani: Afghan finance minister and then president, 2014–21.

Shafi Karimi: journalist who fled to France in early 2021 after receiving death threats.

Fatima: graduate of the American University of Afghanistan who fled to Europe.

Salman: husband, father and former aid worker turned translator.

Omid and **Hanif** are brothers and veteran drivers.

Habibullah is a Taliban soldier serving with their intelligence department.

Mullah Hibatullah Akhundzada: the current leader of the Taliban, 2016–present.

AMERICANS
George W Bush: US president 2001–09.

Donald Rumsfeld: President Bush's Defence Secretary, 2001–06.

Zalmay Khalilzad: US special envoy and ambassador to Afghanistan, 2002–05; negotiated the Doha withdrawal agreement with the Taliban in 2020.

David Barno: Lieutenant-General (retired) who commanded all American forces in Afghanistan, 2003–05.

Louis Fernandez: former US officer and platoon leader who served in Afghanistan and Iraq.

Barack Obama: US president, 2009–17.

Donald Trump: US president, 2017–21.

Joe Biden: US president, 2021–time of writing.

Frank McKenzie: General (retired) and CENTCOM commander at the time of the US withdrawal in August 2021.

OTHERS

Mikhail Gorbachev: Soviet leader, 1985–1991

John Mohammad Butt is an Islamic scholar and co-founder of the popular Afghan radio soap opera *New Home, New Life.*

General Pervez Musharraf: Pakistani military ruler and then president, 1999–2008.

Ed Butler Brigadier (retired) who commanded the first British military deployment to Helmand province in 2006.

Boris Johnson: British foreign secretary and later prime minister.

Osama bin Laden: Saudi-born co-founder of Al Qaeda and architect of the 9/11 attacks.

Timeline
Afghanistan over the Centuries

6th century BCE: The territory that is today Afghanistan is conquered by Darius I, ruler of the Achaemenid or First Persian Empire.

4th century BCE: Alexander the Great conquers Afghanistan after defeating the Persian ruler Darius III.

4th–1st century BCE: Hinduism and then Buddhism are introduced by the India-based Mauryan Empire.

6th–7th centuries CE: The small, and then large, Buddha statues are built in Bamiyan.

7th–9th centuries: A series of Arab invasions introduces Islam.

13th century: The Mongols conquer, destroying Kabul and other cities, but leave the Buddhas intact.

18th century: Afghan Pashtun tribes rebel against their latest Persian overlords. In 1747, Ahmad Shah Durrani declares the Pashtun-led Durrani Empire, laying the foundations for modern-day Afghanistan.

19th and early 20th centuries, 'The Great Game': Britain seeks to control Afghanistan to protect its Indian colony from Russia, leading to two Anglo-Afghan Wars.

1839–42 First Anglo-Afghan War: A British colonial army over-throws Amir Dost Mohammad Khan and installs Shah Shuja Durrani as their puppet ruler. When the British retreat in 1842 in the face of an Afghan uprising, their army is almost entirely wiped out.

1878–80 Second Anglo-Afghan War: Britain installs Abdul Rahman Khan as Amir, making Afghanistan its protectorate. Known as the 'Iron Amir', he uses mass violence to consolidate his power.

1893: Abdul Rahman Khan signs a treaty demarcating Afghanistan's 'Durand Line' frontier with British India.

1901–19: Habibullah Khan – Abdul Rahman's son – reigns as Amir. His son, Amanullah Khan, takes over.

1919 Third Anglo-Afghan War: Amir Amanullah Khan launches a surprise attack on British India, leading to formal independence for Afghanistan in August 1919.

1922–29: Amanullah Khan declares himself king and, in conjunc-tion with his wife, Queen Soraya Tarzi, launches a modernisation programme, partially emancipating women. But he is forced from power after a rural uprising against his reforms. General Mohammad Nadir Shah takes over, but he is assassinated in 1933.

1933–73: Reign of King Zahir Shah (son of Nadir Shah), a period of relative stability. Just 19 when he ascended the throne, his two uncles ruled in his place for the first 20 years.

1947: Colonial India wins independence from Britain. But Afghanistan refuses to accept the 'Durand Line' as its border with the new Pakistan, and the violence accompanying Partition creates lasting regional instability.

1950s: The USSR and the US compete for influence in Afghanistan, with Kabul growing closer to Moscow.

1973–78: Prime Minister Mohammad Daoud Khan – the King's cousin – overthrows King Zahir Shah and declares himself president, establishing close ties with the USSR.

April 1978: Daoud Khan and his family are killed in a coup by Afghan communists. Their brutal campaign to create a so-called 'People's Democracy' triggers a new rebellion and the birth of the mujahideen (holy warrior) guerrilla movement.

1979: Civil war spreads and the Soviet Union invades, provoking a full-scale mujahideen rebellion.

1980s, Soviet occupation: Soviet troops and their Afghan allies hold the cities, while the US and Saudi-backed mujahideen control most rural areas. Millions of Afghans take refuge in Pakistan and Iran.

1980s, Arab volunteers: Saudi millionaire **Osama bin Laden** travels to Pakistan to work with other Islamic ideologues in assisting the mujahideen, recruiting Arab fighters and setting up camps in eastern Afghanistan.

1988: Soviet leader Mikhail Gorbachev agrees to pull out. Osama bin Laden and other Islamist figures form Al Qaeda to expand their 'jihad', or holy war, after the Soviet defeat.

1989: Soviet troops complete their withdrawal in February 1989 and bin Laden returns to Saudi Arabia.

1989–92: Fighting continues between the mujahideen and the Moscow-backed government, which hangs on until Soviet aid is cut off, leading to the government's collapse in 1992.

1992–96 Afghan Civil War: 50,000 people are killed in Kabul as mujahideen factions fight for control.

1994–95: Pashtun mujahideen and ulema, or religious scholars, led by Mullah Mohammad Omar form the Taliban, which expands with help from Pakistan.

1996: Osama bin Laden returns to Afghanistan, assisted by old mujahideen allies and independent of the Taliban. The Taliban seize Kabul and execute the former president, Dr Mohammad Najibullah, before implementing their version of Sharia law.

1998–2000: The United States tries to kill bin Laden with missile strikes in retaliation for Al Qaeda attacks on US embassies in east Africa. The Taliban face international isolation, but resist US demands for bin Laden's expulsion.

March 2001: Taliban leader Mullah Omar orders the destruction of the Bamiyan Buddha statues.

9 September 2001: Al Qaeda assassins kill anti-Taliban resistance leader Ahmad Shah Massoud.

11 September 2001, 9/11 attacks: Al Qaeda operatives acting on bin Laden's orders crash US passenger planes into New York's World Trade Center, the Pentagon and a Pennsylvania field, killing nearly 3,000 people.

October–November 2001: The US and its allies invade Afghanistan, ousting the Taliban regime.

November 2001: President George W Bush orders the US military to make plans to invade Iraq.

December 2001: US-led forces surround bin Laden at Tora Bora in eastern Afghanistan. He escapes. Hamid Karzai is chosen as the new Afghan leader at an international conference in Bonn, Germany.

2004: A new constitution is inaugurated, naming the country the Islamic Republic of Afghanistan and giving women and men equal rights. Hamid Karzai is officially elected president, with an 84 per cent turnout.

2005: Afghanistan holds its first parliamentary elections, as a Taliban insurgency gathers pace.

2006: British forces are sent to Helmand province, provoking heavy fighting.

2009: President Hamid Karzai wins a second term, amid allegations of systematic fraud. US President Barack Obama announces a temporary surge of US troops to reverse Taliban advances.

2011–13: American forces find and kill Osama bin Laden in Pakistan. US reinforcements push back the Taliban in some places, but these gains are reversed as the troops are withdrawn in accordance with Obama's timetable.

2014: Ashraf Ghani and Abdullah Abdullah become president and chief executive respectively through a US-brokered power-sharing deal, after a vote marred by more fraud. The US and NATO say they are stepping back into a support role, giving the Afghan army and police lead responsibility for security.

2016–18: The Taliban step up urban attacks and President Donald Trump orders increased US air strikes, contributing to a rise in civilian casualties.

2019: Ashraf Ghani wins a second term as president, after an election with a record low turnout.

February 2020: In Doha, Qatar, the United States and the Taliban sign a deal for a US withdrawal.

14 April 2021: President Joe Biden orders an unconditional US withdrawal from Afghanistan.

15 August 2021: President Ashraf Ghani flees Kabul and the Taliban take control, prompting an emergency evacuation by the United States and its allies of their personnel and some of their Afghan colleagues.

30 August 2021: As the last US troops leave Afghanistan, the Taliban celebrate victory.

March 2022: The Taliban renege on a commitment to keep girls' schools open.

Overview

A Short History of Afghanistan

Afghanistan – literally, the land of the Afghans – became an independent nation state in 1919. But this young country has a long and complex history, defined by its location and topography.

It is slightly larger than France in area and a little smaller than the US state of Texas. Landlocked between South and Central Asia, China and the Middle East, geographical fate has made Afghanistan a strategic crossroads. It was a key junction on the ancient Silk Road, and a gateway to the Indian subcontinent, via routes such as the Khyber Pass. And with no viable detour around this expanse of territory, empires have competed to dominate it through the ages.

The Hindu Kush mountains that dominate much of Afghanistan, as well as its large deserts, always put outsiders at a disadvantage. Many armies have managed to conquer; few managed to stay. But from the Persians to Arabs, Mongols to Mughals, they have all left their mark in the complex multi-ethnic and multi-lingual country it has become.

The Pashtuns – from which today's Taliban emerged – are the largest ethnic group. They dominate southern and eastern Afghanistan and speak Pashto, which shares some vocabulary with Persian, but is still a distinct language. Next are the Tajiks, who speak Dari, a close variant or dialect of Persian, and the country's most common tongue. The third largest group are the Hazaras, who have both Central Asian and Persian heritage and are mostly Shia Muslims. Their numbers have been decimated by centuries of repression. The many other minorities include Uzbeks, Turkmen, Pashai, Nuristanis, Baluchis, Sayyids and Kyrgyz.

Most Afghans today follow the Sunni branch of Islam. The Buddha statues of Bamiyan (destroyed by the Taliban in 2001) were just one sign of the other faiths that put down roots long before the Islamic religion was introduced by the Arab invasions of the late 7th and early 8th centuries. There had been established Zoroastrian, Hindu and Jewish populations in the country at different times. Until the civil war in the 1990s, Afghanistan was also home to a large community of Sikhs, most of them living in Kabul.

It was after a Pashtun rebellion against attempts by their Persian overlords to impose Shia Islam in the early 18th century that modern-day Afghanistan began to emerge. In 1747, the leader of one of these Pashtun clans founded the Durrani dynasty, going on to create a regional Afghan empire encompassing both eastern Iran and northern India. And while the empire didn't last, the Pashtun Durrani tribal line did, producing many of Afghanistan's leaders since, including one Hamid Karzai.

As the Durranis were beginning to shape an independent destiny for Afghanistan, the country was sucked into a new round of great power competition – this time between the British and Russian empires. In the 19th century, both feared that the other was trying to encroach on their imperial possessions – India in Britain's case and Central Asia in Russia's. Just as Alexander the Great had taken Afghanistan as part of his quest for India more than 2,000 years earlier, Britain now saw the country as crucial to its possession of the subcontinent.

In Britain, competition with Russia for Afghanistan became known as the 'Great Game', a phrase popularised by the colonial-era writings of Rudyard Kipling. Much of this battle for influence was fought by spies and diplomats, but it also led to two Anglo-Afghan Wars, as the British sought to turn Afghan territory into

their own client buffer state. Conjuring up images of faraway impe-
rialists playing chess with their land and lives, it's hardly surprising
that many Afghans resent the phrase 'Great Game'.

These two Anglo-Afghan Wars were fundamentally regime
change operations, as the British sought to install their chosen
strongmen in power. But the first attempt ended in a humiliating
British retreat and the massacre of their army. They responded with
a retaliatory massacre of their own, but the territory of Afghanistan
remained outside their control. The British were more successful
when they invaded again, four decades later, leaving a new Pashtun
strongman in charge, who became known as the 'Iron Amir'. In
return for keeping the Russians out, he received British weapons
and funds. Afghans initiated a third war with colonial Britain in
1919, and that conflict led to Afghanistan winning its independence.

The legacy of Afghanistan's past as a British protectorate endures
to this day. By installing a client dictator dependent on outside
support, British colonialists created what became Afghanistan's
dominant model of government in the years afterwards, making
it harder for more stable and inclusive forms of administration to
emerge. Britain also left its mark in the way it drew the country's
borders, deliberately dividing up the Pashtuns between Afghan
territory and what is now Pakistan. The fractures in the new nation
that Britain had helped to create quickly showed.

Less than a decade after independence in 1919, Afghanistan was
in the grip of civil war and its king had been overthrown. Though
there was a period of relative stability during the long reign of King
Zahir Shah – when Afghanistan became a stop on the Western
hippie trail – his monarchy still survived on aid from competing
powers, including both the USSR and the United States. The country's underlying divisions festered, laying the ground first for the
king's ouster in 1973 and then the violent coup that put Afghan
communists in power five years later. It set the stage for Afghanistan
to become the last major struggle of the Cold War.

After taking power in 1978, Afghan communists launched a ruthless campaign to turn a deeply religious society into a Marxist–Leninist state. Thousands of people were tortured and executed, some as a result of Bolshevik-style purges. It inevitably provoked a backlash, and they were soon facing a nationwide insurgency led by mujahideen rebels, or holy warriors. But when they pleaded for Moscow's help, the Soviet leader, Leonid Brezhnev, initially resisted.

It was the siren call of Afghanistan's strategic location that helped change his mind. Brezhnev's advisers warned him that if they didn't move in to help their Afghan comrades, the United States could carve out a zone of influence there, right on the USSR's southern border.

When the Soviet military invaded in December 1979, the pattern set by the British repeated itself. They took over the major cities with relative ease and installed a new client Afghan leader. But the Soviets couldn't stop mujahideen attacks from the countryside, and their scorched earth retaliation tactics quickly hardened feelings against them.

Washington seized the opportunity to take revenge for its defeat in Vietnam and bleed its rival. The goal, said US officials, was to turn Afghanistan into 'a bear trap' for Moscow. So began 'Operation Cyclone', the CIA's covert programme to arm the mujahideen and use them as a proxy anti-communist army, in conjunction with Saudi Arabia and Pakistan. To disguise US support, only Soviet-made armaments were sent in initially. One source was a stockpile of weapons captured by Israel during its 1973 war with Arab states, which had been armed by the USSR. In the later stages of the conflict, Washington also provided its own Stinger anti-aircraft missiles, to help the mujahideen shoot down Soviet helicopters.

As Soviet losses mounted, the new leader, Mikhail Gorbachev, concluded the war was unwinnable, signing a deal to pull out in 1988. Afghanistan had notched up a new superpower scalp, but the cost to its people and social fabric was devastating. And with the competing agendas they brought to their proxy war, America and its allies had helped seed yet more conflict – and the blowback would eventually reach US soil.

What mattered to the CIA was not the beliefs of the mujahideen factions it had been arming, but how good they were at 'killing Russians'. It had played down the reports that came in of mujahideen human rights abuses.

The military-led government in Pakistan acted as America's quartermaster, or arms distributor, while pursuing its own local agenda in Afghanistan. It used its control over the weapons pipeline to build up a select few Pashtun mujahideen commanders who it hoped would eventually take power in Kabul and support its interests, at the expense of other factions.

Pakistan was taking a page from the British handbook of divide and rule, and in response to the British separating the Pashtuns with the way they drew the Afghan–Pakistani border. Past Afghan governments had refused to recognise the frontier line, and Pakistan feared the prospect of Pashtun tribes on both sides breaking away and creating an independent 'Pashtunistan'.

Pakistan's generals also feared their main rival, India, gaining influence in Afghanistan, leaving their country squeezed from both sides. And as they leveraged the flow of weapons for their own security interests, the generals favoured hard-line Islamists. More moderate figures, including the leaders of Tajik- and Hazara-majority factions, were largely sidelined.

Saudi Arabia added further complexity, directing support to its own favoured leaders. When Osama bin Laden, the son of a Saudi construction tycoon, began to use his family wealth to assist the mujahideen, he was carrying out the official policy of the kingdom and, by extension, the United States.

Still in his twenties when he first arrived in the region in the mid-1980s, bin Laden paid for Arab volunteers to fight alongside the mujahideen. He was a marginal figure at first. But, over time, he turned these foreign fighters into his own private army, with goals far beyond Afghanistan. He had aligned himself with a new genera-tion of radical Arab Islamists who called on the 'ummah', the global Muslim community, to unite across borders and rise up against foreign domination. Liberating Afghanistan from godless communism was, in their view, just one of many essential battles in a new 'jihad',[1] or holy war, which also included eliminating the state of Israel.

By the time Gorbachev had agreed to withdraw, bin Laden and his allies had built a network of bases and training camps across eastern Afghanistan, filled with battle-hardened Islamic warriors. It was that same year that he co-founded Al Qaeda.

After first the British, and then the Soviets, were humbled in Afghanistan, commentators started to call the country the 'graveyard of empires'. It is not clear who first coined the phrase. But while it can sound like a term of respect, it represents a skewed, outsiders' point of view.

Calling Afghanistan the graveyard of empires overlooks the fact that it was itself the foundation of empires, including that of its own 18th-century Durrani dynasty. The term is also inaccurate. While both Britain and the USSR were badly mauled in Afghanistan, that wasn't the reason their two empires came to an end. Most important of all, the term ignores the reality that it is Afghanistan rather than its invaders that has always paid the heaviest price, becoming a grave-yard for its own people. And that pattern continued after the Soviet withdrawal in February 1989.

Though the US-led anti-Soviet coalition had achieved its objec-tive, the fighting didn't end, as all sides continued to back their respective clients. It was the collapse of the USSR that broke the

---

[1] In the Qur'an, a 'jihad' refers to the 'struggle' to promote right and prevent wrong. Many Muslims still use it in this capacity, but it is now also widely used by both Muslims and non-Muslims as the word for an Islamic 'holy war' against infidels or non-Muslims.

stalemate, when Moscow cut its support to Mohammad Najibullah's government in late 1991, opening the way for the mujahideen to seize Kabul the following year.

Yet instead of leading to peace, Pakistan's ethnic power play ensured the conflict would metastasise again. Unhappy at the make-up of the new interim government – which included those mujahideen factions it had snubbed during the war against Moscow – Pakistan urged its favoured Pashtun commander to seize power. That triggered the civil war that tore through Afghanistan from 1992 to 1996.

It was from within the ranks of another of Pakistan's client mujahideen groups that a new opposition movement emerged, determined to restore order. They were Pashtuns from the south and they were partly inspired by a purist school of Islamic thought known as Deobandism, first espoused by Indian Muslims resisting 19th-century British colonial rule. For their title, they chose the name 'Taliban', which translates as 'the students'.

Their uncompromising tactics, which included hanging warlords from tank barrels, soon began to deliver results. Just as important a factor, the US academic Barnett Rubin points out, was the Taliban's success in using Islam to attract support, channelled through the backing of mullahs, or religious scholars. Pakistan's powerful intelligence agency, the ISI, shifted allegiances in response, and threw its weight behind them.

There was no connection between Osama bin Laden and the Taliban when he first returned to Afghanistan in May 1996. Old mujahideen allies helped him enter, with the United States on his tail – and in his sights. Fighting the Soviets had been just the first stage of a wider battle, bin Laden said.[2] America had always been, in his words, the bigger peril. He had also fallen out with Saudi rulers, after condemning their request for US protection after Iraq invaded Kuwait in 1990. Bin Laden said it should be his fighters

---

[2] https://www.pbs.org/wgbh/pages/frontline/shows/binladen/who/edicts.html

protecting the 'Land of the Two Holy Mosques', not an infidel American army.

Just weeks before the Taliban seized Kabul, the now undisputed leader of Al Qaeda issued a call for Muslims to join him in a global jihad against the United States, in his 'Declaration of War against the Americans'. He also gave a preview of his tactics, saying that because of the 'imbalance of power', Al Qaeda would have to work in complete secrecy to fight a 'guerrilla war' against the United States and its allies.

He took aim at what he called the 'crusader–Zionist alliance'. Though later forgotten, the goals he set out then were, in his words, to eject American forces from Saudia Arabia and to 'liberate' the Al Aqsa mosque in Jerusalem from Israeli control. All civilians from these countries were legitimate targets, he told his followers.

A series of suicide bomb attacks on US embassies and military installations followed. Inside Afghanistan, bin Laden built Al Qaeda into an unofficial Islamic army, with a brigade of foreign fighters providing shock troops for the Taliban. He also created a specially picked unit to plan the 9/11 attacks. The rest is history.

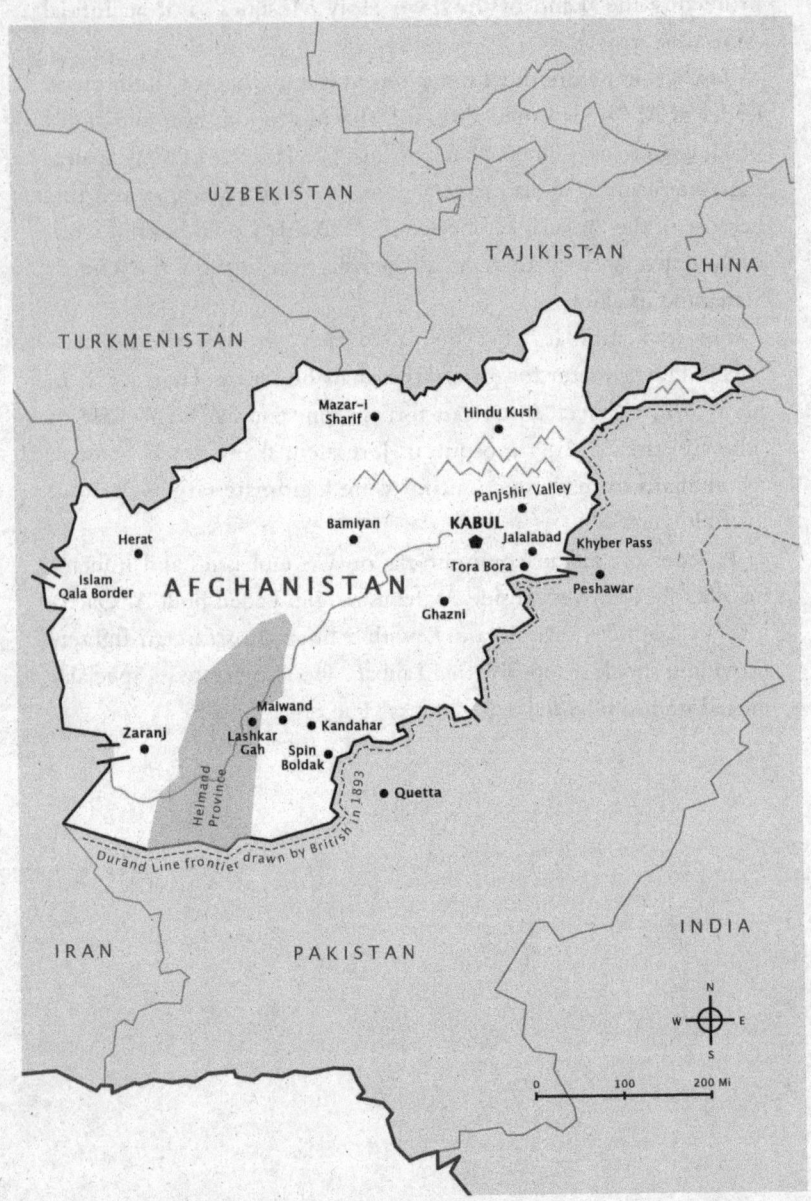

UZBEKISTAN

TAJIKISTAN

CHINA

TURKMENISTAN

Mazar-i
Sharif •   Hindu Kush

Panjshir Valley

Bamiyan •   KABUL ⬟
Herat •   Jalalabad
                         Tora Bora •   Khyber Pass
Islam   AFGHANISTAN   Peshawar •
Qala Border   Ghazni •

                    Maiwand
           Lashkar • • Kandahar
Zaranj •   Gah   Spin
                  Boldak •
                                • Quetta

          Helmand Province

          Durand Line frontier drawn by British in 1893

IRAN   PAKISTAN   INDIA

                                    N
                              W ⊕ E
                                    S

                    0   100   200 Mi

Chapter 1

9/11 and the Kabul Hotel
That Britain Built

The Intercontinental seen from the Bagh-e Bala palace.

On the north-western edge of Kabul, a large and angular-looking building stands proudly on a ridgeline, silhouetted against the sky at sunset. It is the Kabul Intercontinental hotel, and it has its own chapter in recent Afghan history.

Built by the eponymous UK-based global hotel chain in the late 1960s during the reign of King Zahir Shah, it is symbolic of that period of calm in Afghanistan. It was lauded as the country's first five-star luxury hotel. Photos from the time show women in Western-style swimsuits sunbathing around its pool. But it also exemplifies the complacency of that era, when internal fractures were ignored or papered over while the King and his advisers courted external powers to sustain their own. The ideological contest of the Cold War provided the perfect conditions, and the Afghan monarchy played off both sides.

While British hoteliers were overseeing the completion of the 200-bed hilltop Intercontinental, the then French prime minister, Georges Pompidou, arrived in Kabul to lay the foundations for a new lycée. King Zahir Shah had begun his education at the French school's earlier incarnation. The Americans had already left their mark with a large dam and irrigation project in the south-western province of Helmand. It was Soviet engineers, though, who had constructed the airport everyone used to fly into Kabul, as well as the nearby airbase at Bagram, and many of Afghanistan's main roads.

The Soviet invasion at the end of 1979 marked the beginning of turbulent times for the Intercon, as the hotel became known. Its British owners cut all ties but it kept going under the same name during the Soviet occupation, albeit without the original wine selection.

The hotel became a front line during the subsequent civil war. Rooms with a view became sniper positions, and parts of the building were destroyed as mujahideen factions battled for control of the city. The Taliban did little to fix up the ruin they inherited, but at the time of the 9/11 attacks, a skeleton staff was still offering service in the less-damaged parts of the hotel. Members of Al Qaeda were guests from time to time.

* * *

Abdul remembers the party he and his family held to celebrate his younger brother's marriage in September 2001. It was the quietest he had ever been to.

The Taliban had been in power for nearly five years at the time. Music and dancing remained strictly banned, labelled as sinful under the regime's religious code. But for Abdul and his family, there was an extra risk. Their apartment was in a complex of Soviet-era buildings known as Mikrorayon, and the neighbour immediately above them was a senior officer in the Taliban's feared intelligence service. If he heard music leaking up from below, not only would the family's covert wedding celebration be over, but Abdul and his brother could be flogged.

Tall and powerfully built, the Taliban intelligence officer was a forbidding presence whenever he appeared in the building's communal areas. Abdul tried not to catch his eye. What he knew about his neighbour came through his wife, who sometimes chatted with the Talib's spouse at the building's shared water pump outside. That was how they had discovered his job.

Though not long out of his teens, Abdul was the head of the family, and would preside over the marriage ceremony. His father had died of a heart attack at the height of the civil war. As the eldest son, Abdul had to step up and take care of his mother and siblings, as well as his own wife and two young children. The Taliban forbade women from working, increasing the pressure on him.

To provide the family with an income, he had set up a small cafe near their home, where they made and sold 'sheeryakh', or ice cream, and fresh juice. Depending on the season, their menu included watermelon, apple, orange, carrot and the country's national fruit, pomegranate. When available, they also brought in mangoes and bananas from neighbouring Pakistan.

If they didn't close up quickly enough when the muezzin at the local mosque gave the call to prayer, the Taliban's religious police sometimes shut them down for several days. Abdul had been beaten several times. Yet the business did well enough to allow him to attend to his medical studies at Kabul University in the mornings.

On the evening of the wedding, Abdul was on his guard as the family tried to celebrate, listening to how much noise they were making and constantly looking at the door. Understandably, the party didn't last long. After their few guests had left discreetly, Abdul switched on the family's radio for a nightly ritual – listening to the BBC World Service news in Pashto. The headline that evening instantly grabbed his attention.

The newsreader announced that there had been a catastrophic attack on America, using hijacked passenger aircraft. The twin towers of a skyscraper complex called the World Trade Center had been brought down in New York City, while another plane had hit America's defence ministry on the edge of Washington – apparently housed inside a pentagon.

A fourth hijacked plane was thought to have been aiming for a building called 'The White House' or the one housing its national assembly, but it had crashed before reaching its target. The reports said that US officials suspected that Osama bin Laden had ordered the attacks from his base inside Afghanistan.

* * *

Live footage of black smoke streaming from the first World Trade Center tower to be hit had spread around the world by the time the second aircraft struck. At that moment, Bilal Sarwary was coming to the end of his day working in a hotel gift shop, and happened to glance up at the lobby television carrying CNN. The hotel was in Peshawar, the north-western Pakistani city that forms the eastern gateway to the Khyber Pass. It is a place of smugglers, spies and exiles, forever on a tightrope between its past and present ties to Afghanistan.

Bilal, 18 at the time, was born in Kabul. But he had been living with his family in this frontier city for the past eight years, among millions of other Afghans forced into exile there. His first few years as a refugee were spent living in a draughty tent and looking for ways to make money to help support his family, an experience that provided many early lessons: 'It taught me to size people up, to be careful, but also how to win them over.'

At first, Bilal sold things like sweets and bottled water, before graduating to working with some of the city's traders, acting as a broker for duty-dodging consignments of Afghan fruits and carpets. His earnings and those of his siblings allowed the family to start renting a proper house. In his early teens by then, he was finally able to return to school. He also started paying for lessons for himself at one of the city's English language colleges.

One day in early 2001, he got talking to a man who owned the gift shop in Peshawar's best hotel, the Pearl Continental. He offered Bilal a job. Bilal's English wasn't good, but the shop owner's was non-existent, and he thought Bilal could sell more carpets to foreigners.

With his combination of natural charm, improving English and an ability to read people learned on the streets of Peshawar, Bilal was soon proving his new employer's instincts right. Diplomats from the city's various consulates were frequent customers. He quickly noted who would try to bargain and who would pay the most. 'The Japanese were the most generous,' he said, 'the British and the French the least.'

Bilal plied his trade amiably, making green tea for his customers and befriending many of them. And then came 11 September 2001. 'I remember seeing a flash on the screen and then fire shooting out of the other tower,' Bilal recalled. 'At first, I didn't understand what had happened. And I had no idea then that it would change my life.'

* * *

Few people had access to CNN, but at that moment, people across Afghanistan were tuning in to the BBC just like Abdul's family, some listening in Pashto, others in Dari. The country had no publicly accessible internet connection and the only other local information source was the Taliban's 'Voice of Sharia' radio, whose content was evident from its title. There was some irony in the fact that the BBC's evening news bulletin had come to be known as the 'sixth prayer' of the day.

Among those listening that night in another part of Kabul was a teenager called Jahan. Like Bilal in Pakistan, Jahan had had to spend his childhood doing odd jobs to support his family, and at the time he was working as a shoeshine boy. His uncle was listening with him, and he turned to him for answers. Jahan hadn't heard of America and he asked him where New York and Washington were. His uncle did not know, but he thought that New York must be a country.

Inside his Kabul apartment, Abdul was listening to more reports from eight and a half time zones away. He began to realise there had been a harbinger to the attacks inside Afghanistan itself. The day before, they had heard that an iconic mujahideen commander called Ahmad Shah Massoud had been assassinated at his base in northern Afghanistan. For his supporters across the country it was a huge blow and, for the Taliban, an important windfall.

A member of Afghanistan's ethnic Tajik community, Massoud had won his reputation fighting Soviet troops in the 1980s from his home turf in the Panjshir Valley, north of Kabul, earning him the title the 'Lion of Panjshir'. After the Taliban took power, he became the best known figure in the so-called Northern Alliance, a coalition of militia groups resisting their rule, employing the same skills he had used to defy the USSR. Five years after the Taliban had seized Kabul, they had still not been able to dislodge him from his remaining redoubts in the north, preventing them from claiming full control of Afghanistan.

It later emerged that two Arabs sent by Al Qaeda, posing as journalists, were responsible for the suicide attack that killed Massoud on 9 September. Abdul was sure there was a connection. 'I thought war must be coming,' he said.

From the signs Abdul picked up the next day, so, too, did the Taliban. His neighbour the intelligence officer left with unusual urgency with his driver that morning. And as Abdul passed through the city centre on his bicycle, the Taliban soldiers guarding roadside checkpoints and government buildings seemed jittery and hyper-alert. The pleasing smell of meat grilling in nearby streetside cafes still hung in the air, but people walking by were more careful than usual to avoid catching the guards' eyes.

On his shoe-shining round the next day, Jahan also sensed the impact of what he had heard on the radio the night before. He lived in a cramped mud-and-straw, cob-brick cottage in one of the many densely packed neighbourhoods that climb Kabul's hillsides. A few minutes' walk away was the somewhat wealthier area of Mikrorayon, where Abdul had his home. Jahan knew Abdul's cafe and often stopped there to find clients, carrying his wooden foot box, which doubled as a container for his cloths, brushes and polish. Sometimes customers bought him ice cream.

On 12 September, Jahan was hunting for business in the nearby district of Wazir Akbar Khan, going from house to house offering to clean shoes. It was known as the city's diplomatic quarter and many of its high-walled villas were occupied by officials from the Taliban regime, as well as their Pakistani backers and Al Qaeda Arabs. Many had their families with them, too. 'I didn't know what Al Qaeda was then, or understand why they were there,' said Jahan. But his shoe-shining round gave him an unusual window on the balance of power.

Among Jahan's clients were several members of the Taliban's cabinet. One was Sher Mohammad Abbas Stanikzai, who would become deputy foreign minister when the Taliban returned to power 20 years later. His wife sometimes came to the gate to give him and other boys food, even gifting them cake during Eid.[1]

A handful of foreign aid organisations and news agencies also rented properties in Wazir Akbar Khan for their staff to live and work, including the BBC. And even if they didn't want their shoes cleaned, they would usually at least give Jahan some money if he knocked on their doors.

Seldom did he get business from the Arabs associated with bin Laden. They came and went in large sports utility vehicles, at a time when most Afghans couldn't afford petrol, let alone a car. But one day, an Arab man stopped Jahan in the street to have his shoes cleaned and warned him not to work for 'kafirs',[2] a derogatory term for non-Muslims. 'He said he would shoot me in the head if he saw me doing it again,' said Jahan. After that encounter, he never polished shoes on the street again, always asking his clients if they would let him come inside their homes.

But Jahan and other boys doing street jobs in Wazir Akbar Khan often ended up playing football with the children of these Arab families. 'They knew we needed to earn money, so they paid us to play,' he said.

Jahan had been his family's main income earner since he was around six years old, when his father was paralysed by a stroke. As was the case in Abdul's family, his mother and sisters couldn't work. It was a harsh childhood. At first, Jahan's mother sent him out with a bucket and sponge to wash car windscreens, or to sell small felt handicrafts she and her daughters made. Despite his efforts, they mainly subsisted on old bread and often went hungry.

After a few years of doing these odd jobs on the street, a kindly Italian doctor working for the Red Cross took Jahan under his

---

[1] Eid al Adha and Eid al Fitr, the two most important Muslim holidays.

[2] An Arabic word, 'kafir' literally means non-believer or 'denier', as in someone who denies the truths of Allah.

wing, enrolling him in a school he had set up for street children. The doctor bought him the shoe-shining kit, allowing him to earn better money.

Shining shoes in the afternoons paid him enough to support his family, allowing him to go to class in the mornings. By 2001, Jahan was attending a government school. And there was another educational benefit to his street work: through his interactions with the journalists and aid workers in Wazir Akbar Khan, he had started picking up English.

In the days after 11 September, however, Jahan's work abruptly dried up. Many of the neighbourhood's residents were getting out, anticipating America's retaliation. The urgent clang of metal gates opening and the growl of four-wheel-drive engines starting up defined the mood. And on the hill above his own neighbourhood, Jahan saw Taliban fighters preparing anti-aircraft guns.

* * *

I was working at the BBC's London headquarters at the time of the 9/11 attacks. That day, I got back from lunch to find all the newsroom television monitors showing the same CNN live shot of the crippled Twin Towers that Bilal had been watching on the other side of the world.

At first, I didn't realise that the small dark shapes falling from their upper floors were people giving up hope and jumping. The shock of seeing the planes ploughing into those burning skyscrapers, and the thought of the passengers and people in the buildings just before impact, never left me.

'The world has changed today,' my editor said that afternoon. By the evening, I was on my way to the airport with other colleagues, ready to fly to the United States. But there was no way to get there as the airspace above North America had been closed to most flights.

We spent the next two days at the airport waiting for the ban to be lifted. In the meantime, the BBC clubbed together with other media organisations to charter a Boeing 747 to fly everyone there in one go. When our media jumbo was finally allowed to take off, there were some 300 people on board, from all the main British broadcasters and newspapers.

But we actually touched down in Canada, arriving at the smaller of Montreal's two airports, the one place we were allowed to land. The handful of taxi drivers outside suddenly found themselves overwhelmed by customers demanding to go to New York. I went against the flow and asked my driver to head for Boston, from where the two planes that struck the Twin Towers had taken off. I had worked in the city in the past, and my editor wanted me to find out what I could about how the hijackers had carried out their attack. Focused on gathering the news, I had only just begun to digest the enormity of what had happened, and its potential consequences. I was in a country seized by grief and shock.

Across the globe, the dominant response to 9/11 was one of sympathy and support for the United States. Many other countries had citizens among the dead. But it was also clear that, even among America's allies, more than a few people felt a tinge of schadenfreude and believed US foreign policy was partly to blame for the attacks. Such sentiments enraged mainstream America. Any calls for introspection were condemned as treason and appeasement.

By turning jetliners into jihadi weapons, Osama bin Laden had used America against itself, smashing into its identity and shattering its sense of security. Political divisions were put aside. People held impromptu rallies and lined up outside military recruiting offices to volunteer. As Louis Fernandez, one of those who enlisted at the time, put it, 'Everyone wanted revenge.'

* * *

After an $800 taxi ride to Boston, my reporting took me to a former industrial town north of the city, called Peabody. One evening, a few days after the attacks, I watched several hundred residents come together around a monument commemorating another American crisis moment, its own civil war.

Parents with toddlers in their arms grasping tiny flags mingled with pensioners waving the Stars and Stripes. One man had a cardboard banner reading 'Honk if you're proud to be an American'. Some people wiped away tears. Holding candles, young women in crop tops and baseball caps urged on the crowd. 'U-S-A! U-S-A! U-S-A!' they chanted, drivers joining in with their horns. There were many meanings in those three letters: heartbreak and loss; fear and anger; resolve, and a deep need for retribution.

When President George W Bush visited the ruins of the Twin Towers at 'Ground Zero' in New York, the rescue teams working at the site greeted him with the same raw chant of 'U-S-A! U-S-A! U-S-A!' It was a moment he never forgot. Bush recalled afterwards: 'There was kind of a palpable bloodlust.'[3]

It was a twisted expression of that desire for retribution which had brought me to the Peabody area. There had been several Islamophobic attacks in the vicinity, part of a nationwide trend. Several local mosques had been vandalised; so, too, had a community centre for Iranian-Americans and an Arab-American food store.

Ignorance meant that it wasn't just American Muslims who were the victims of this backlash. At the local gurdwara, the 'granthi', or priest, told me that male Sikhs in the area were staying indoors because they had been threatened by people who thought that, because of their turbans, they were Muslims. In the state of Arizona, a gunman hunting for Muslims shot dead a Sikh gas station owner.

---

[3] 2011 Interview with President George W Bush on National Geographic/ Disney.

President Bush condemned the violence at home, but his attitude towards the international community – and that of his close aides – was hardening. 'Every nation, in every region, now has a decision to make,' he announced, as he addressed a joint session of the US Congress on 20 September. 'Either you are with us, or you are with the terrorists.'

I was in Washington by then, reporting on the administration's response to the attacks. Bush's speech spelled out US demands for the Taliban to turn over bin Laden and shutter his camps in Afghanistan. But it was the demand for loyalty that stood out – and for which his speech would be most remembered.

Most governments around the world had rallied to America's side after 9/11. None other than Russian President Vladimir Putin was the first foreign leader to call President Bush, offering condolences and support. America's NATO partners pledged their backing on the same day, invoking the alliance's Article 5 mutual defence clause for the first time.

In his remarks, Bush highlighted the freedoms he said Al Qaeda was trying to destroy, including the right to 'disagree with each other'. But no one, apparently, could disagree with America. That speech formed the ideological blueprint for what became known as the 'war on terror'. It was then that Bush first used that ill-defined phrase: 'Our war on terror begins with Al Qaeda, but it does not end there,' he said. 'It will not end until every terrorist group of global reach has been found, stopped and defeated.'

From those words would flow actions such as the creation of the Guantanamo Bay prison camp, the use of kidnapping and torture, and the United States' invasion of Iraq, as President Bush set about remaking the region. US lawmakers had already given him unlimited authority to launch military action in a near-unanimous vote. A lone Congresswoman who voted against the legislation – which was later used to authorise the attack on Iraq – was widely dubbed a traitor and subjected to a stream of death threats and hate mail.

But around the country, the mood on Main Street echoed what I had seen in Peabody, and Bush reflected their feelings. Before 11 September, his presidency was on the slide. After the attacks, his approval ratings surged.

* * *

Farzana was 10 years old when Al Qaeda attacked the United States. Her sole memory of that time was of her parents celebrating. They were sure that America's response would spell the end of Taliban rule. 'I didn't understand what had happened,' she said. 'I just remember my parents saying again and again: "We're going home. We're going home."'

That home, Afghanistan, was a place that existed for Farzana only in snatches of her parents' conversations. In September 2001, she lived with her sister in a two-room hut on the edge of the Iranian capital, where they were born. Her parents had fled Afghanistan in the 1980s as fighting between Soviet forces and the mujahideen engulfed their village.

Life was hard in Tehran. To try to deter other Afghans from coming, the Iranian government barred them from working or putting their children in schools, forcing them to live a semi-underground existence. But Farzana's family had faced even worse discrimination back in Afghanistan once the Taliban took over. They were from the minority Hazara community, whose members were routinely subjected to Taliban violence.

In Iran, Farzana's parents made a tenuous living working informally for a plant wholesaler. Their hut was one of his sheds, and she grew up immersed in the damp smell of flower beds and compost. But her overriding childhood memory is of being expelled from multiple schools, simply because she was Afghan.

Despite the official restrictions, her parents didn't give up on trying to get her an education. 'Every time the principal came to the class, I thought, "Oh, they're kicking me out again." That's how I got to know that I'm not from here and I'm different,' she said. 'It shaped my life.'

For months at a time, Farzana and her sister Shireen would be home-schooled by their mother. She was strict, making sure they studied hard and learned to read and write. But as the Taliban became entrenched back in Afghanistan, her parents decided they had to find a solution to secure a formal education for their daughters in Iran. Their answer was to procure black market identity documents to pass them off as Iranians. 'It was a huge thing,' said Farzana. 'I mean, they were faking IDs, and it cost my parents all the money they'd saved.'

Her mother found a school where the girls were not known, warning them beforehand to keep quiet when she took them to meet the principal. 'I remember my heart booming when we were in her office,' Farzana said. But she stayed silent, and by the time of the 9/11 attacks, she was going to school every day, like any Iranian girl.

One day, Farzana and Shireen came home from class and found their parents singing and crying. From what they had heard on the radio they were convinced that America was going to invade. 'They were playing old Afghan songs and telling us: "Our country is going to be free."'

* * *

There were no Afghans among the 19 men who hijacked the planes on 11 September. All of them were Arabs, most, like bin Laden, from Saudi Arabia. The man who masterminded the plot, Khalid Sheikh Mohammad, was from Pakistan. And there is no evidence that the Taliban were involved in planning the attacks, or that bin Laden told his hosts about them beforehand.

Ironically, it was not the Taliban but some of the United States' former mujahideen allies who had originally helped bin Laden return to Afghanistan when he needed a refuge. The Taliban leader, Mullah Mohammad Omar, inherited the Saudi as a kind of sitting tenant and initially tried to control him, asking him to stop issuing fatwas calling for a jihad against America.

But his uninvited guest made himself useful, building a new fortified compound for his host in Kandahar and deploying Al Qaeda fighters to protect the Taliban regime against Ahmad Shah Massoud's Northern Alliance. And when faced with US demands to turn bin Laden over, the enigmatic Mullah Omar said his religious faith barred him from handing over a fellow Muslim to an infidel, even with his survival on the line. 'I don't want to go down in history as someone who betrayed his guest,' he said in an interview in late 2001. 'I am willing to give my life, my regime.'[4]

* * *

Nearly a month after the 9/11 attacks, on the night of 7 October 2001, Jahan was up late. He had finished his shoe-shining rounds and was at home playing a board game called 'carambol'[5] with his uncle. Fearing war was about to break out again, most of his family had moved to their ancestral village outside Kabul, but he had stayed behind to keep earning.

The game is played by knocking discs into corners of the board. Jahan was taking aim when he heard a low whistling sound, followed immediately by a powerful explosion. It was so strong it threw him and his uncle to the floor, and the door blew in. Twenty-six days had passed since the 9/11 attacks and the United States and its allies, including Britain, had responded with 'Operation Enduring Freedom', the first round of its war on terror.

---

[4] Interview with Mullah Omar conducted by journalist Rahimullah Yusufzai, 2001, quoted by Peter Bergen.

[5] Known as 'Carrom' in India, where it originated.

The Taliban had a Soviet-era anti-aircraft gun on the hill above Jahan's home, and it was one of the coalition's first targets. Fearing a second strike, he and his uncle ran for a relative's house further down the hill. Debris from the destroyed weapon and the missile lay scattered in the alley outside.

This was a different kind of invasion, though. The United States had no boots on the ground except for small groups of CIA and special forces operatives, who had co-opted the Northern Alliance and other anti-Taliban militia forces to act as its infantry. America was their air force.

Jahan had narrowly missed being killed by that first wave of strikes, but in the days that followed, the war had little immediate effect on day-to-day life. He continued to spend his days hunting for shoe-shining jobs in Wazir Akbar Khan. In fact, he worked more than usual as he was on a break from school, waiting to be summoned for an annual exam to decide if he would move up a grade.

At this early stage, the Americans even said they were having trouble finding targets. 'Much of the country is rubble,' US Defence Secretary Donald Rumsfeld told a press briefing. 'They have been fighting among themselves. They do not have high-value targets or assets that are the kinds of things that would lend themselves to substantial damage from the air.'

His remarks also betrayed the way that the Bush administration saw their campaign in Afghanistan as an entirely new war, with no connection to the 23 years of conflict before, in which the United States had played an indirect but fundamental role.

At his cafe, Abdul found he still had customers and enough supplies. It was pomegranate season, and they filled Kabul's markets, taking over from the sweet summer melons. The only impact on his day-to-day life was that the university had delayed reopening, so he spent more time running the cafe with his brother.

Things were starting to change for Bilal, however.

Soon after the US began its strikes, the Taliban granted permission for a television crew from Abu Dhabi TV to travel overland from Peshawar to Kabul. As their translator, they chose a quick-thinking young man they had hired from the souvenir store in their hotel. The day rate they offered Bilal was as much as he earned in a month selling carpets, plus expenses. Still only 18, he jumped at the chance to become, as he later put it, 'an accidental journalist'.

When Bilal arrived in Kabul with the Abu Dhabi crew, he found them rooms at the dilapidated Intercontinental. Dinner was eaten in the dark when the generator ran out of fuel, but the hotel was once again a power centre. Taliban leaders used the Intercon as a meeting place and hosted news conferences there for the handful of journalists in the city. They also had an important local base nearby, inside an ornate building further along the same hill.

Known as the Bagh-e Bala[6] palace, it was built in the 19th century as the summer residence of Amir Abdul Rahman Khan, the tyrant Britain installed to run Afghanistan after the second Anglo-Afghan War. Distinguished by its blue cupolas and white walls, it had somehow survived the factional warfare of the 1990s. The Taliban had then taken over the complex and by 2001, it was also being used as a base by their Al Qaeda allies.

After hearing that an Arab TV news crew had checked into the hotel next door, their Al Qaeda neighbours became regular visitors, flanked by bodyguards. They assumed the channel would be sympathetic to their cause. Bilal could hear them talking in the dining room for hours at a time. He couldn't understand most of their conversations as they spoke in Arabic, but there was one word he kept hearing: 'Sheikh', the honorific that Al Qaeda and the Taliban used for Osama bin Laden.

---

[6] Bagh-e Bala literally means the 'garden on top' in Dari.

He learned that the Al Qaeda delegation wanted the Abu Dhabi news team to travel to a secret location to interview their leader. The state-controlled channel's editors turned the offer down, fearing the wrath of the Americans if they gave the terrorist leader a platform. Their Al Qaeda visitors then offered a tape of bin Laden speaking, Bilal discovered. That, too, was rejected.

At night, Bilal heard the crackle of a Soviet anti-aircraft cannon the Taliban had set up in the palace grounds, responding to the sound of US and British warplanes overhead. To him, it seemed a pointless show as the aircraft were far out of range. But the Taliban officials who came to the hotel to speak on Abu Dhabi TV were defiant. Bilal translated their words from Pashto to English for his colleagues to re-translate into Arabic. 'If the Americans come,' said one Talib, 'we will go to the mountains and then we'll come down and fuck their wives.'

The inhabitants of the hotel and palace soon realised the Americans must have informers relaying details of their comings and goings. One night, the anti-aircraft fire became more intense, the red trails of tracer rounds slicing through the darkness. Bilal and the team had just returned to their room after doing a live broadcast on the roof when he said they heard 'what sounded like a helicopter, or maybe a small plane'. Seconds later, there was an explosion outside which shook the windows. Their rooms overlooked the palace garden, and it appeared that something had been hit there by a single, targeted missile.[7]

When Bilal and the Abu Dhabi crew tried to reach the blast site the next morning, Taliban guards blocked the way. Later that day, one of them whispered to him that an important Al Qaeda member had been killed in the strike.

* * *

---

[7] It is possible that this was one of the early US drone strikes, as it was at this time that the Americans first started using armed drones.

Governments that rule by fear and force have no foundation. Once their capacity to intimidate is gone, they collapse like derelict buildings. Afghanistan has a history with such regimes, which usually end when those in charge either switch sides or take flight.

Abdul saw it happen to the Taliban one afternoon in the second week of November 2001. Looking out from his apartment's balcony, he spotted a vehicle he recognised near the entrance: the Toyota Hilux pickup belonging to his neighbour, the Taliban secret policeman.

Then his wife and two young daughters hurried out, enveloped in long black cloaks, followed by his son and the man himself, a Kalashnikov in his hand. Abdul had never seen him carrying a weapon before: 'He was too important.' His fear of his neighbour evaporating, Abdul called down to him: 'What's happening?' He looked up and their eyes met. But then he climbed into the front seat and drove away. Abdul never saw him again.

Jahan noticed the Taliban's sudden departure too. His mother had returned to Kabul and as he accompanied her to buy food one morning, he saw the Taliban guards at a nearby military hospital had gone and the gates were open.

Bilal witnessed a mass exodus of Taliban and Al Qaeda fighters from the Intercontinental and the adjacent palace base. The nearby main road into the city was clogged with convoys of shell-shocked fighters who had abandoned their positions on the Shomali Plain,[8] a plateau of fields and farming villages that forms the northern gateway to the capital.

Three weeks into the invasion, the Americans had changed tactics, sending B-52 bombers to pound Al Qaeda and Taliban units on the Shomali and the approaches to other major cities. The onslaught had precipitated a nationwide Taliban collapse.

---

[8] Literally, the 'Northern Plain' as the word 'Shomali' is derived from the Dari word for 'north'.

Paradoxically, the very success of the US war strategy now exposed its flaws. With the Taliban's retreat, the way was open for the CIA-backed Northern Alliance to advance out of their redoubt in the Panjshir Valley and take Kabul – to the alarm of both the Bush administration and General Pervez Musharraf, Pakistan's military ruler.

The Northern Alliance was dominated by ethnic Tajik militia-men from the Panjshir Valley, loyal to their late leader Ahmad Shah Massoud. They were commonly referred to as 'the Panjshiris'. There were fears both in Washington and among some Afghans that the Panjshiris would ignite a new round of communal violence, in order to avenge Massoud's assassination two months earlier.

Panjshir Valley

In Pakistan, Musharraf and his ISI intelligence service feared a disastrous loss of influence across the border. Having starved Massoud of assistance during the anti-Soviet war, they had turned the late commander and his Panjshiri forces into long-time opponents, and now it looked as though they would seize power unopposed.

The Americans were hoping another old CIA contact could provide balance by fomenting an anti-Taliban uprising in the Pashtun heartlands in the south. Hamid Karzai had clout as the leader of an important Pashtun clan. But his first attempt to stir up a revolt went awry, and the Americans had to rescue him. That left the way open to the Northern Alliance to take power. Having outsourced its ground war to them, the United States could hardly now expect Panjshiri commanders to halt at the gates of Kabul.

* * *

On the second morning after his secret policeman neighbour vanished with his family, Abdul was woken by automatic gunfire outside. Edging carefully towards the nearest window, he looked out to see several Panjshiri soldiers down below, firing their Kalashnikovs. With their camouflage fatigues and shorter beards, they were easily distinguishable from the Taliban and Al Qaeda. It was 13 November 2001, and Kabul had fallen yet again.

Memories from five years earlier came to mind, when Abdul had witnessed the lynching of President Najibullah by the Taliban. Then it was the Panjshiris who had been forced out. Now they were back, as Afghanistan's revolving door to power turned once more.

In Wazir Akbar Khan, Jahan watched as looters had descended on houses previously occupied by Taliban officials, Arabs and Pakistani spies. They carried away blankets, clothes, shoes, bags of rice, and even sheep. He recognised many of them as people from his own neighbourhood further along the hill.

Jahan looked enviously at the stolen livestock; his family hardly ever had meat. But when he told his mother, she admonished him. 'These are not gifts,' she said, forbidding him from joining in. Over at the Intercontinental, Bilal also saw looters arriving in search of anything in the hotel they could take away.

After the gunfire had subsided around Abdul's home, he went out with one of his brothers to test the mood and check their cafe was secure. On the street was the corpse of an Arab-looking man, his wounds still fresh. The two brothers assumed he had been shot by the Panjshiri men they had seen from the window. The Northern Alliance was acting as the security force, hunting down remnants of Al Qaeda who had been left to fend for themselves as the Taliban fled. By the afternoon, its troops had taken over all major government buildings and the airport, as well as the Intercontinental.

There were reports of Panjshiris executing Arabs and Taliban they captured and mutilating their corpses. Reports later emerged of another US ally, Uzbek warlord Abdul Rashid Dostum, suffocating hundreds of Taliban fighters who had surrendered.[9] But the rampage some had feared in Kabul did not materialise, and the Panjshiri troops were facing men trained to kill themselves rather than surrender. Later that same day, Abdul saw another Arab fighter blow himself up with a grenade when he was surrounded.

Simultaneously, celebrations were erupting across Kabul as word spread that the Taliban really were gone. The sounds of Afghan dance music filled the streets, rattling out of long-hidden cassette players. Children were flying kites in the street again, another popular activity the Taliban had outlawed. Cautiously, women began to appear without head-to-toe burqas. Outside Abdul's local barber shop, the line of men waiting to have their beards shaved went round the block. 'I had to wait until the next day to get mine done,' he said.

From America's point of view, its invasion had been a triumph of modern warfare. In less than two months, it had ousted the Taliban using only air power and a few hundred US personnel on the ground, at minimal cost in its own blood or treasure. On 5 December, Hamid

---

[9] Reported by Carlotta Gall in December 2001 https://www.nytimes.com/2001/12/11/world/a-nation-challenged-prisoners-witnesses-say-many-taliban-died-in-custody.html See also p.18 in her 2014 book, *The Wrong Enemy*.

Karzai was named as the chairman of a new interim Afghan administration at a United Nations-led meeting in the German city of Bonn[10] – though his tenure almost didn't last the day.

When he learned of his appointment, Karzai was in southern Afghanistan, after being infiltrated back into the country by US forces, when a misdirected American bomb aimed at stalling a Taliban attack narrowly missed him. Many of his Afghan and US guards were killed. Just a day later, the Taliban had melted away from Kandahar and their other bastions in the south, many of them making for the borderlands of Pakistan.

He may have been named as Afghanistan's interim leader, but Karzai could not exert his authority across the country. The result was that old warlord figures were free to rotate back into their old fiefdoms, regardless of the wishes of the Afghan people, or Karzai himself. As it happened, most of these Afghan strongmen were current or past CIA allies.

Swift invasions followed by protracted power struggles have a long history in Afghanistan. But people wanted to believe that this time was different, especially those in the cities, and there was a sense of change and opportunity in the air. Many regarded the Bonn meeting that named Karzai as leader as a peace conference.[11] But while Afghans were looking for an end to war, the Americans were in the country because they had just started a new one. Their priority was not peace in Afghanistan, but winning their war on terror, however that was defined.

Despite this mismatch in perspectives, the Americans' arrival was a chance for those with means and entrepreneurial spirit to

---

[10] Karzai was initially nominated by Dr Abdullah Abdullah of the Northern Alliance, not by the US, according to Zalmay Khalilzad, who was part of the US negotiating team at Bonn. (Interview with the author.)

[11] Interviews by the author with a range of Afghans in the early 2000s. See also Barnett Rubin interview for Foreign Policy podcast series *The Afghan Impasse* (2024) and his chapter 'The Two Trillion Dollar Misunderstanding' in the Scandinavian Journal of Military Studies.

make some money, after years of war-induced poverty and Taliban austerity. The first battalions of Western soft power were arriving.

Diplomats were returning to reopen long-shuttered embassies. Humanitarian agencies were arriving to distribute aid. Afghan exiles were starting to come home as well in a trickle that became a torrent. And hundreds of journalists were flowing in to cover the global story of the moment. They needed somewhere to stay, translators to communicate and drivers to get them around – and they all had plenty of cash.

Abdul had an old Toyota van. Though he had hardly driven it in years because petrol was too expensive, it was useful now and he decided to offer his services as a driver. He heard that the Kabul Intercontinental was the place to go. As the Taliban moved out, it had filled with international journalists. There was so much demand that they had even occupied many of the rooms damaged during the civil war.

But as Abdul arrived hopefully at the hotel, Bilal was leaving it, under very different circumstances. He had just been placed under arrest as a suspected terrorist collaborator.

Chapter 2

Mission Unaccomplished: Letting Osama Leave and the Warlords Return

The Tora Bora hills and the White Mountains.

Bilal had always had a way with words and a knack for winning people over. It was how he had landed a job in TV, and it had made him pretty good at selling carpets, too. But his charms were no help in the aftermath of the fall of Kabul in mid-November 2001.

Soon after taking control of the Intercontinental, Panjshiri soldiers with the Northern Alliance arrested Bilal, alleging that he was a Taliban

61

agent, and locked him up in a jail on the other side of the city. Some of the hotel staff were working as informants for the Northern Alliance's intelligence department. Having watched Bilal talking to Taliban and Al Qaeda figures in the course of his work, they had decided he was with them. It was a moment that encapsulated Afghanistan's divisions.

Everything about Bilal made him suspect in the eyes of the Northern Alliance's agents. He didn't have an Afghan identity card and, after years as a refugee in Pakistan, where he spoke Pashto and Urdu, he had forgotten much of the Dari he had learned as a child – the language of the Panjshiris who dominated the Northern Alliance. Further complicating his situation was the fact that he was originally from Kunar, a Pashtun-majority province near the Pakistani border which was both a source of Taliban recruits and a bastion of Al Qaeda supporters.[1]

It was a terrifying situation for any 18-year-old to be in, and Bilal had no connections with the new authority in Kabul who could help. Finally, his Abu Dhabi TV employers asked the government in the UAE to intervene with Northern Alliance leaders. A week after he was taken prisoner, Bilal was brought out of his cell to find himself in front of a senior Panjshiri official who had been one of the late Ahmad Shah Massoud's closest advisers.

The official wrote a letter of authority for Bilal to show in the event of any further problems. His name was Dr Abdullah Abdullah. A few weeks later, at the UN gathering in Germany, he was named foreign minister in Afghanistan's interim government.

By then, Bilal's fortunes had changed again. He was camped out in a spectacular mountain valley in eastern Afghanistan, now reporting for the BBC on the hunt for Osama bin Laden.

* * *

---

[1] Some Arab Al Qaeda followers settled in Kunar and married local Afghans, helping to spread the group's 'Salafist' ideology.

Six days after the 9/11 attacks, President Bush was asked by a reporter if he wanted Osama bin Laden dead. 'I want justice,' he replied, before pausing a moment and adding: 'There's an old poster out west as I recall, that said: "Wanted: Dead or Alive".'[2] Less than three months later, American forces located the Al Qaeda leader and his entourage at one of his old bases in a complex of caves called Tora Bora, situated in the eastern province of Nangarhar, just across the border from Pakistan.

Having witnessed the fall of Kabul, Bilal was about to have a window on the next key moment in America's war. Before the Taliban abandoned Kabul, he had met a BBC news team at the Intercontinental who had just been allowed into the country. After his release from Northern Alliance custody, he linked up with them again and he was added to the BBC's roster of translators to work with the surge of journalists it was bringing in.

At the time, Bilal saw it as a useful short-term job. He thought he would stay a few weeks then go back to Pakistan and open a shop. But the chase and challenge of finding stories energised him. Another spur was the competitive pressure from his fellow translators, all of them older and with more fluent English: 'Surviving in that job was like swimming with sharks.' When the bureau chief asked for volunteers to cover the hunt for bin Laden in eastern Afghanistan, he saw his chance. None of the others wanted to go and he was an ideal fit: Pashto, his first language, is the region's main tongue.

To capture bin Laden, the Americans reprised the tactics they had used to oust the Taliban, deploying small teams of special forces and intelligence operatives around Tora Bora and hiring local Afghan forces to provide infantry manpower, as US warplanes bombed the caves from above. Britain and Germany also deployed elite units

---

[2] President Bush during a visit to the Pentagon on 17 September 2001.

to assist. But even with these reinforcements, the actual number of Western personnel at Tora Bora was small. It meant the Americans had once more severely limited their ability to control events on the ground. But this time their agenda did not really overlap with that of their local Afghan allies.

The Tora Bora caves are set in a remote, wooded valley beneath the snow-dressed peaks of the Spin Ghar, or White Mountains, which form the border with Pakistan. It is an area of stunning beauty.

To reach the valley and the caves from Kabul, you first pass through the Nangarhar provincial capital, Jalalabad. When the BBC team stopped there, in early December 2001, Bilal got into an argument with the manager of their hotel. The row had to do with renting some vehicles. More significant was the manager's identity. He turned out to be a relative and close aide to Hazrat Ali, one of the militia commanders on the US payroll. Bilal deployed his charm and turned their clash into friendship, leading to an introduction to Ali himself.

That chance encounter in a hotel lobby opened doors for Bilal and the BBC team, ensuring a better view of Tora Bora for their camera and a flow of information. In turn, it also gave him access to the two other commanders, Haji Zaman Ghamsharik and Haji Zahir, and an insight into the operation's inherent weaknesses.

The Americans had contracted out their manhunt to three warlord figures with a track record of switching allegiances. Their résumés had more than a few warning flags and in late 2001, the priority for the three commanders was not rooting out Al Qaeda, but rebuilding the power and wealth they'd lost during Taliban rule. And though they were officially partners in the Northern Alliance, they were bitter rivals in Nangarhar. Bilal witnessed them arguing himself.

Hazrat Ali was the highest profile of the three men and the most controversial. Tall and thickset, he usually wore a traditional round woollen hat known as a 'pakol' perched at an acute angle on his head. Ali had built his reputation and power base as a local mujahideen commander during the anti-Soviet war, but had been accused of using that position to build up a local criminal empire, with links to the cross-border trade in drugs. He was widely feared in the region.

A member of the Pashai minority, Hazrat Ali was unwilling to trust his two fellow commanders, who were Pashtuns. He also feared they would be able to get the better of him in negotiations with the Americans over money, because one of the other commanders spoke English. Hazrat Ali didn't. Sometimes he asked Bilal to translate for him when they met their US paymasters at Tora Bora.

Aware of the divisions between the three Afghan militia leaders, the Americans asked Bilal to appeal to them to put their differences aside: '"We need you to be on the same page," they asked me to say. "We need results."' It was a convoluted way to communicate, ripe for misunderstandings.

The Americans, dressed in local Afghan clothes and wearing pakol hats themselves, were paying for the commanders' services in hard cash. They brought in the money packed inside boxes of Oreo cookies. Bilal didn't know what an Oreo was, but he never forgot the deep blue colour of the boxes and the logo, with the photo of America's signature sandwich cookie beneath. Inside were shrink-wrapped bundles of 100-dollar bills. Given the size of each box, there must have been hundreds of thousands of dollars in each. Oreos had become the unofficial brand of the hunt for Osama.

Chatting with the commanders' foot soldiers, Bilal was struck by their casual approach: 'Often they were smoking right next to stores of fuel the Americans had brought in.' The more important takeaway from these conversations was that the militiamen and their commanders did not regard bin Laden as their enemy. Indeed, for many, he was a friend and guest.

Over the years, bin Laden had built up a reservoir of influence and goodwill in the Melawa Valley that surrounds Tora Bora. He had put money into the economy by hiring locals to expand the cave complex, build other bases and improve local roads. Al Qaeda fighters settled in the valley and married local women. When the Pashtun militiamen who made up the commanders' ranks talked to Bilal about bin Laden, they referred to him as the 'Sheikh', just as the Taliban had done.

Many were also disturbed by the destruction the Americans were visiting on the Melawa Valley. Hundreds of people had had to flee their homes as US bombs crashed down, some containing as much as seven tonnes of explosive apiece. One village in the area was flattened by the onslaught, with dozens of residents killed. Bilal came across many local refugees.

The Pashtun militiamen understood the Americans' desire for retribution, versed as they were in the principles of their tribal code, Pashtunwali. But this was not their feud. And few believed that the 'Sheikh' was responsible for bringing down two American skyscrapers. Moreover, in Pashtunwali, protecting a fugitive is just as important as taking revenge. As they pocketed US cookie box dollars, the militiamen were still talking to bin Laden's men.

British personnel quickly realised the odds of catching bin Laden at Tora Bora were poor, given the challenges of the mountain terrain and doubts about the loyalty of their Afghan allies. 'There was a lot of frustration,' recalled one British special forces operative who was in Afghanistan at the time.[3] 'The plan was to "capture or kill" bin Laden. But once they saw the scale of everything, they said, "This ain't fucking happening."' What was needed, said another Western

---

[3] Author interview.

operative in the country at the time, was a mass deployment of US ground troops 'to seal off the whole area.'[4]

CIA and US special forces officers were, in fact, sending urgent requests for reinforcements, but they were rebuffed. History again weighed on the decision. Donald Rumsfeld was determined to maintain a light footprint, arguing that a more overt US presence would be seen as a Soviet-style occupation by Afghans and trigger a backlash.

The frustrated American and British units at Tora Bora could not know that there was another factor influencing decision-making at the time. In late November 2001, about two weeks before the operation targeting bin Laden got under way and only a week after the fall of Kabul, Rumsfeld had instructed the US military to start working up plans to invade Iraq.[5] He asked for the incorporation of lessons from 'the use of special operations forces learned in Afghanistan', almost as if America's war there was already over.

While the Bush administration was moving on, so, too, was its most wanted man. Sometime in mid-December 2001, bin Laden and an unknown number of associates stole away from Tora Bora, taking advantage of a ceasefire they had negotiated with the three US-allied Afghan commanders.

In Washington, the administration quickly pivoted, playing up its triumph over the Taliban and playing down the significance of bin Laden's escape. Some officials and generals also tried to sow doubts about the intelligence that had placed him at Tora Bora. It was true that the United States had uprooted Al Qaeda from its Afghan base.

---

[4] Author interview.

[5] General Tommy Franks, commander of Centcom, which oversaw Afghanistan and Iraq operations, said in his memoir that Rumsfeld told him to start planning to invade Iraq in a phone call on 21 November 2001. See *American Soldier*, Tommy Franks, 2004.

But finding their leader had still been the primary US goal, and the failure to achieve it during the initial invasion had long-term consequences. While President Bush had been clear he wanted bin Laden 'Dead or Alive', he was vague on his plan for Afghanistan.

In the cities, many Afghans hoped the Americans would follow up their lightning removal of the Taliban's theocracy with a comprehensive effort to rebuild the country and bring peace. The reality was that the White House was still more interested in what it called the counter-terrorism mission, tracking down remnants of Al Qaeda as well as bin Laden himself. Key figures like Rumsfeld were ideologically opposed to any larger-scale intervention that smacked of 'nation building'. In the early months after the Taliban's collapse, he was true to his beliefs, resisting calls for the deployment of a Western-led stabilisation force.

The compromise was the establishment of a small United Nations-authorised stabilisation force in the Kabul region, initially led by Britain. The problem was that the new interim government led by Hamid Karzai didn't actually have much power, because the country's institutions had been so hollowed out by years of war. And in the power vacuum beyond the capital, the other local strongmen who had been enabled by the US invasion were consolidating their grip.

* * *

Tora Bora was a pivot point for Bilal as well. He didn't return to Pakistan to open a store. He decided, instead, that he wanted to keep doing this peculiar, unpredictable job which allowed you to turn up anywhere, ask people questions and then tell a lot more people about what you'd seen and heard. If it felt like it was meant to be, perhaps that's because he was not entirely an 'accidental' newsman.

When Bilal was growing up in Peshawar in the 1990s, the Afghan language programmes of foreign broadcasters like the BBC were essential listening. Its reporters were household names in the refugee settlements, and people stopped what they were doing to listen to the main evening bulletins. What they said helped decide whether it was safe to return. Seeing the difference that reporters made inspired Bilal. He told his father he wanted to be one, too, when he got older.

But in the summer of 1994, the BBC had to report on itself when its most famous journalist in Afghanistan, Mirwais Jalil, was murdered while covering the civil war.[6] When Bilal's father heard, he decreed his son's journalism career over before it had even begun. 'I don't want you to end up like Jalil,' he said. But he still wanted his son, a sometimes-recalcitrant student, to get a decent education. He persuaded Bilal to study agriculture at a local college, because he thought it would be useful if they returned to Afghanistan.

So, when Bilal had been picked to work with Abu Dhabi TV and then the BBC, it had been the fulfilment of a long-held dream. But in the aftermath of the bin Laden hunt, he learned about the fickleness of news organisations. Afghanistan was no longer making headlines daily and the BBC wanted to slim down its news-gathering operation. Bilal was told he was no longer needed.

'I was furious at first, after all my work for them in Tora Bora,' he said. But, while he had been there, he had made more contacts – including with the US network ABC. And within days of being fired by the BBC, he had signed on with the ABC bureau, on better pay. His journalistic career was far from over.

* * *

Back in Kabul, the hard pinch of a high-altitude winter had descended. The Afghan capital is one of the highest in the world, its downtown area nearly 6,000 feet, or around 1,800 metres, above sea

---

[6] Gunmen suspected of ties to one of the militia groups abducted and murdered BBC correspondent Mirwais Jalil in Kabul in July 1994.

level. It is surrounded on all sides by barren, sharp-edged mountains that rise even higher, and it is not uncommon for temperatures to fall below minus 20 degrees Celsius.

For those Afghans returning from abroad, that winter felt especially harsh. Kabul was starting all over again, but still saddled with the destructive legacy of the civil war. Swathes of the city were a ruin. There were several different versions of the Afghani, the national currency, in circulation. People had no electricity or running water. Many burnt trash to keep warm, and the fumes hung heavily over the city – trapped by the cold air pressing down like a lid.

Even Hamid Karzai had to layer up when he started work that winter in the dilapidated and unheated rooms of the Arg presidential palace. He dealt with the cold by wrapping himself in several of his trademark striped cloaks.

It was the worst time of year to be going door to door on a shoe-shining round. But as he made his way through Wazir Akbar Khan, Jahan knew there was one place where he was welcome to stop. Next to the former home of the Taliban minister whose wife sometimes gave him cake was the house that served as the BBC's local bureau. Jahan had become a well-known face there, and was regularly invited in. When the broadcaster rented a second house to accommodate the slew of journalists now coming in for short-term assignments, Jahan did small jobs like collecting groceries and local newspapers.

The permanent bureau was in a two-storey stone house enclosed by high walls. It served as both office and home for its resident English language correspondents. Some of its local staff had worked there since it opened in the early 1990s, keeping the operation going through the worst days of the civil war. The building often became a refuge for their families when fighting enveloped their own neighbourhoods.

By late 2001 onwards, Jahan's association with its staff was opening up a new future for him. Still only around 14, he couldn't have an official role. But by helping out occasionally at the bureau, he was becoming absorbed into the fold and picking up more English, too.

As the new year arrived, Abdul also felt his prospects were improving. Reviving his Toyota van and looking for work driving journalists had paid off. He'd picked up plenty of clients and then been taken on by the BBC, with his brothers keeping the cafe going. Though restrictions on women were beginning to ease, there was still no prospect of his sisters helping out there. In Afghanistan's conservative society, it would still be frowned on to have women working in a street-side cafe serving unknown men.

Abdul planned to do his driving job for a year, save some money, and then return to his long-disrupted medical studies. Although he still had anxieties about the power of the old warlords, he felt that, on balance, the situation was positive.

At the bureau, as he waited between driving jobs, Abdul was introduced to a visitor he recognised as one of the shoeshine boys who sometimes hung around his cafe. The more junior Jahan addressed him as 'Kaka Abdul', using the Dari word for 'uncle', commonly employed as a term of respect for an older man. But Jahan was fast leaving his days as a shoeshine boy behind. Soon after, I met them both.

* * *

As my plane taxied from the runway to Kabul airport's Russian-built terminal building, I felt both excitement and trepidation. I had finally made it to Afghanistan, the country that had fascinated me for so many years. But now I was here, I felt tense and overwhelmingly aware of my own ignorance. Ahead lay a vertiginous learning curve.

It was early spring in 2002, and I had come in on a United Nations flight from Pakistan. No commercial airlines would risk the journey then. One reason was right below me. Men in protective clothing were probing the ground beside the runway for mines.

Many of the devices they were looking for dated back to the Soviet occupation. Unexploded ordnance from US air strikes the year before had added a new danger. Scores of red markers indicated the substantial areas the de-miners still had to cover. It was a promising sign that finally the work had begun.

The carcasses of destroyed warplanes added another element to the backdrop, some emblazoned with the communist red star. Various modern military aircraft parked on the side aprons were there to support the British-led stabilisation force.[7] The peaks which fringed the airport's northern boundary had been part of the story, too, often serving as firing positions in the past. Now their treeless flanks looked tired and worn.

I was only a visitor so I stayed in the new temporary house, not the old bureau. My bed was a sleeping bag on the floor in a shared room. But, as an outsider working for a well-funded foreign organisation, I was insulated from most of the challenges Afghans faced. We had diesel generators and stacks of imported bottled water.

My biggest problems were timing and communication. I had committed to delivering a long radio piece for the upcoming weekend, but I had lost the first part of the week after being stuck in Pakistan because of bad weather. Pilots couldn't land in Kabul without a clear view of the runway. With no internet or mobile phone service in Afghanistan, you couldn't set things up in advance. The only way to see anyone was to drop round in person and hope they were in, or send someone to arrange a meeting.

As I was scrambling to gather ideas and work out what I could achieve in the too-short time left, Jahan offered to help. 'Let me know if you want me to take a message to someone,' he said. I was very grateful. It meant that while he passed on requests for meetings, I was able to make reporting trips out of the city.

---

[7] Officially called the International Security Assistance Force (ISAF), established through a UN resolution and taken over by NATO in 2003.

Preparations were under way to give the interim government some legitimacy after its rushed birth in Germany that past
December. The plan was to organise a consultative assembly of key
power brokers to provide the equivalent of a confirmation vote,
filling the gap until a new constitution had been drawn up and
nationwide elections could be held.

Around two-thirds of the 1,500 delegates were due to be chosen
in a two-round voting process, to inject some democracy into the
proceedings. The remainder would be appointed, with 160 seats
reserved for women. It was a long way short of a representative
election, but it was the first time Afghanistan had held any kind of
nationwide vote in more than 30 years. This gathering – known
as a loya jirga[8] – would cement the foundations of the new power
structure, and it was hotly contested.

While Jahan helped me set up meetings, Abdul drove me into the
countryside to cover the rollout of the vote. I tagged on to a small
convoy of election monitors who were inspecting the first round of
voting in the district of Bagram on the northern edge of the Shomali
Plain, about an hour's drive from Kabul. Though it was still only
spring, a warm haze blurred the detail of the snow-capped Hindu Kush
mountains, which loom over the far, northern side of the plain like an
impenetrable wall, rendering them into an amorphous white mass.

Bagram district is home to the Soviet-built airfield of the same
name, which had by then become the main US base. The sun-
baked husks of Soviet-era tanks and armoured personnel carriers
abandoned in ditches and fields told the story of how many battles
had been fought in this area over the past decades. It was here that
the Northern Alliance had faced off with Al Qaeda's death-seeking
zealots only a few months earlier.

---

[8] A 'loya jirga' is a Pashto phrase that translates as 'great council' or 'grand
assembly' when elders meet to choose leaders or make decisions according to
Pashtunwali, the traditional Pashtun social and legal code.

'Will that be the last battle to take place here?' I asked myself, as we bumped along the old road north. Dust crept inside the car, itching our noses.

Abdul swung the steering wheel back and forth to avoid the cavities in the surface. He was a thickset man, with strong shoulders and big hands and there was something reassuring about the way he muscled past the obstacles. Dark circles around his deep-set eyes, like tree rings, spoke of the burden of taking on responsibility for his family when he was still so young.

Crossing a stretch of fields between two villages, we saw a man with a Kalashnikov waving us down from his checkpoint, which consisted of an unsteady-looking wooden cabin, a length of tank track laid across the road as a speed bump and a piece of frayed rope hooked to a post.

Abdul stiffened before reaching around to make sure the doors were locked. As we came to a halt at the tank track, we saw a second man inside the cabin lifting himself from his seat, one of those stackable, metal-framed chairs used in a million schools around the world. But he was unarmed. They had one gun and one chair between them. When Abdul opened the window, letting in a cloud of wheel-churned dust, they asked apologetically if we had any food or water.

'Where is he from?' one of the roadside guards asked Abdul, nodding towards me. 'Englestan,' he replied, the Dari word for England, though it was not clear they registered Abdul's answer. The man with the gun responded with a thumbs up and a gap-toothed grin as he said, 'Amreeka good.' Abdul passed them a couple of bottles of water, and we carried on.

In the Bagram village where the voting was taking place, candidates, supporters and onlookers had assembled under the shade of some mulberry trees. Though it was still spring, it was hot in the sun. The aroma of meat and rice being cooked for the meal that would follow drifted over the gathering.

As two victors were announced, a few men in the all-male crowd shouted 'Allahu Akbar', the Arabic phrase that means 'God is the greatest', but there was no enthusiasm in their voices. The first name to be declared was Abdul Sattar, a prominent local mujahideen commander and member of the Northern Alliance. The other winner had the same profile.

There was no alternative option, one man explained quietly through the election monitors' translator: 'We were told to vote for them.' The two commanders were aided by the fact that the electorate had been reduced by 50 per cent, because women had been discouraged from exercising their own right to vote. It was a man's job, the translator explained, when I asked why women were not casting ballots. 'They will vote as their husbands tell them, so what's the point?' Even though women were entitled to put themselves forward for seats as well, none from this village had.

But then there was a surprise. Organisers annulled the result and ordered a new vote. This time, the two commanders were barred from standing again. A meeting, or 'shura',[9] of elders was convened, purportedly to agree on alternative candidates. Sitting on carpets laid out under the trees, the oldest among them were dressed in turbans and long, blue-and-green-striped chapans, while the younger men wore pakols.

Commander Sattar may have been scrubbed from the ballot, but he hadn't gone away. At one point he gave a speech to the elders, their deferential body language making clear who was boss. A bulky man dressed in a luminous chapan, he agreed to an interview, flanked by several bodyguards. I saw their eyes tighten when I used the word 'warlord' in my question.

Sattar was indignant that his first-round win had been cancelled. 'I won because I have been serving my people through all the

---

[9] 'Shura' is originally an Arabic word meaning council and used in both Dari and Pashto in Afghanistan.

years of fighting,' he said. As he saw it, power was his right after battling the Soviets and then the Taliban, and he was not going to let it go. When two delegates were selected in further rounds of voting, Sattar and the other commander ensured it was their loyalists who won.

It was another sign of the old mujahideen establishment that the Taliban had unseated making a comeback. And this pattern was repeated across the country, with some commanders resorting to violence and intimidation if anyone opposed them. With no government or international authority to fill the void, there was no one to stop them.

* * *

Less than 100 miles from Kabul, in their village of Sahak, Naqibullah and his family knew nothing about the 9/11 attacks, even after the United States had begun to invade their country.

Sahak is on the high-mountain plateau that runs through the south-eastern province of Paktia. Despite its relative proximity to the capital, the village could have been on the other side of the world for all the connection it had with events there. 'In those days, if something happened in Kabul, people only heard about it a month later,' Naqibullah laughed when we talked years later. The family never even went to the nearby provincial capital, Gardez.

He first heard about Osama bin Laden when a flurry of posters bearing his name and photo landed in and around their village, more than a month into the invasion. US aircraft were dropping hundreds of thousands of such leaflets – like 'snowflakes in December in Chicago', said Rumsfeld at the time – over areas where they thought bin Laden and his deputy, Ayman al Zawahiri, could be hiding. The Americans were offering a $25 million reward for their capture. But Naqibullah and his family didn't understand why the two men were wanted, or who was dropping the leaflets.

Paktia is a majority Pashtun province, and the district around Sahak had been an important source of recruits for the Taliban. So, the one bit of news that had reached the village quickly was of the Taliban regime's collapse in November 2001, as its fighters came through fleeing south. Yet life in Sahak, which consists of a cluster of high-walled compounds surrounded by fields, didn't really change in the immediate aftermath.

Naqibullah's family routine was set by his father's role as the local imam, or priest, overseeing prayers at the village mosque five times a day. Gul Mohammad had inherited the post from his own father, and that entitled him to 'ushr', a 10 per cent tithe of the produce of local farmers. The grain, vegetables, meat and milk the family received was usually more than enough, and so they sold the surplus to cover other needs.

Naqibullah was part of a large family, a common feature of rural Afghanistan, where many men also had more than one wife. He had an elder sister, but as the eldest son, he received the most attention from his father. Gul Mohammad took Naqibullah with him to the mosque, where he learned to read and write, and recite passages from the Qur'an. It was there that he heard from other worshippers that the Americans had put someone called Hamid Karzai in power in Kabul. But then in the spring of 2002, as preparations were getting under way for the loya jirga gathering in the capital, the war came to them.

Naqibullah was 11 years old at the time. His father had hired local labourers to assist him in building an extra room on their house. 'I wanted to help, and I liked climbing up their ladder,' he said. After constructing the walls from cob bricks and plastering over the cracks, they had started laying the roof.

One of the labourers fell off the ladder as he was reaching down for a tool. He picked himself up, but as he did so everyone's attention was drawn to the fast-approaching sound of an aircraft. Though planes passed overhead every day, they were always so high up that no one paid much notice. This one was flying low enough for everyone to see its shape. 'It was the first time I'd really seen an aircraft,' Naqibullah said. Moments later, they heard the first of a series of deep, thundering explosions in the distance.

It was the start of a major new US-led offensive, dubbed 'Operation Anaconda', aimed at what the Americans believed was a large group of Al Qaeda and Taliban fighters taking refuge in an old mujahideen base in the Shah-i-Kot mountains, to the south-east of the family's village. Negotiations to try to persuade the Taliban to give up their foreign comrades had failed, and the US-led coalition was attacking from the ground as well as from the air.

Keen to avoid a repeat of the Tora Bora debacle, the US military deployed a force of nearly 3,000 troops to besiege the Shah-i-Kot area. Most of them were Americans and Afghan militia on their payroll, but many allies also contributed forces, including Australia, Britain, France, Germany and New Zealand. B-52s were brought in again, to pummel the Shah-i-Kot mujahideen base, with helicopters bringing in special forces to attack from the ground.

Hundreds of local people fled the area during the two-week battle, as homes and livestock were caught in the barrage, some taking refuge in Sahak. 'Everyone was talking about the smell of all their dead animals,' Naqibullah said.

It was a traumatising experience for a remote Afghan village community with scant understanding of why Western forces were in their country. And for those who remembered the last foreign army to come to Afghanistan, it conjured up terrible memories. 'We feared they would be like the Shuravi again,'[10] said Gul Mohammad, referring to Soviet forces.

---

[10] 'Shuravi' is a Dari word derived from the Arabic word 'Shura' for council, and became common parlance among the mujahideen to refer to the Soviets during their occupation in the 1980s.

The imam had been in his twenties when Moscow's troops had descended on the area. They became notorious for their collective punishment tactics, routinely wiping out whole villages if any resident was suspected of sheltering the mujahideen. His older brother had been martyred, as he put it, while fighting Soviet soldiers near their village.

When the offensive at Shah-i-Kot ended, the overall US commander declared it 'an unqualified and complete success'.[11] But seven US servicemen had been killed and one of their helicopters shot down, while many of the rebel fighters escaped, including their leader. Later reports suggested US intelligence had also overestimated the numbers there.

More significantly, the battle gave the Taliban a powerful narrative to exploit, while the onslaught coloured local perceptions of America's presence. The effect was compounded over the months that followed as US forces launched a series of follow-up raids in the area. They proved to be far from discriminating as to who they picked up.

* * *

A panorama of the Afghan people was on display as the assembly got down to the business of choosing a transitional government in the summer of 2002, inside a giant, air-conditioned tent, specially constructed for the event. Officially, the meeting was called the 'Emergency Loya Jirga', and it looked like every tribe, group and creed was fully represented in the colourful mix of traditional clothes worn by the delegates for the occasion. But the optics were misleading.

---

[11] General Tommy Franks, the Centcom commander, who also oversaw the initial 2001 invasion.

The Panjshiris and their allies had packed the tent with more of their own supporters by strong-arming the organisers into adding another 500 seats – thus allowing back many of those who had been excluded during regional voting. More than half the seats reserved for women had to be filled by appointment, because in many areas they were too scared to stand, if they even considered the idea at all. In most rural districts, it was still too much of a break with tradition for people to accept having a woman represent them. And the primary qualification for the cabinet posts being selected was not ideas or policies, but identity, as this was essentially an ethnic carve-up.

The loya jirga did mark a final chapter for the Afghan monarchy. The elderly former king, Zahir Shah, had returned from his exile in Rome and his supporters hoped he would be 're-throned'. But he was persuaded to step aside and given the title 'Father of the Nation'. Hamid Karzai was duly confirmed as the leader of a new transitional government. However, the atmosphere during the week-long gathering was often tense and ugly. There were walkouts and confrontations. Sometimes weapons were drawn.

Bilal was following proceedings for his employers, the ABC network. And he was back at the Intercontinental hotel, which served as the assembly press centre. The scene there was more revealing than at the loya jirga, with warlords rolling up to the entrance in Land Cruisers surrounded by armed bodyguards with bandoliers across their chests. This was not the new Afghanistan he had been hoping for. 'Everyone wanted something for themselves or their faction,' said Bilal. 'No one had a vision for Afghanistan.'

Short-term interests came first. No one was content with the distribution of power, but the Panjshiris clearly came out on top, retaining control of the foreign and defence ministries as well as the intelligence service. Relative to their numbers, the Pashtuns came out worst and their most important faction – the Taliban – were not represented at all. Lakhdar Brahimi, the UN special envoy to

Afghanistan who steered both that loya jirga and the original Bonn agreement that had installed Karzai as interim leader, later called the failure to include the Taliban in the political process 'the original sin'.

One opening to include them may have closed around the same time that the Bonn deal was being signed in early December 2001. On the day that Karzai learned that he had been appointed as Afghanistan's next leader, not only did he just avoid being killed in a 'friendly-fire' US air strike. He also met a delegation of senior Taliban leaders in the Kandahar district of Shah Wali Kot, carrying what is now believed to have been a conditional offer of surrender.

It came in a letter that some say was signed by the Taliban leader Mullah Omar himself.[12] At the very least, it was issued with his authority. One informed source I have spoken to says it was about 'the transfer of power from the Taliban to the interim government', adding that it 'did not contain anything else'.[13]

Speculation has continued, however, that the letter also included an offer from the Taliban to lay down their arms and stop fighting, as long as they were allowed to return to their homes without being pursued or arrested. The source said the text did acknowledge 'acceptance of the new order'. But no one can be sure of the exact wording because Karzai returned the letter to the Taliban delegation, and no copy has ever emerged.

That moment was an opportunity, according to Zalmay Khalilzad, President Bush's special envoy to Afghanistan, who had also acted as Washington's point man during the loya jirga gathering. The envoy said he only learned about the letter years later, when Karzai told him that he had handed it back to his Taliban interlocutors.[14]

The former Afghan leader has never given a clear explanation for his actions. But Khalilzad acknowledged it would have been hard

---

[12] See p.34, *The Wrong Enemy*, Carlotta Gall.
[13] Interview with the author.
[14] Interviews with the author.

for Karzai to do a deal with the Taliban. The message Karzai had heard from Rumsfeld was that Taliban leaders should be brought to justice; anger over 9/11 was still at a peak in the United States. The Northern Alliance leader, Mohammad Fahim, was also opposed to working with the Taliban. Whatever happened, Taliban leaders were not satisfied with Karzai's response and they disappeared, with US forces on their tail.

It was not just the Taliban who felt sidelined. So, too, did their long-time backers, Pakistan. Officially, General Musharraf had severed ties with the Taliban in the weeks after the 9/11 attacks and pledged support for the US war on terror – in return for billions of dollars in US aid. But for Musharraf and the ISI, the rationale for assisting the Taliban had never gone away.

They still wanted a say in who ran Afghanistan, for the same reasons they had manipulated the flow of arms and aid to the mujahideen in the 1980s. There was their perennial concern about Pashtuns on both sides of the border coming together and dismembering the Pakistani state, as well as their fear of India expanding its presence and influence in Afghanistan. To Musharraf's alarm, the new power balance in Kabul gave Delhi an advantage; India had close ties both to the Panjshiris and to President Karzai, who had been educated there.

History had taught Pakistan's generals another lesson: that the United States was a fickle friend. After spending billions to support both the mujahideen and the Pakistani military, in pursuit of its Cold War objectives, Washington had left Islamabad to handle the fallout after a hobbled USSR withdrew from Afghanistan. The United States had then imposed sanctions on Pakistan, in response to its nuclear ambitions. The generals never forgot. Jump forward again to late 2002, and the US focus on Afghanistan was again starting to wane. The Bush administration was moving on to Iraq. Musharraf needed an insurance policy.

The ISI had never actually cut ties with the Taliban, having given sanctuary to their leaders and many of their fighters after they were forced from power in 2001. The Pakistani border city of Quetta had already become the main hub for the Taliban regime in exile. Now the ISI started to expand its contacts again, helping the movement to rebuild as a fighting force.

It was the start of what became known as Pakistan's double game. In some cases, Musharraf would help the United States, tracking down Al Qaeda followers who had taken shelter inside Pakistan's borders, and providing bases for US drones. But at the same time, wherever there might be a benefit for Pakistan or, to be more precise, for its generals, it was also working with America's enemies.

Chapter 3

London and Cuba: Two Faces of the West

The old fort in Gardez, originally built by Alexander the Great's army.

It was not in Kabul that I first met Bilal, but London. It was late 2003 and he had been flown to Britain by the BBC for training. Bilal had been working for the British broadcaster again for the past year, after his previous employers shrank their Afghanistan office to focus on Iraq. It had brought him back as the bureau's local producer and translator. He had won the battle with the sharks.

I was supposed to have been working with him in Kabul by then, after being appointed as the resident correspondent for Afghanistan earlier that year. Instead, I was recovering from a strange paralysing illness I had contracted that summer, after spending the first part of the year in Iraq covering the US-British invasion. Known as Guillain-Barré syndrome, it's a sudden auto-immune disorder that attacks your nerves and can be fatal. In my case, it was my facial muscles that were worst affected. By the time I was admitted to hospital, I could barely say a word or form an expression. The neurologist who treated me had warned me my speech might never recover – a bit of a deal-breaker for an on-air job with the BBC.

Weeks after being discharged, I was still off work and struggling to talk and wondering if I would even make it back to Afghanistan. But as I waited to see if my face would recover, Bilal and I had the chance to get to know each other, meeting up in central London. With the difficulties I had talking right then, I was grateful he had plenty to say. And it was fascinating to see my own home through Bilal's eyes.

London was a place where identities were hard to pin down, with its mix of people from everywhere – especially when they were all crowded together in an underground train. 'This is not Britain's city,' Bilal declared during one ride on the Tube, shouting over the noise. 'This is the world's city.' He was struck by the city's architecture; admiring the 'glass palaces' that lined the Thames and the grandeur of the Leicester Square cinema where we watched a film, declaring it better than Karzai's Arg.

Despite the turmoil America and Britain had unleashed in Iraq, Bilal still thought they offered the best hope for fixing his own country. Being in London made him reflect on what was possible. George Bush and Tony Blair were being pilloried because of the failure to find weapons of mass destruction in Iraq, but Bilal turned the controversy into one of his signature quips. 'We've had your weapons of mass destruction in Afghanistan, your B-52s,' Bilal said. 'What we want now are all your weapons of mass construction.'

When we first met, Bilal was surprised at how young I looked. I was surprised at how young he was. Still barely 20 then, you would have believed him if he had said he was more than 30, and he had a wisdom to match. 'We Afghans are old before we are young,' Bilal said.

It meant a lot to him that the BBC had flown him to London for this training and to meet his bosses. Only with their support could he get the necessary British visa, which involved no small amount of bureaucracy for an Afghan passport holder. Even more important, though, was the broadcaster's capacity to offer security and stability for his family.

But Bilal's instinct was still to be cautious. It was not just because the BBC had previously fired him, but the lessons from his past life speaking – having to flee his childhood home and start all over again as a refugee. 'If you're from Afghanistan, you learn nothing is permanent, everything is temporary,' he told me. During the weeks we were together in London, he often said, 'I hope we will still work together when you come.'

It was a lesson for me, too – highlighting how the forever war experience of so many Afghans had bred an ultra-short-term approach to life. Assuming I made it to Kabul, the idea that I would try to replace Bilal as soon as I got there hadn't crossed my mind. But I hadn't been forced to earn money to support my family before I was 10. I'd grown up in the cocoon of the West. I didn't know what it was like to spend every day worrying about tomorrow.

Walking along the Thames one day after lunch, we wandered towards the former power station that had been turned into London's Tate Modern art museum. I'd read about a large installation of an artificial sun that the museum had set up inside what had once been the Turbine Hall. I suggested we take a look.

It was impressive. The artist Olafur Eliasson had created an orange light emitting from a semi-circular screen, which combined with mirrors on the ceiling and mist in the air to create a convincing illusion of a huge setting sun. Just as arresting, though, was the sight of scores of visitors on their backs, gazing up at their reflections far above and partially silhouetted against the orange shine from the polished concrete floor. They were an installation of their own. Some had formed themselves into shapes and letters and were giggling happily at their reflections. Couples were enjoying the atmospheric gloom to snuggle up.

For a second, I felt unsettled, unsure how Bilal would react. Thinking of everything he had been through, the stories he had told me of his life, would he be annoyed by people who could spend an afternoon lying in the glow of a make-believe sun? But in this moment, there was also security and freedom, things Bilal longed to see in his homeland. He loved it. 'Will we ever have things like this in Afghanistan?' he said. 'Maybe in 30 or 40 years. I hope so.'

* * *

It was a crisp winter's morning in Kabul, the snow on the mountains gleaming in the sun. Along the big sweep of the city's Darulaman Road, the colours shone; the red awnings of the street-side food stalls, the yellow of the city's taxis and even the blue-grey of the road. The spots of little kites being flown above nearby rooftops danced in the sky.

I was probably 30 metres away from the policeman. At first, I didn't recognise the dark, football-sized object that he was prodding with the tip of his boot. But as he turned it over, I caught a flash of charred skin and blood, and I realised it was a head. A sheet had been stretched over the corpse it was once attached to. Two military jeeps stood abandoned in the middle of the avenue's inbound lane, the front of the lead vehicle blown out of shape.

The head belonged to a lone suicide bomber who had launched himself at a patrol of Canadian troops serving with ISAF, the NATO-led peacekeeping force, after they left their base nearby. An

Afghan and a Canadian soldier had been killed in the attack and several passers-by injured by the shrapnel and flying debris. As we arrived, amid the squawk and wail of sirens, an ambulance accelerated away.

Canadian soldiers bulked up with body armour and ammunition pouches had formed a cordon around the blast site. But their agitated shouts of 'Get back!' had the opposite effect. Many people simply froze where they were, probably fearing they would be shot. They didn't understand English, and the soldiers spoke no Dari or Pashto. 'Get the fuck back,' one young soldier bawled in frustration, his gestures finally making his meaning clear.

It was late January in 2004. I had arrived back in Kabul a week earlier to start my posting. I had made a full recovery and was hoping to have a quiet start, meeting people and getting my bearings in the city. That clearly wasn't going to happen now. I could see several missed calls on my mobile from the news desk in London, asking for an update.

Bilal was nearby, a phone clamped between his shoulder and ear, speaking rapid-fire Pashto. Two more mobiles were ringing, one in each of his hands, and he was deciding which to answer next. 'There's been a statement from the Taliban saying it was them,' Bilal told me when he got off the phone. He switched into Dari as he took his next call.

The day before the Canadian patrol was attacked, Bilal and I had been at the Arg palace to watch President Karzai sign Afghanistan's new constitution. It was a landmark moment, bringing the country's transitional government to an end and inaugurating what was now called the Islamic Republic of Afghanistan. This new constitution called for equal rights for women and men. Across the country, girls were going to school again. Many older women were signing up for classes too, seizing their first chance to be educated.

The highway linking Kabul to Kandahar, in the south, had just been rebuilt with US and Japanese funds. Hundreds of thousands of Afghan exiles were streaming back into the country from across the region and the rest of the world. New businesses were opening, and for the first time that anyone could remember, the capital had traffic jams. Along Kabul's Jada-e Maiwand, the ruined old city boulevard that had long provided a reliable backdrop of war-torn decay for television reporters and photographers, cyclists, cart pullers and pedestrians were being edged out by a noisy surge of vehicles.

There were warning signs, too. The gridlock was most stressful when convoys of blacked-out Land Cruisers tried to push their way past, ferrying around newly empowered warlords. Their bodyguards followed, leaning out of their windows, yelling at drivers and brandishing their weapons. There had been a slow but steady increase in violence, with the Taliban the main cause.

When they spoke about the country in public, US and British officials employed phrases like 'encouraging progress', 'steady gains' and 'better than expected', only throwing in an occasional 'fragile'. But at a British Foreign Office briefing I had attended before leaving for Kabul, there was no such spin from the head of its Afghan unit. My notes from the meeting read: 'Things are on a knife edge. Security worsening. The whole thing could unravel, and because of Iraq, there are no more troops or resources available.'

There was rarely a day when Bilal didn't receive at least one or two calls from his contacts detailing a bombing, shooting or rocket attack somewhere in the country. Sometimes, it involved attacks on isolated US bases and the Americans responding with artillery and air strikes. Usually, the casualties were in single figures, but the numbers were climbing.

As most of these incidents occurred in the south and east, far from the capital, they rarely made headlines. In Kabul, people reached for more palatable explanations, saying that these incidents were caused by local disputes, not Taliban bombs. But in the weeks before the Canadian patrol was hit, known Taliban spokesmen had phoned the BBC and other media organisations, saying that their suicide bombers had infiltrated the city and vowing to attack the fledgling government and foreign troops.

Before 2001, in more than two decades of war, there had never been any reports of suicide attacks in Afghanistan. The mujahideen fought to the death, but they still wanted to live. Turning humans into bombs was a foreign concept, introduced by Al Qaeda and first deployed to kill Ahmad Shah Massoud two days before the 9/11 attacks.

And then, in early 2003, Osama bin Laden released a tape from hiding calling for 'martyrdom operations' against Western forces and their Afghan allies. Two suicide bombings followed later that year, killing German troops and officers with the new Afghan army.

The day after the attack on the Canadian patrol in January 2004, Bilal and I were reporting on the aftermath of a second suicide attack in Kabul – this time targeting British soldiers serving with the peacekeeping force. The bomber had driven an explosives-packed taxi into their convoy. The attack claimed the life of 23-year-old Private Jonathan Kitulagoda, making him the first British soldier to be killed in combat in Afghanistan since the early 20th century.

The Taliban promised more attacks 'until the foreign infidel forces leave our country'. But they were not in sync with what most Afghans felt right then. As Bilal and I reported on the reaction to the attacks over the following days, the mood in Kabul was summed up by a university student called Mirwais, whom we interviewed. 'Suicide is against the Qur'an. It will not be forgiven even by Allah,' he said. 'The foreign soldiers are here on the will and invitation of the people and the government of Afghanistan. We do not want them to go.'

I hadn't heard anyone say things like that in Iraq, where there was far greater resistance to the US invasion from the start. And it would, in fact, be months before the Taliban managed to carry out another headline-grabbing attack in the Afghan capital. They didn't have the capacity, yet. But in stumbling on the grisly aftermath of the attack on the Canadians, it turned out that Bilal and I had witnessed the first in a deadly pattern.

In the suicide bombings the year before, the explosives had been delivered by Arabs suspected of ties to Al Qaeda. Many people believed that Afghans would never resort to blowing themselves up. But when the full report came out on the suicide attack on the Canadian patrol, it was confirmed that the head on the road belonged to a man from Khost, one of the Taliban's old recruiting grounds, near the border with Pakistan.

* * *

There are so many unforgettable journeys in Afghanistan, but the road from Kabul to the south-eastern province of Paktia always stood out for me. You feel as if you are departing one world and entering another.

I first experienced it after a typically jarring drive south from the capital later that winter in 2004. We left while it was still dark, the acrid tang of household stove fumes compressed by the chill lingering in our nostrils even as we left Kabul behind.

The first sun revealed neat villages beside compact fields irrigated by the winding flow of the Logar River. Then we started climbing steeply to the Tera Pass, the high mountain air seeping into the car and cleansing the staleness inside. Suddenly, at the top, the next world stretched out before us: a high-altitude plain more than 2,000 metres above sea level, guarded by another range of peaks on the far side. Beyond them lay the city of Khost.

From this bridge between worlds, it is easy to look backwards in time. Alexander the Great passed this way more than 2,300 years ago with his Macedonian army, en route to the Indian subcontinent. On the plain below the Tera Pass is a hilltop fort with foundations that were laid by his soldiers. And what is today the small city of Gardez, the capital of Paktia province, grew up around it.

In fact, Alexander would not get that much further east after this. Far from home, his armies had begun to tire by the time they reached the Indus River that runs through today's Pakistan. But with his hilltop redoubt at Gardez, the Macedonian emperor had created one of many way stations for future conquerors. The British took over the fort in the 19th century, followed by Soviet troops a century later.

As we passed by in early 2004, we could see a little thicket of US military communications masts poking up above its walls. American combat forces had been in the area for nearly two years by then, since launching Operation Anaconda. The Shah-i-Kot mountains, the gathering place for the suspected Taliban and Al Qaeda fighters who were the target of the two-week air and ground assault, lie just to the south of Gardez.

On that day, the plain was carpeted in snow, making it look like a vast white desert, dotted here and there with clusters of Pashtun residential compounds. With Abdul driving, Bilal and I were on our way to follow up a story that had seemed almost unbelievable when we had first heard about it. We had come to meet a boy from one of these villages who had been detained by American troops and then sent to the US prison camp at Guantanamo Bay in Cuba, when he was just 11 years old. He had spent nearly two years incarcerated there and had just been released. He was Naqibullah.

We stopped in Gardez for a quick breakfast of eggs, bread and green tea. It was also where we had agreed to link up with Kamal Sadat, a colleague who had travelled over from Khost. At the time, he was covering the eastern provinces for the BBC and Reuters news agency. It was his local connections that had provided us with the necessary security guarantees to make the journey, and which led us to Naqibullah.

After Gardez, we left the tarmac behind, heading for Naqibullah's home village of Sahak, part of a large district called Zurmat. The roads now were trails in the snow; the path decided by whoever had gone first. With Kamal in the lead car, Abdul followed behind, making sure not to deviate, however much we were thrown around inside the car.

Small red flags poked through the snow cover in some places, warning of mines or other volatile war debris. In other places, we saw clusters of wispy flags on spindly poles, marking graveyards. Many of the flags were white, indicating Taliban fighters were buried there.

Sahak wasn't on any map. Bilal, Abdul and Kamal had travelled through the area the week before to find Naqibullah and ask his father if he would meet with us. But with new snow, no signs and few obvious landmarks, today they had to start over.

They navigated the traditional way, pulling up each time they saw a person, testing the directions given by the last and checking that we were still on the way to Sahak. Pashto was the lingua franca here, so the Dari I had started to learn was no help.

In rural Paktia, you don't see houses when you enter a village, but high, mud-and-straw cob walls. Every dwelling is encased by them, reflecting the Pashtun imperatives of protection, privacy and purdah. If we saw a woman on the road, she was always enveloped in a head-to-toe burqa and accompanied by a close male relative or 'mahram'.[1]

When we reached Sahak, our first stop was at the local mosque to find Naqibullah's father, Gul Mohammad. Bilal and Kamal emerged from the one-roomed mosque building with an elderly-looking man dressed in an impressive white turban, his body tightly wrapped in a woollen 'patu', or shawl, against the cold.

Bilal directed him to the front passenger seat, using the honorific 'Mawlawi Sahib'[2] rather than his name. Abdul did the same, as he

---

[1] 'Mahram' is an Arabic word widely used in Dari and Pashto referring to a family member with whom marriage is prohibited.

[2] 'Mawlawi': an honorific for Islamic scholars and commonly used as a term of respect for religious officials. Sahib: 'Sir'.

turned to shake the man's hand, asking after his health and family, before both men touched their right hand to their chests. Even when they are by necessity quick and functional, the rituals of Afghan greeting should never be neglected.

Oil-starved hinges whined as Gul Mohammad let himself in through the door to the family compound. We didn't need to be told to wait outside, while he went ahead to check his wife and daughters were out of sight of the visitors. But his son came out to greet us, giving me a shy handshake as he said, in English, 'How are you?'

Naqibullah was around 13 by then, having spent the start of his teenage years in American captivity. His disturbing journey began in the aftermath of the 2002 Anaconda assault. Rather than delivering the decisive blow that US commanders claimed at the time, it had marked the beginning of a new round of conflict, with the Taliban using the battle to catalyse support for their incipient insurgency.

At the time, most of the movement's leaders and much of its rank and file were taking shelter across the border in Pakistan, recovering from their drubbing in 2001. At Shah-i-Kot, they again sustained heavy casualties, though not as many as the Americans had initially claimed. When word spread through Taliban circles that their comrades had shot down a US helicopter and inflicted heavy losses, it had a rallying effect. The previously little-known leader of the Taliban force at Shah-i-Kot gained iconic status after his escape, earning the nickname 'Black Dragon'.[3] He had won by not losing.

Some Taliban leaders later said that the new jihad began at Shah-i-Kot. And the American response often played into their hands. As they hunted for pockets of Taliban and Al Qaeda support, US operatives launched a series of large-scale raids across the Zurmat district, adopting a dragnet approach.

In the autumn of 2002, Naqibullah was in a nearby village called Musawal, visiting his uncle with his mother. While his

---

[3] Saif-ur-Rehman Mansoor.

mother was inside, he was watching local men on horseback playing a popular local game called 'saange', which involves trying to knock a small object along the ground with a long pole or spear while racing past at speed.

But late in the afternoon, the attention of both horsemen and spectators was distracted by American helicopters overhead, followed by the throb of diesel engines on the ground. Musawal had been surrounded by US soldiers and troops from the new Afghan army.

'They were shouting with loudspeakers, telling everyone to put down their weapons,' Naqibullah said. Most households in rural Afghanistan keep at least one gun for self-defence, so the order was standard practice. With American soldiers standing guard, their Afghan allies proceeded to go through several homes. From what Gul Mohammad later learned from his wife, they were hunting for militants allegedly hiding in the village.

That is not how the raid looked to Naqibullah. 'They took out anyone they felt like arresting, including my uncle. His boys were too young. So, they arrested me. I think they suspected me because I was standing next to some men who had guns,' he said. 'I told them I was innocent, that we were just visiting. I didn't even know how to use a gun.'

His mother was powerless. After binding the boy's hands, the Afghan soldiers pushed her 11-year-old son into one of their vehicles, along with another boy around the same age and several dozen men. For older people there, the raid was reminiscent of a past Soviet tactic of rounding up whole villages if any resident was suspected of sheltering the mujahideen.

The Americans and their Afghan allies applied a similar lens to Zurmat in 2002, seeing it as axiomatic that most people in the district would be on the Taliban's side. It was true that many local men had joined the Taliban – after previously fighting against the Soviets – and some served as officials in its first regime. But in the early 2000s, it was more complicated than that.

Gul Mohammad insisted that he had never been a member of the Taliban himself. In any case, at that point, so soon after the Taliban's defeat, attitudes in the villages were in flux. The narrative that had spread about the battle of Shah-i-Kot had given the Taliban a boost, but they were still a long way from regaining their previous influence and control. Zurmat's inhabitants wanted peace. They were as sick of war as Afghans anywhere in the country. And as Gul Mohammad pointed out, the foreign troops didn't come looking for him or his son. Naqibullah was in the wrong place at the wrong time.

I thought of Bilal's experience as I watched him talking with the imam and his son. He, too, had been detained after being in the wrong place at the wrong time when Kabul fell. For a while, he, too, had been labelled an enemy, partly because of his Pashtun identity. What happened afterwards had depended on his other identity as a budding journalist with connections who could vouch for him.

Naqibullah and his family had none of those connections. When his son was abducted, Gul Mohammad had no idea where he had been taken or even whom to contact to press for his release. His son had simply disappeared.

The Americans who had taken him were motivated by their own cause and narrative: righteous revenge, and the need to protect their homeland against another attack. That they were a foreign force in a foreign land, dealing with people for whom 9/11 meant little or nothing, was a secondary concern, if they thought about it at all. And with that outlook, it was easy to see everyone in a community with a history like Zurmat's as a potential enemy.

Scores of civilians had already died in US air strikes on other Pashtun areas, because of bad intelligence or lack of knowledge of Afghan customs and habits. In one incident in July 2002, pilots killed at least 50 people at a wedding in the southern province of Urozgan, claiming that they had interpreted celebratory gunfire as a Taliban attack on their planes.

The differing motives of their Afghan allies, already demonstrated at Tora Bora, often added further poison to American raids. By the time Naqibullah was captured, a new pattern had emerged, with Afghan commanders exploiting American ignorance of local dynamics to serve their own agendas. They bad-mouthed their rivals, telling the Americans that they were working with the Taliban or Al Qaeda so they would be placed on a US target list.

What prompted the raid on Musawal is unclear. Perhaps the American unit had a lead that there were Taliban there. But as he was being driven away, Naqibullah heard a telling conversation among his Afghan captors. 'They said: "We have picked up a lot of people, we need to let some go." But their commander said: "No, take them to the Americans. Hand them over to them and let them do whatever they want."'

The priority for America's Afghan allies was to please their paymaster, and keep its largesse flowing. There was little incentive either for US military or intelligence officers to second-guess their local helpers. If the wrong person was arrested or killed as a result, US personnel seldom paid any price. The cost to them of *not* acting, on the other hand, if that led to a new attack on the United States, was incalculable. It created an almost unbridgeable chasm in priorities and motives, incentivising aggressive action and ensnaring many other Afghans beside Naqibullah.

Initially, he was held at a joint US and Afghan base in Gardez, where he was kept with other older detainees and suffered regular beatings at the hands of Afghan guards. They also subjected their captives to sleep deprivation. Then he was flown by helicopter to Bagram airbase, where the Americans had converted a Soviet-built aircraft repair hangar into a jail, housing people who had been detained across Afghanistan.

Inside, Naqibullah was interrogated multiple times. One of the American demands was for information on the whereabouts of the Taliban leader who had escaped from Shah-i-Kot. He said he was often beaten and slapped. 'They would ask me the same questions each time and if I said something different the next time, they beat me.' What made the experience even more terrifying for the 11-year-old was that he couldn't see his captors; they always kept him blindfolded in their presence.

By the time we were talking to Naqibullah and his father, details of worse abuses had emerged. Not long after he was held at Bagram, two prisoners died from torture there. In 2003, a man who had voluntarily handed himself in to US forces was beaten to death by a CIA contractor.[4]

After what he thinks was a few weeks at Bagram, Naqibullah was bound and blindfolded once again. He heard the sound of aircraft and helicopters on the base flight line as he was taken out of his prison and then manhandled on to a plane. He had no idea where he was going.

Through whispered conversations, he learned that the other boy captured with him in Musawal was on the plane as well, along with another youngster detained elsewhere. 'Once we stopped somewhere,' said Naqibullah, 'we felt the plane land and someone asked the translator: "Where is this?" And he said: "Turkey."'

The next time the aircraft doors opened, Naqibullah felt a wave of tropical heat wash over him. 'I didn't see anything until they put me in a cell and took my blindfold off.' He was in Cuba.

* * *

Over the course of 2002, the US military coalition conducted many other operations against remnants of the Taliban and Al Qaeda. While the Pentagon resisted deploying NATO-led peacekeeping troops outside Kabul in this early period, it expanded its counter-terrorism forces, concentrating on the Taliban's heartlands in the

---

[4] David Passaro was charged and convicted of the fatal assault, serving six years in jail.

belt of Pashtun majority provinces in the south and east. But it was not all air strikes and raids. In some areas, the coalition took a more deliberative approach, and encountered little or no opposition.

Small units of special forces, from Britain, France and other allied countries, as well as the United States, were deployed in rural towns to build ties with local communities and gather intelligence. Some lived in rented houses with light defences to maximise their contact.

'We were encouraging local people to get involved in the loya jirga process,[5] building schools and all the hearts and minds stuff,' said a former British special forces soldier who served in one of these teams. He was sent to a former Taliban stronghold in southern Afghanistan, wearing local clothes and growing a beard to blend in. They had also been given another task: to look for Stinger missiles, so they could buy them back.

The CIA gave hundreds of these anti-aircraft missiles to the mujahideen to blunt the Soviets' advantage in the air. They had a devastating effect, downing many of their helicopters. But years later, an unknown number of Stingers were still in circulation and the CIA was trying to retrieve them, fearing that now they would be used to shoot down US aircraft.

The British unit put the word out that they were offering $80,000 a piece, and two were handed in. The seller was a former mujahideen commander. The British special forces were the middlemen, passing on the Stinger missile kits to be verified by their US colleagues, before handing over the cash.

More significant, in hindsight, was the reaction to their presence. 'Everywhere we went we had a good reception,' the soldier said. 'We never got into any fights. We never used our weapons.' When the Soviets invaded, they encountered violent opposition from the start; by the equivalent point in their occupation, they were facing a nationwide uprising. But at this stage, despite the counter-productive

---

[5] The 2002 Emergency Loya Jirga gathering.

methods in use in places such as Zurmat, the US-led coalition was not facing popular resistance. Much depended on how this new foreign army behaved next.

* * *

Situated on the southern coast of Cuba, the US prison camp at Guantanamo Bay and its anomalous legal status is a by-product of America's antagonistic relationship with the island nation. The official US position is that it is leasing the land on which the prison sits, under a deal it effectively forced on Cuba in 1903. But when Fidel Castro took power, he called it an illegal occupation, and Havana has refused to cash Washington's cheques ever since.

This unresolved legal tangle made Guantanamo the perfect place for the US military to incarcerate people it captured in its 'war on terror', but whom it refused to recognise as prisoners of war. Instead, they were classified as 'enemy combatants' who could be detained indefinitely and without charge. It also provided the legal space to torture detainees, using what were euphemistically called 'enhanced interrogation measures'. Locked away on the Caribbean coast, prisoners were beyond the reach of anyone's courts. Naqibullah's visit to his uncle had turned into a one-way ticket into a judicial Bermuda triangle.

The three boys were separated from the older prisoners and locked up in a different compound called 'Camp Iguana', so named for the giant lizards roaming the shoreline outside the wire-mesh perimeter. Beyond was open sea. 'We could see nothing else,' he said. 'Not a dry place, or a mountain. There was no way to escape.'

As Naqibullah answered our questions, his sharp, inquisitive eyes were fixed on Bilal. He was dressed in a neat white cap and wore a fraying coat over his long shirt and pants. A little teenage fluff was starting to grow on his lips and chin. He recounted most of his experiences with a calm maturity probably born of his experiences.

But as he remembered his early days at Guantanamo, his composure began to crumble. 'I couldn't believe what had happened,' he continued. 'I didn't understand why I'd been chosen to go there. That was the worst time.' As Naqibullah described how frightened he had been, and how much he missed his family, his father, the imam, nodded in sympathy. But his expression also conveyed a certain pride.

It was while he was being interrogated in his faraway seaside prison that Naqibullah first understood what 9/11 was about and how it had brought the Americans to his country. 'It was the first time I'd seen the video of the towers being attacked by planes,' he explained. Early interrogation sessions would always start with a screening, he said. 'They would say: "These people have done this, and they are in Afghanistan, and that's why we invaded. They killed so many people."' Then they would ask him where the Taliban fighters were.

'They would attach equipment to my fingers and say, "This can tell if you lie."' The Americans could be threatening, but he said he was never beaten or otherwise physically harmed at Guantanamo. It soon became clear that the three boys had little useful information, but this did not lead to their release. And it was only six months after his son was captured that Gul Mohammad learned that he was on the other side of the world, via a letter delivered by the International Committee of the Red Cross, who had been given access to the boys.

But Naqibullah said his treatment did improve. He was moved into a shared cell with the two other boys. A Pashto-speaking teacher was brought in to give them lessons, including some instruction in English.

Then, one day in January 2004, Gul Mohammad got another message from the Red Cross, telling him to make the journey to Kabul to collect his son. When Naqibullah and his cellmates landed at Bagram airbase, Afghan Interior Ministry officials were also there to meet them. They gave the boys a final warning, telling them not to get in touch with the Taliban.

Naqibullah had been back home in Sahak a week when we discovered he had been freed, and Bilal and Kamal tracked him down. In line with normal procedure, the Red Cross had kept the boys' release quiet, but the Americans were also worried about the negative publicity. They had less to worry about than they may have feared.

Gul Mohammad left us for a moment, saying that he was going to find a chicken from among the flock in his yard. He insisted that we stay for lunch. But the bird he selected had other plans and ran for its life, with the imam in hot pursuit. For a moment, Naqibullah's extraordinary story was forgotten as attention switched to the chase, and everyone broke into laughter.

When his father returned with the hen's lifeless body, Bilal asked him how his son's experience in US captivity had affected him. His response was unexpected. 'He has learned to speak English,' Gul Mohammad said, with some satisfaction. 'He has come back with an education. He knows about things.'

If Gul Mohammad was angry about his son's treatment, he didn't say so. Perhaps he thought it safer to withhold his criticisms for his foreign visitors. But he seemed sincere when he said of his son: 'He behaves better with his sisters and brothers, and he shows me more respect.' Naqibullah had seen the world, he continued, travelling to Kabul and to Cuba. And his son even said he missed some aspects of his prison time in Guantanamo. 'The food was good,' he said, 'and they let us play football every day.'

We asked Naqibullah to take us around his side of his village. He tried out a few more of the English words he had learned in his Guantanamo classroom. A crowd of other boys from the village followed us. Attracted by our presence, they had been waiting outside. Everyone had heard about the imam's son who had seen the sea.

One of the boys scooped up some snow and lobbed it at Naqibullah, who sent another snowball sailing back. Soon, they were all careening around a nearby field, alternately ducking or taking aim with another handful of snow. They were dressed alike, in baggy long tops and trousers with crisp white caps on their heads. But Naqibullah was different now. He was a local celebrity. Having had a glimpse of the world beyond Paktia, his outlook had changed. 'I want to go to the city,' he said, before adding that he thought the Americans should compensate him for his imprisonment. 'I want them to help me become a doctor.'

If you transplanted Naqibullah's experience into an American or British context, there would have been few limits on the compensation demands his family could have made for his abduction and illegal imprisonment. They never even received so much as an apology.

Naqibullah and Bilal's stories were very different. Bilal was older, he had learned English, and he was in Kabul, with incomparably better opportunities. Yet the contrast in their experiences was still stark. Both of them had been flown across the world by Western powers, one to be locked up in prison, the other to progress to the next stage of his career.

In that moment, despite the miscarriage of justice they had experienced, the battle for hearts and minds wasn't yet lost on Naqibullah and his family. They still seemed prepared to give the latest foreign army to come to their land a chance to make amends for imprisoning him without charge.

Their ambivalence matched the mood in the rest of the district. Despite Zurmat's reputation as a pro-Taliban area, we had been able to travel there. Afghanistan's black, red and green tricolour – resurrected by the new US-backed Republic – flapped in the breeze on Gul Mohammad's roof – and on many others in the village. It may have been for show. Arguably, it was also a sign of people waiting to see which way the wind would blow.

In the years after we met Naqibullah in his snowbound village, Bilal and I tried to keep in touch, to find out how he was faring and what happened to him next. Through Kamal's contacts, we heard that he had returned to school.

But it became harder to get any message through. Even after mobile phone companies started to extend their service nationwide, places like Zurmat were not a high priority. And as the Taliban stepped up their insurgency, phone masts became one of their targets. Sometimes, they simply switched them off. Within a few years of our visit, the Taliban's white flag was flying again in parts of Zurmat, and it became too risky for us to make the journey there.

Chapter 4

The Kabul Bureau and a View on the Past

The Darulaman Palace in Kabul in the early 2000s, destroyed during the civil war in the 1990s.

Haji, the night guard at the BBC's Kabul bureau, had just shut down the generator and he was walking back from the rickety, open-sided shed at the far end of the garden where it lived. With the noise gone, I could hear the music playing from the radio he held in his hand.

The power cuts in Kabul were as bad as ever. More electricity was being generated, but demand outstripped supply with so many people returning. But it was the end of the day, the load on the grid was falling and so the city power was back. I was settling down with a book on the back terrace of the house, overlooking the garden.

It was always a relief when we could switch off the bureau generator. Its squeaky, diesel-powered engine produced oily fumes that floated into the house and a head-splitting roar that made it difficult to talk, even inside. 'It's as old as Noah's Ark,' was Haji's regular complaint, whenever he asked why the BBC wouldn't upgrade to a newer model.

Before he became the night guard, he was the office driver and a skilled amateur mechanic, so he also took a certain pride in keeping the machine going. Replacing the generator or installing some soundproofing around the shed were always on my to-do list when I lived there, but somehow I never got round to it.

As the background hum of the Kabul streets and Haji's music replaced the diesel roar that summer evening in 2004, there was a succession of screeching noises, then three explosions somewhere in the direction of the US embassy and the presidential palace. Haji paused to listen. 'Rockets,' he said. 'It's nothing.' Then, with a shrug, he carried on back to his room by the front gate, his sandals slapping rhythmically on the stone path.

There had been a series of similar attacks on the centre of Kabul in the weeks before, causing several casualties. Some thought it was the Taliban; some blamed recalcitrant mujahideen factions, unhappy at their stake in the new power balance. Elections were due later that year. No one was sure who was responsible, and no one claimed responsibility. But it was hardly surprising if Haji was unmoved.

When he had first been hired by the BBC, during the civil war in the early 1990s, the city was being rocketed and shelled all day long. You sensed Haji's past in his business-like demeanour and piercing dark eyes, his face framed by a white cap and a carefully tended, intense white beard. Originally from central Afghanistan, he had fled his home during the Soviet occupation. 'There was so much fighting, it was impossible to live,' Haji said. After reaching Kabul, he had found work as a taxi driver.

Though he had a full name, he had been called simply 'Haji' for as long as anyone could remember, as a mark of respect. After the fall of the Taliban, bureau staff clubbed together to pay for him to perform the pilgrimage, so he could make his title official.

While helping past colleagues report on the civil war, Haji had sometimes had to turn his car into an impromptu ambulance to carry away the injured and the dead. In 1994, it was he who had retrieved the body of his colleague, correspondent Mirwais Jalil, after the journalist was murdered.

It was during those years that the BBC had first rented the house in Wazir Akbar Khan to serve as its Kabul bureau, situated on Street 10, a few blocks in from the main road. Only the upper floor was visible from outside, because the building was surrounded by a high stone wall topped by a spiked-iron fence.

Two solid metal gates, with peeling blue paintwork, opened to a parking bay. There was a separate, adjacent pedestrian gate, fitted with a shuttered observation panel and a heavy metal bolt as thick as a large man's thumb. The doorbell ringtone was a tweeting bird. I still hear its chirpy rise and fall when I think of the outside of the house – followed by the sight of Haji's intimidating glare appearing in the frame of the observation window, as he looked out to see who was at the gate.

With its flat roof and spacious back garden, the house was typical of the villa-style homes that lined the neighbourhood's neat grid of streets, most of them built in the peaceful times before the overthrow of King Zahir Shah. It escaped major damage during the wars that followed and although the building's exterior and interior were chipped and faded by the time I lived there, it still retained the aura of better days.

Our generator may have been old, but most people in Kabul dealt with the all-day power cuts without one. In a country in turmoil, the house was a privileged and sometimes claustrophobic bubble. The bureau employed a cook, a housekeeper, a gardener and handyman, two drivers and a guard, as well as Haji covering the evenings and nights.

Happenstance had brought together a group of men of very different backgrounds, from within Afghanistan as well as abroad. As I got to know my co-workers better and heard more about their life stories, they gave me a personal window into their country's revolving history.

The neighbourhood around us provided a reminder of its scope. It was named after Akbar Khan, the man who led the uprising against Britain's colonial garrison in Kabul after its first 19th-century invasion. He was the Wazir,[1] or chief adviser, to his father, Amir Dost Mohammad Khan, whom the British had overthrown, and so his desire for revenge was personal. And it was Wazir Akbar Khan who arranged the massacre that followed, after tricking the British into thinking he would give them safe passage.

Most of the roughly 16,000-strong garrison sent in by the British East India Company were Indians, including the sepoys, or soldiers, and so-called 'camp followers' or support staff, along with their families. All but a couple of hundred were killed or perished from exposure during the retreat, in one of the biggest British military disasters in history. But the colonial administration quickly followed up with a revenge massacre of its own, sending an 'Army of Retribution' to sack Kabul and nearby villages. Thousands of Afghans were killed.[2]

---

[1] Can also be translated as 'minister'. Akbar Khan was the crown prince to Dost Mohammad Khan.

[2] For a full account of the First Anglo-Afghan War launched by the British East India Company, and the resulting massacres – both of the invading British-led force and during its subsequent retaliation – see *Return of a King* by William Dalrymple.

When the Taliban official who lived next door left, the neighbouring house was taken over by one of Zahir Shah's sons. The old elite was moving back in – and so was the new. Ministers in the new government soon settled into other villas in Wazir Akbar Khan.

A large tract of undeveloped land in the adjacent Sherpur district had been snatched up by the warlord class and others with the right connections. Some called the area 'the town of thieves'. Ostentatious mini-palaces with Graeco-Roman-style columns and tinted glass had sprouted up, many funded by profits from drugs smuggling and reselling weapons provided by the West during the anti-Soviet war.

Inside our Street 10 compound, the front door to the house led to a low-ceilinged hallway. The light through a frosted glass panel in the outside wall illuminated a flecked marble staircase, as well as our modern addition to the hallway furniture – a plywood rack filled with helmets, body armour and bulky green battle-zone medical kits. Three doors led off the hall: one to a combined dining and living room, one to the office with its satellite phone and other broadcasting paraphernalia and one to the kitchen, which also had another door leading out to the room used by Haji and the drivers.

Abdul always did the later driving shift so he could study in the daytime, as he had returned to medical college. In the office, Bilal had a desk beneath a set of shelves set into the wall where he kept lists of all his contacts. By 2004, Jahan was carving out a role as office assistant and he was now officially on the payroll. I taught him the basics of using a computer, but he was soon showing me shortcuts and began to help with tasks like compiling the bureau's monthly accounts.

The living and dining room gave out on to a covered terrace and a garden, the anti-shatter film on the glass giving the view a mirage's shimmer. The door to the outside had a stiff catch, and prising it free made the film-covered windows rattle in their metal frames. That sound also had another meaning. It was often the first signal that a bomb had exploded, when the blast wave slapped against the glass.

The back terrace was a place of escape, and my favourite part of the house. We had several charpoys, or rope beds, set up there, covered with carpets and thick cushions known as 'toshaks'. The space served multiple functions: a reception area for guests and a meeting room to discuss a story and plan a trip, and a classroom when my language teacher came. When it was quiet, I went there to read or think, with a glass of green tea.

From my place on the charpoy, I looked out on the roses and geraniums that our gardener brought into bloom each spring around Nowruz, the new year in the Persian calendar. In summer, the terrace was the best place to escape the heat. When it got colder, we huddled round the flames in a fire pit made from a cut-down oil drum. And, over the years, the terrace was also the place where I heard about the past lives of my friends and colleagues.

* * *

Abdul was just old enough to have a faint memory of his country at peace. His early childhood was spent living in a hillside village near Kabul, where his father was a respected local doctor. He couldn't forget the moment everything changed, when he had to flee home in the middle of the night. It was the spring of 1980, during the early stages of the Soviet occupation, when he was about six.

He remembered being woken by his mother pulling his hand in the dark. His sister and other brother, a year or two older, were already awake. In a whisper, Abdul's mother told them to be quiet and follow her and their father out through the window in their room and on to the roof. Everyone was dressed already. They slept in their clothes because it was still cold at night.

From the front gate, Abdul heard shouts. Someone was kicking on the door, and demanding entry. Abdul's parents helped him and his siblings cross a gap between their house and the one next door, owned by relatives, before dropping down into their yard. They were saved by the traditional high walls around their home. The intruders couldn't see them from outside. They had got out just in time.

Several armed men broke down the gate and then ransacked the house. 'They collected everything in our yard and set it all on fire,' Abdul said. 'My parents told me that later. I just remember being very scared and my mother holding our hands, telling us to stay quiet.'

The intruders were from a local mujahideen cell. They had come to find and kill Abdul's oldest brother after hearing that he had signed on with the Moscow-supported Afghan army as a cadet. He was in Kabul at the time, but the mujahideen hadn't given up pursuing the family. The next morning, Abdul's father found a so-called 'night letter' – a warning – pinned to the broken gate, ordering him to pay the equivalent of $50 in local currency, a lot of money in 1980. Otherwise, they would return for him as well.

Abdul's village lay at the foot of some of the highest mountains around Kabul, in an area called Paghman, known for its orchards of pomegranates, apples and almonds, and elegant groves of poplar trees. Historically, it was also a popular retreat for Afghan monarchs, including Zahir Shah. One of his predecessors, Amanullah Khan, who secured Afghanistan's independence from the British, had an elaborate hillside garden constructed there in the 1920s.

Inspired by a visit he made to France, it featured an ornate entry arch modelled on Paris's Arc de Triomphe. King Amanullah's garden was emblematic of other Western-influenced changes he wanted to make, including improving the rights and living conditions of women.[3]

His wife, and later Queen, Soraya Tarzi, both spearheaded many of these changes and came to symbolise them. Educated abroad, she

---

[3] King Amanullah's reforms included outlawing forced and child marriages and dowry, restricting polygamy, making veil-wearing optional and promoting female education.

campaigned for girls to have the same access to schooling as boys and spoke out against mandatory dress codes for women, including being veiled outside their homes. Queen Soraya often dressed in Western-style clothes and also challenged the long-standing precedent that women should not be seen by unrelated men by appearing, unveiled, with her husband in public.[4] But King Amanullah's architectural follies in the shadow of the Hindu Kush also came to symbolise the dangers of trying to change Afghan society too quickly.

He made public access to the Paghman garden conditional on wearing Western-style clothes. When he called a special assembly there in 1928 to discuss his reform agenda, he demanded the same dress code for all the delegates coming from across the country. Queen Soraya was there, too. Conservative rural clerics were enraged, and it sparked a violent uprising, leading to Amanullah's overthrow a year later. Just over a half-century after that, Paghman became a locus of rebellion yet again, this time against the Soviet occupation.

In the view of the mujahideen, Abdul's family were local collaborators who had sided with the infidel enemy by allowing their eldest son to join the Soviet-backed Afghan army. Many Afghans had indeed taken the communist side, for ideological reasons. Abdul's father was no communist. But, as the head of the family, he felt trapped by bad options. 'He didn't like the Russians and didn't want

---

[4] Queen Soraya's precedent-breaking public appearance did not endure. Some 70 years later, when the US-backed Republic government was in power, it remained politically and socially risky for male Afghan leaders to appear with their wives in public. On the few occasions that Zinat Karzai, the wife of former President Hamid Karzai, did actually show her face, she was not with her husband and always wearing a hijab. https://www.bbc.com/news/world-asia-21699353 Rula Ghani, the wife of former President Ashraf Ghani, is a Christian (from Lebanon), making her more controversial in the eyes of conservative Muslims. She was slightly more prominent, but would not appear with her husband at major public events, such as election rallies.

them in our country,' explained Abdul, as we were talking one day about his childhood years. But neither did he want the US-backed mujahideen running his life and deciding his family's future.

The group the family believed had targeted them was led by a hard-line Islamist[5] known for keeping several young wives. He would later give refuge to Osama bin Laden and back the Taliban. The bulk of his fighters were men from rural areas linked by kinship and tribe.

They may have been able to recite many verses from the Qur'an, but few could read or write, and they didn't impress Afghans from an urban, educated background, including a Kabul-trained doctor. 'My father saw the mujahideen as illiterate people who were against progress,' said Abdul. They had reinforced that impression a few weeks before invading the family's home, when they abducted and murdered a local teacher and dumped his body in a well.

Even before Soviet troops and advisers arrived, the Afghan communist regime had embarked on a campaign to remake Afghan society, introducing compulsory universal education. Dress codes for women were also abolished and child marriage banned. But it was accompanied by violent repression, stirring up the same kind of aggressive culture war that King Amanullah had faced. Mujahideen leaders depicted communist reforms as an atheist battering ram pummelling Afghan traditions and Islam itself. Teachers therefore became a target.

For the Reagan administration, then stepping up its aid to such mujahideen groups in cooperation with Pakistan, these were small

---

[5] Hezb-e Islami Khalis, led by Mawlawi Mohammad Yunus Khalis. He studied Islam at the Darul Uloom Haqqania seminary in Pakistan, from which many Taliban figures would later emerge. One of his sub-commanders was Mullah Mohammad Omar, the Taliban founder. In 1987, President Reagan received Khalis at the White House along with Zalmay Khalilzad https://www.youtube.com/watch?v=c9RWtx8myQc

details that mattered little relative to the big picture priority of bleeding Moscow. The US was not weighing their positions on gender equality and education.

'We supported the most extreme elements because we believed they fought the hardest and they would fight the longest,' acknowledged Zalmay Khalilzad, who was part of the team overseeing US policy on Afghanistan at the time. And most of the world – outside the Soviet bloc – saw the conflict as a straightforward moral struggle, with the Afghan mujahideen 'the good guys', defending their country against Russian-led imperialism.

After the arson attack and the warning letter on the gate, there could be only one response for Abdul's family. Within hours, they were on the winding road down from Paghman to Kabul, taking refuge with other members of their extended family. They spent the next few years living in a relative's house, before his father was able to afford a new place of their own.

Inside the bubble of Soviet-occupied Kabul, the war was far away, in the countryside. But Abdul and his family lived in a ruthless police state, enforced by the Afghan KGB, known as the KHAD. Its leader at the time was a charismatic and ambitious physician from the eastern province of Paktia. Mohammad Najibullah never actually practised medicine, and he had earned the sobriquet of 'the butcher' because of the thousands of Afghans who had been detained, tortured and executed on his watch.

But in the classic formula, if you stayed out of politics, you were left alone. And as he grew older, Abdul decided that he wanted to be a doctor, following in his father's path.

* * *

Bilal was born sometime in 1983, a bit less than a decade after Abdul, but still in a period when the country was under communist rule and Soviet occupation. Yet that police state gave him a relatively comfortable childhood, living with his parents, two brothers, one sister and paternal grandparents. 'We had everything we needed. Enough food, and electricity. My family didn't support the communists. But we felt safe.'

His father had a decently paid job as an administrative official at Kabul University, which allowed him to save and build a two-floor home for his family. 'I had my own room and a television. I remember watching cartoons,' said Bilal, reminiscing one afternoon on the terrace at Street 10. The war was something that happened in the adults' conversations, or on the airwaves. But the words and phrases he overheard became the lexicon of daily life and, as he got older, the war also got closer.

The West referred to the mujahideen as 'rebels' and 'freedom fighters', who were defending their country against Soviet imperialism. On the bulletins from state-controlled Radio Afghanistan, Bilal heard them described as terrorists and gangsters. It was the Soviet-backed Afghan government that was 'fighting imperialism', the station's listeners were told, because of the West's backing for the mujahideen, who 'were drinking the people's blood'.

The communist regime's statements were all lies, his grandfather told him. 'He also warned me never to repeat that to anyone outside our family.' Bilal's family got their information from foreign broadcasters. The whines and whistles of shortwave radio as his father and grandfather searched for the best signal were the backdrop to Bilal's childhood during the communist era. And they had to gather close, not just because of poor reception, but to avoid being overheard.

Their listening habits were a taboo subject outside the home, because the BBC and other foreign broadcasts were banned by the communist regime. Bilal's father told him about two relatives who had been detained and beaten by the KHAD in the past, after agents had received a tip-off from one of their ubiquitous informers.

At school, Bilal received a daily dose of pro-Moscow messaging. 'Before lessons, we had to sing Soviet songs and praise Lenin. We were taught that communism will give you land and a house.' American democracy, on the other hand, was simply the 'gun and the dollar'.

His classes were mixed, as the communists had outlawed gender segregation, and boys and girls wore European-style clothes. When he got back home, Bilal would change into the baggy cotton shirt and trouser combination he was used to. When his grandfather heard that he was being forced to sing communist hymns, he told him not to join in. But Bilal had no choice. He learned to keep secrets, and move between different and often diametrically opposed worlds.

While Bilal had an urban childhood, his family had rural roots. His mother came from a Dari-speaking Tajik community in the north. His father was born in a village in the majority Pashtun province of Kunar, in eastern Afghanistan. Bilal's grandfather was a prominent elder in one of the major tribes there, though regarded as a relative liberal for someone in his position. He was the first from the village to be educated and later won a scholarship to study in India. And while he opposed the communists, he persuaded fellow elders in his district to open classrooms to local girls for the first time.

By the time Bilal was in his second year at school, the conflict had become a proxy civil war on all sides. With the departure of the last Soviet troops in February 1989, the Americans, Pakistanis and Saudis had achieved their goal of ejecting the USSR, but they still wanted their mujahideen allies to overthrow the communist regime in Kabul, now led by Mohammad Najibullah. Moscow was equally committed to propping him up, airlifting in arms, fuel and food, as well as leaving behind military advisers. Other neighbouring states, including Iran, and regional powers such as India, were also arming and funding their own proxies.

Najibullah gained the upper hand, repelling a mujahideen bid to seize the eastern city of Jalalabad. This put the United States and

Osama bin Laden on the same, losing, side, as the Saudi took part in the battle with his own Arab fighters. The CIA and Pakistan's ISI were incensed by the defeat, and even more determined to finish off the Afghan strongman. 'We want to see Najibullah strung up by a light pole,' was how one CIA operative is reported to have put it at the time.[6] Words that would prove grimly prophetic.

Three years later, the wily Najibullah was still clinging on, having repackaged himself as an Afghan nationalist defending the country against malign Pakistani influence. It was this period that rebuilt his reputation in the eyes of many Afghans, thereby also making him a sworn enemy for Pakistan's generals. The implosion of the Soviet Union cut off Moscow's support and grounded the Afghan air force, which had been critical to blunting the mujahideen's advance. After that, Najibullah's days in power were numbered.

It has become conventional wisdom, even among many Afghans, that the nation can unite only against an invader. Once the threat is gone, they return to fighting each other. When Najibullah was overthrown in April 1992, mujahideen leaders proved this stereotype wrong, as a majority of them signed an accord for a peaceful transition of power and an interim unity government. It could have worked, if not for the influence of Pakistan's ISI.

Under the deal, their closest mujahideen ally, the hard-line Islamist Gulbuddin Hekmatyar, would have become prime minister. But that was not good enough for his Pakistani patrons, because the powerful defence minister's post was allotted to the commander they most feared, Ahmad Shah Massoud. Hekmatyar refused to sign the accord.

---

[6] 'Light pole' meaning lamp post or street light in British English. As told to US journalist Robert Parry https://consortiumnews.com/2013/04/07/hollywoods-dangerous-afghan-illusion/

It was around that time that Abdul was told that he had won a scholarship to study medicine in India. War had never stopped him from trying to plan for peace. 'It was my dream,' he said. 'Before the exam, I used to wake up at 3 o'clock in the morning and study until 7 o'clock. My father was so happy when I told him I was going to India.'

While preparing for the exam, he had lived in dormitory accommodation at Kabul University on the western side of the city. He stayed on there while he lined up the necessary paperwork to travel to Delhi.

But then one night, he was jolted awake by the crack and whistle of gunfire nearby. Then he heard shouting and crashing sounds. Seconds later, a band of heavily armed mujahideen burst into his dormitory, ordering all the students out of bed at gunpoint. They had overrun western Kabul and were on the rampage. 'They took everything, all the money we had and anything else they thought was valuable,' said Abdul. 'They just left us with our clothes.'

Having refused to sign the power-sharing accord, Hekmatyar had attempted to seize control by covertly infiltrating his forces into the city, prompting other factions to advance when they realised what he was doing. The battle for the capital had begun, and Abdul and his fellow students were caught up in it. 'We will march into Kabul with our naked sword,' Hekmatyar was heard telling Massoud in a radio call, when the latter tried to persuade him to hold back.

Abdul and his fellow students were incredibly lucky to be spared. He was from a Sunni Pashtun background, and the group that overran his dormitory were Shia Hazaras. Within months, ethnic clashes between Hazara and Pashtun mujahideen would leave carnage in the streets.

When it got light, Abdul walked to the house where his sister lived with her husband and young children and told them what had happened. He was devastated. 'I knew there would be no trip to Delhi,' he said. His sister gave him some money so he could get home.

In Bilal's part of the city, the takeover was less violent, but just as sudden. One morning, the main road near their home was filled with columns of tanks and armoured vehicles carrying hard-faced men with thick beards. 'Many people went out on the streets to welcome them,' Bilal remembered. 'But we were worried too.'

The suspicion was mutual. The European-style clothing that had become commonplace among Kabulis under Najibullah's rule – men in suits and ties, women in dresses and even short skirts – looked alien to the mujahideen, who had been fighting in the countryside for years.

Few had ever been to Kabul, the epicentre of the godless communism they had been waging jihad to destroy. The atmosphere changed quickly. Many women stopped going to work. Bilal's sister stopped going to school, staying at home to help their mother instead. Suits and dresses were put away in favour of more traditional clothes.

The mujahideen takeover left Kabul divided into ethnic and sectarian blocks, demarcated by checkpoints decorated with posters of their leaders. The Tajik-dominated forces under Massoud had a dominant position, controlling most of the strategic heights and government buildings, which lie closer to the northern gates of the city, from which they entered. They were also well armed with massive quantities of Soviet weapons that they had captured as they overran Bagram and other communist bases during their advance on the capital.

Hekmatyar's forces, by contrast, were far from the centre in the southern and eastern suburbs. But in the summer of 1992, he launched another bid to seize power, urged on by the ISI, letting loose volleys of unguided rockets on the city's tightly packed neighbourhoods.

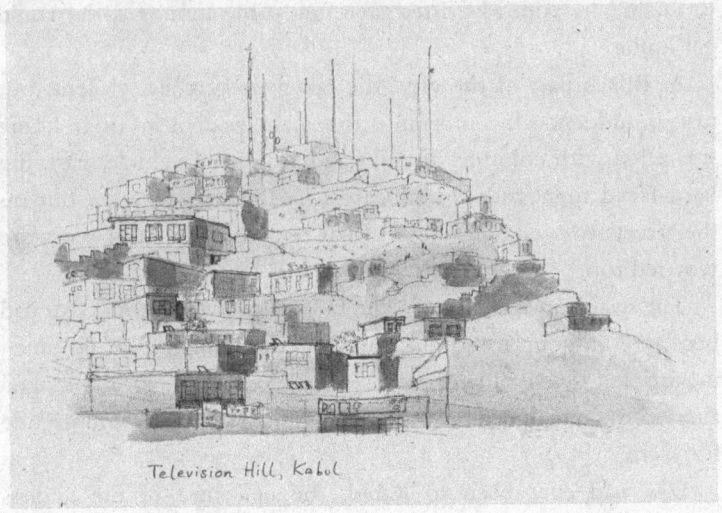

Television Hill, Kabul

Massoud's forces hit back from Television Hill, which bisects the city. The Uzbek warlord Abdul Rashid Dostum controlled the airport and joined in with captured Soviet warplanes, while a Saudi-sponsored commander went to war with Iranian-backed Shia Hazara factions in western Kabul. The Kabul Intercontinental was a key battleground. Around a dozen different factions were involved, many of which switched sides as the fighting progressed.

Front lines changed like tides, suddenly leaving civilians from one ethnicity stranded and at the mercy of vengeful fighters from another. Women and both girls and boys were routinely raped. The city was trapped in a spiral of Hobbesian terror, each new atrocity provoking the next.

Over nearly a decade of Soviet occupation, Kabul had sustained only minor damage. Just a year into the mujahideen's victory, large areas of the city had already been flattened, leaving thousands dead and many more homeless and maimed. But after years of micro-managing Afghanistan's fate, Moscow and Washington had lost interest and turned their backs.

The location of Jahan's house left him and his family dangerously exposed. The mujahideen rocket position on top of the hill above the family cottage had a commanding view over eastern Kabul, looking towards the airport. Everyone had used it at some point: Indian sepoys under British colonial command and Soviet soldiers in the 1980s. And in the early 1990s, the hill was a constant target of rival mujahideen factions.

The unguided Soviet rockets they fired could land anywhere. A relative's house was destroyed by one barrage. 'Three boys living near us were killed in another attack,' Jahan said, shaking his head. The family retreated to a makeshift bomb shelter near the city's military hospital. He was a child then, but he remembers being there day after day, never leaving.

Like Bilal, Jahan comes from a mixed Pashtun and Tajik background. Years later, when we talked about his experience of living through the civil war, Jahan refused to take sides and ascribe blame. 'We have a saying: "With one hand, we cannot make a sound." It means we cannot work alone; we have to work together.'

Abdul was less forgiving. 'It was the mujahideen who brought this thinking about different groups to Kabul – Pashtun, Hazara or Tajik,' he said. 'Before that, we were all just Afghans.' Not everyone would agree with that – Afghanistan's ethnic fault lines had existed before. But there is no doubt that they became more pronounced during and after the civil war. And it was the civil war that spelled the decline of Kabul's once thriving Sikh community, which could trace its origins back to the 15th century. Most of its estimated 200,000 members fled around that time, and only a few thousand later returned.

After being driven from their home in Paghman, Abdul's family suffered a second time at the hands of the mujahideen. Another brother was killed when the plane he was travelling in with four other family members was shot down by mujahideen fighters in eastern Afghanistan in 1988, just a year before the Soviet withdrawal.

Abdul and his family spent the early period of the civil war hunkered down at home. For days and sometimes weeks at a time, they didn't leave the house, interpreting the sounds of the conflict so they knew when to run for the shelter. When the noises subsided, they ventured out to see if they could find any shops still selling food and other essentials.

On the other side of the city, Bilal and his family were living the same fragile, day-to-day existence. 'We stored as much food as we could as we didn't know how long it would be before we could get out again,' said Bilal. The fighting was all around them, and he lived in a state of almost constant terror. Though many of the people they knew had fled to Pakistan, his father and grandfather wanted to hang on. They were praying the situation would improve.

The rest of Afghanistan fragmented as well, with commanders carving out mini-statelets around the country. Helped by their superpower-donated arsenals, many built up sizeable criminal empires with multiple revenue streams; selling off surplus weapons, smuggling drugs, timber and minerals, or robbing travellers at road-side checkpoints. They were the law.

Within two years of Najibullah's ousting, Kabul's population had fallen by three-quarters, to fewer than 500,000. Most first fled to Peshawar, where the ill-fated peace accord had been signed, adding to the vast numbers of Afghan refugees already there. Yet again, Pakistan felt the impact of its neighbour's wars, and of its own role in fuelling them.

Sometime in 1993, Bilal and his family joined the flight from Kabul as well. Once they crossed the border, the UN Refugee Agency gave them a tent, some bedding, and a few other essentials to get going. Local Pakistanis also helped out. But it was soon clear that this would not be enough and that even though he was not yet 10, Bilal had to find work.

Bilal, Jahan and Abdul recounted these memories during many conversations at the Kabul bureau in the early and mid-2000s over many cups of tea. It was an education for me and I found it humbling to listen to their stories, imbued with so many layers of psychological trauma, yet also with their determination to survive and move on.

That finely tuned instinct for survival was lodged in the soul of anyone who had endured the civil war. There were negative consequences, too; promoting a short-term mindset that tended to exclude or downgrade longer-term thinking. It also entrenched the narratives of different ethnic and militia groups, polarising communities even after the fighting was over. But what also struck me about the stories Bilal, Jahan and Abdul told me was how little Western governments paid attention to that period of Afghanistan's story, even as they were trying to reset and rebuild the country.

After its trauma was effectively exported to the rest of the world with the 9/11 attacks, Afghanistan was habitually labelled a 'failed state'. But there was rarely much effort by the outside world to understand how it had become so, and to design policies accordingly. Even though the United States had been involved in that past, what mattered was the humbling of the Soviet Union and the new war that started in 2001. The civil war in between, which dominated Afghan consciousness, was treated by Westerners as an interlude.

It was a selective reading of history and another example of the 'graveyard of empires' mindset, reducing Afghanistan to a stage on which the interests of larger powers played out, not those of its people. But it was Afghanistan that had become the graveyard, and those past years of darkness would condition many Afghans' outlook in the decades afterwards.

* * *

In early 1994, the BBC funded the creation of a radio soap opera for Afghan audiences whose title translates as *New Home, New Life*.

Loosely modelled on *The Archers*, the broadcaster's long-running domestic radio drama about life in rural Britain, it swapped a fictional English farming community for three Afghan villages. The characters included families and individuals who represented a cross-section of society and experience – among them refugees, a widow and her sons, and a cantankerous landlord.

Like its UK counterpart, *New Home, New Life* combined entertainment with education, but with a more life-and-death edge. Its storylines frequently hinged on avoiding landmines and reducing child mortality. The broadcast format was particularly well suited to Afghanistan, with its high levels of illiteracy. At its heart, it was about 'telling engaging stories to solve real-life problems,' said John Butt, the soap's energetic co-founder and early driving force.

Tall and gregarious, with an infectious chuckle and voluminous white beard, John Mohammad Butt, to give him his full name, was a story himself. He was born in the West Indies, packed off to a Catholic boarding school in Britain aged nine, and then became a hippie, criss-crossing South Asia before studying at an Islamic seminary in India and becoming its first and only Western-born mullah. He remembers spending his first trip across Afghanistan in 1970, then aged 20, travelling in the boot of a post bus filled with hay.

After settling for a few years in Pakistan, where he formally converted to Islam, he picked up Urdu and Pashto. He then returned to Afghanistan in the mid-1970s, where he learned Dari, and he was beginning his studies to become a mullah when he was thrown in jail.

King Zahir Shah had been overthrown the year before and the new regime was reflexively suspicious of this young British Muslim convert on his own in Kabul. 'No one could believe that an Englishman could become a mullah without being a spy,' Butt said. After 18 months inside, where he initially earned his keep by cooking for fellow inmates, local diplomats secured his release. He admitted he could have called for their help earlier. 'I was being very idealistic, and I said, "I'm not going to call the British Embassy."'[7]

After boarding school – which he had tried to run away from – Butt had felt that taking to the hippie trail was his only option. The precepts drummed into him by his Jesuit teachers also put him on the path to embracing Islam. 'Who made the Pope infallible? These were things that I had doubts about, growing up at a Catholic school in England, and I found that the Qur'an addressed these questions in a way that struck a chord.'

He spent six years studying Islam at the Deoband seminary in India, the intellectual wellspring of the purist Deobandi school of thought that the Taliban would later claim as their inspiration. The seminary has dissociated itself from Taliban ideology, however, and Butt is no fundamentalist, as ready with a line from a Bob Dylan song as the pages of the Qur'an.

After graduating as a mullah from the seminary, in 1984, he became a journalist, seeing a natural overlap between reporting and the storytelling traditions of Islam, such as the hadiths (the sayings of the Prophet Muhammad). In 1992, as Najibullah's regime fell, he was in Kandahar reporting for the BBC's Pashto service. When the BBC advertised a job to set up a radio soap opera in Peshawar, Butt's idiosyncratic résumé made him the perfect candidate.

As he built up his roster of actors and writers for the Afghan *Archers*, he had the pick of Afghan talent to choose from. Much of Kabul's cultural community had ended up in Peshawar, among the hundreds of thousands of new refugees pushed out by the civil war.

It was at an early meeting in the city to solicit ideas from aid agencies that the soap's title was born, Butt recalled. 'This man came up to me at the end and said, "Your new programme is called *New Home, New Life*." It was perfect, but then he left. I don't know who

---

[7] Interviews with the author.

he was, and I never saw him again,' he said. 'The beginning of *New Home, New Life* was very much like that: on a wing and a prayer.'

Within months, it had become appointment listening across Afghanistan and in border refugee communities such as Peshawar. Crowds gathered to listen whenever it was on, around anyone who had a radio. And it had a measurable impact; an early storyline covering landmines led to a dramatic drop in injuries.

The series began with a family of Afghan refugees deciding to return to their village after the mujahideen had finally taken over in Kabul. But on the way they end up being robbed and fleeced at gunpoint by one of the many mujahideen factions robbing travellers. For many listeners, Butt explained, it sent the message that it was still too early to think about returning.

New Home, New Life became part of Afghan life. One day Butt met a former mujahideen commander who had ended up aligning with the Taliban. 'He was laughing and he said, "Oh, you run that show, do you? That *New Home, New Life* ruined us commanders!"' Butt realised that the commander was referring to the episode in which the returning refugees were robbed.

The soap opera format provided Afghans with a mirror on their lives, said Butt, allowing them 'to see themselves in the characters and laugh at themselves'. By the time the Taliban took power in 1996, surveys showed that some 14 million Afghans, or around two-thirds of the population, were regularly tuning in to the thrice-weekly broadcasts in Pashto and Dari. When one character, Khair Mohammad, had to be killed off because his real-life actor was moving on, the production team received stacks of condolence letters and many people held mourning ceremonies.

John Butt learned from Taliban contacts that some hardliners wanted to ban the soap, unhappy about many of the storylines, and at hearing so many women's voices. The reason they lost the battle, Butt believes, is because of one particularly influential fan. 'I was told by one source that "people in the highest echelons of the Taliban leadership are listening to it." My source did not mention him by name, but I inferred that he meant Mullah Omar.'

After the Taliban were overthrown, *New Home, New Life* came home itself, with the actors and production team moving to Kabul and the stories reflecting the new times. Now, the characters were discussing the benefits of taking part in the loya jirga and elections. By then, John Butt had moved on, but many of the voices Afghans knew so well were still there.

I visited the team in the early 2000s, while I was living in Kabul. Watching the *New Home, New Life* actors recording another episode through the glass of the studio control room was a profound experience when you realised the role they played in bringing Afghans together across linguistic and ethnic divides.

Haji and other long-time staff in the bureau had been avid listeners since the beginning. But after the fall of the Taliban, listenership to *New Home, New Life* had started to decline. Tastes were changing and the programme was facing growing competition from the host of new media outlets that had started up.

Sitting on the terrace of the house at Street 10, I was more likely to overhear music from one of the new commercial stations coming from Haji's radio. It was a new era and new stories were being told.

Chapter 5

Trapped by Britain's Bequest: The Divide between Kabul and Afghanistan

Farzana's Tehran childhood in the cottage that her parents rented from their plant and flower seller employer was damp, cramped but also musical. They tuned in to local radio stations broadcasting Iranian music, and they had a collection of songs by Afghan singers on cassette.

One of their favourites was a wistful old ballad called 'The Flower Seller Girl', about an Afghan girl trying to find buyers for her blooms in a city street. 'My parents always used to sing along when they played it, or hum the tune to themselves,' Farzana said. 'It's one of the sounds of my early years.'

It was a song from Afghanistan's past and, for her parents, a constant, present connection to home. In 2004, Farzana and her sister Shireen at last got a chance to understand that pull for themselves.

Her parents had been listening to the entreaties of relatives and friends who had already returned, who told them: 'Come. It's safe.' They had also been following the news and listening to *New Home, New Life*, as the soap covered the experiences of the latest returnees. With Afghanistan's first presidential elections due later that year, their parents decided it was time to join them. At last, they could dispense with their daughters' fake identity cards. Farzana and Shireen could be Afghan again.

The route they took to their parents' birthplace in the southern province of Ghazni meant going through Kandahar, long known as the home of Afghanistan's national fruit. 'My dad had told me so much about the pomegranates there, and then he bought us some.' They were the best Farzana had ever had.

However, life on the edge of Ghazni's provincial capital was not so sweet at first. They arrived in summer, and although Farzana was used to hot temperatures in Tehran, she found the heat and dust of the semi-desert plain surrounding Ghazni oppressive. She kept falling ill.

Farzana's struggle to adjust led to an early taste of Kabul. Her parents sent her to stay with an uncle who lived in the capital with his family and to go to school there, hoping her health would improve in the higher altitude climate.

To be sent to Kabul, after hearing so much about it, sounded like a fairy tale to Farzana. The actual sight of the broken capital, not so much – especially for someone who had come from the metropolis of modern Tehran. But Farzana was buoyed up by the mood.

'We all believed then that Afghanistan had a prosperous future; that we were done with all those years of war. I remember my schoolteachers wearing bright clothes and make-up. They were relaxed and open, wearing their headscarves around their necks when they were teaching.' Farzana didn't wear a scarf at all and, like many other girls in her part of Kabul, regularly went out dressed in jeans and a T-shirt – unthinkable just a few years earlier. The signature touch to her look was a pair of purple sunglasses that her father had bought for her. Farzana wore them everywhere.

* * *

More than 3 million Afghans had returned home by 2004. Most had made the journey from across the border in Pakistan or Iran. But there were many others who left behind settled lives further afield, drawn by the pull of home and the hope that it would become freer and more stable. Saad Mohseni, along with his brothers and sister, was among them.

They were representatives of the first big 20th-century Afghan exodus, provoked by the Soviet invasion. As a schoolboy, he had witnessed the communist coup in 1978, narrowly escaping injury in the fighting. By the time Russian troops overran Kabul two years later, he was in Tokyo, where his father was serving as a diplomat. He then won asylum for his family in Australia, and by the time of the September 11 attacks, Saad had become a successful banker there.

But along with his siblings, Saad Mohseni had an itch to return to the country they had only known as children, to help it rebuild. 'When you have two brothers, and one is sick, you tend more to your sick brother than your healthy brother,' Saad said in an interview at the time. 'We love both countries, but Afghanistan needs us a lot more than Australia does.'

They set up a media company which launched the country's first 24-hour commercial music and talk radio station. Called Arman

FM – which translates as 'hope' or 'wish' – it offered a mix of Afghan, Indian and Western music, and entertainment news and gossip, delivered by male and female DJs. It was soon winning large audiences. 'People had been deprived of entertainment,' said Mohseni, 'and Afghans have a zest for music and joking and storytelling.' He was a natural storyteller himself. With his signature shock of curly hair, he had become a fixture of the new Kabul scene.

Younger Afghans made up the bulk of their new listeners – with more than two-thirds of the country's population under 25, that was hardly surprising – but they attracted older age groups too, happy to have Afghan music on the radio again. Haji and other colleagues in the Kabul bureau were among them. When the station added call-in shows and invited song requests, a novelty for Afghan audiences, they asked Jahan to write up their choices and drop them in at Arman's offices. Nostalgia was back. He said: 'They were always asking for songs by Ustad Hamahang,' an Afghan singer who had become famous in the 1970s.

Mohseni and his team then launched a television channel called Tolo, Dari for 'Sunrise'. It broadcast hard news, locally produced dramas and Indian soaps, albeit with the midriffs of the actresses pixelated. Later, they added a *Pop Idol*-style talent show.

Other new commercial channels joined the fray, transforming the Afghan mediascape, but there was a backlash. Conservatives were outraged by the sound of male and female hosts chatting and laughing together on Arman FM. Opposition crystallised around an attempt by the state broadcaster to freshen up its own output by screening 1960s-era tapes of performances by Afghan female singers.

The scratchy, celluloid footage that Radio Television Afghanistan (RTA) dug out of its archive was certainly not risqué. The artists wore body-covering dresses and headscarves and looked away from the camera as they sang in front of soft-landscape backdrops. But religious traditionalists on the Afghan Supreme Court – brought into being as a result of the Western-backed constitution – painted the broadcasts as a threat to Islamic custom, public morals and social harmony, and demanded RTA pull them from their schedule.

Mohseni batted away criticism that he was lowering standards, and pointed to their surveys showing that listeners preferred the 'colloquial banter' of the station's presenters over the more formal styles of the state radio channel or the BBC. If people didn't like it, 'they could just switch it off.'

The dispute over the old singers' tapes attracted the attention of an Afghan diva among the new returnees, who spoke out to condemn the Supreme Court move. More than a half-century earlier, Mirmen Parveen had featured in a milestone moment for the state broadcaster when it invited her to become the first Afghan woman to sing on air.

It was only Radio Kabul then, the signal limited to the capital region. And Mirmen Parveen was actually her stage name, because it was seen as dishonourable in Afghanistan's patriarchal culture for her to use her real one, Khadija Rahim Ziayai. But the name Parveen stuck and she went on to become a local celebrity, performing on television as well when it started up, and at concerts in India and Russia.

'She is the sound of my past,' was the comment of the wife of an Afghan friend when I asked around for opinions before going to meet Parveen. 'Please tell her, "Everyone loves her."' When the civil war broke out in the 1990s, she fled to Peshawar, like many other members of Kabul's artistic community, before returning soon after the fall of the Taliban.

Mirmen Parveen was into her eighties by then. But when Bilal and I arrived at her home, she appeared undimmed either by age or her prodigious smoking habit. The odour greeted us at the door before she did, and she was never without a cigarette while we were there. That, too, was atypical for Afghan women.

The song that Parveen chose for her first outing on Radio Kabul was 'Dokhtar Gul Ferosh' or 'The Flower Seller Girl', the same song Farzana would listen to growing up in Tehran decades later. And as well as putting the song on the path to becoming an Afghan household ballad, it helped pave the way for other women to sing and take on other public-facing roles at the broadcaster, such as reading the news.

Perched on a floor cushion during our interview, Parveen was sure history was on her side now as we discussed the opposition to the state TV channel showing its archive of old performers. 'It's just some old men hanging on to the past,' she said, her big eyes twinkling as she fired up another cigarette. 'It won't last.' And then she took a drag, tapped off a bead of ash and, with a still lusty voice, launched into an entrancing rendition of her most famous song.

* * *

When such optimism was expressed by someone who had lived through so much, it was easy to be beguiled and miss the bigger picture.

Mirmen Parveen represented a select slice of Kabul society. She was distantly related, on her father's side, to Amir Abdul Rahman Khan, the Pashtun strongman installed by British colonialists after the second Anglo-Afghan War. The singer had been part of the capital's elite that orbited the last king, Zahir Shah. He had awarded her with a medal for her singing. If you were part of that set, you inevitably had a narrow and Kabul-centric view. But she also reflected a general divide between the lives and expectations of people in the capital and the rest of Afghanistan.

It was her 19th-century ancestor and his British sponsors who laid the foundations for this schism. The British provided the Amir with money and arms in return for him serving as their regional policeman and keeping their imperial rival, Russia, away from India. He had big ambitions of his own – to bring all of Afghanistan under his control and forge it into a nation state. It was he who built the 'Arg' presidential palace in Kabul. With his coffers filled with British funds, he governed as a dictator, using force and patronage to manipulate the country's mosaic of tribes and ethnicities. That record earned him the title of the 'Iron Amir'.

When Hazara tribes in central Afghanistan resisted, he responded with genocidal violence. Tens of thousands were killed and more than half the Hazara population were forced into exile in neighbouring countries. The man Britain was paying to act as a bodyguard for its Indian colony told his soldiers to make towers of the heads of their Hazara victims.[1]

His rule resulted in a highly centralised state in Kabul, but one largely disconnected from Afghanistan's rural majority. It didn't tax them in any organised way because it could rely on foreign funds, and neither did it offer them any services. This entrenched a semi-feudal system whereby Pashtuns, Tajiks, Hazaras and other ethnic groups lived according to their own social codes. As long as they didn't challenge the Amir's authority, local tribal leaders could impose their own levies and operate their own patronage networks.

British colonialists had first tried out this method for controlling Afghanistan when they invaded in 1839, putting another Pashtun tribal chief into power. Shah Shuja Durrani had previously ruled the country in the early 1800s, when he had first built ties with the British, before being unseated. Like the Iron Amir, Shah Shuja also had a startling penchant for violence, chopping off the body parts of servants who displeased him.[2] Visitors to his court found most of his staff were missing ears and noses, and many were castrated.

None of this was any surprise to the British when they decided to make him their Amir, because Shah Shuja had made a habit of

---

[1] *The Life of Abdur Rahman: The Amir of Afghanistan* by Sultan Mohammad Khan.
[2] *The Return of a King* by William Dalrymple.

such punishments while he was in exile under their protection in colonial India. He continued to treat his retinue this way even after the British colonial army had installed him in Kabul, undermining what little chance he had of regaining the respect of his compatriots. It was just one of many factors that contributed to the British occupation ending with the disaster of their retreat from Kabul in 1842, when most of their army was wiped out.

The second time around, the British learned from their failures and found in Amir Abdul Rahman Khan a more astute tyrant who could protect British interests while pursuing his own. They had no qualms about the brutality with which he ruled his own domain. In one case, the British also inveighed the Iron Amir to destroy one of Afghanistan's most important ancient sites, in Herat, in case the Russians took over the city.

The Musalla complex included a mosque, madrassa and mausoleum, surrounded by 20 towering minarets, and was built in the 15th century, when Afghanistan was part of the Persianate Timurid Empire. It was the creation of Gawhar Shad, wife of the Timurid ruler, Shah Rukh, and she reportedly insisted on female students being admitted to the madrassa, challenging the conventions of the time.

Four centuries later, in 1885, the British feared the Russians would exploit the Musalla complex as a base and firing position, and ordered that most of the site be dynamited, including 11 of the minarets. But the crisis dissipated, and the Russians never came.

Earthquakes, neglect and the anti-Soviet war brought down several more minarets.[3] When I was last in Herat, just five remained, several of them leaning hazardously to one side. As a cultural crime, Britain and the Iron Amir's destruction of the Musalla complex ranks alongside the Taliban's destruction of the Buddhas of Bamiyan 116 years later.

---

[3] https://tolonews.com/arts-culture/ancient-minaret-herat-verge-destruction

In 1893, the Amir did another deal with the British, receiving a colonial official called Sir Mortimer Durand in Kabul to demarcate the country's main border. With a few more pen strokes on the map, they also created the odd-looking finger of Afghan territory that you see on maps poking east into China, now known as the Wakhan Corridor. Its sole purpose was to ensure the Russian empire's southern extremes did not touch British India at any point.

Those borders and Afghanistan's power structure have been a lasting British bequest. Today, Afghans still refer to the frontier with Pakistan as the 'Durand Line', and the country has been ruled by a leader dependent on foreign funds almost ever since, with only a few exceptions. The Americans re-established the model by installing President Karzai.

Many of the CIA's allies among the former mujahideen were a modern expression of this system. They mostly came from rural backgrounds and ran their own semi-feudal patronage networks. One example was Ismail Khan, the veteran commander in Herat who took over again as governor after the Taliban's fall. As the Supreme Court was ordering the state broadcaster to pull female singers off television, he had already instructed his militiamen to confiscate videos and cassettes of female singers in the province.

The self-styled 'Amir of Herat' had established a quasi-independent dictatorship there, funded by the customs fees collected each year at the province's busy border crossing with Iran – fees which were supposed to be going to the government in Kabul. When Ismail Khan appeared in public, you could mistake him for the ruler of a country not a province, the immaculate white in which he always dressed contrasting with the richer colours of his personal honour guard.

On one visit to Herat, I watched Khan receiving petitions for help from local residents at a weekly audience he held in the ornate, marble-floored hall that adjoined his office. As he took their slips of paper, he didn't even turn to look at them.

The roads were better in Herat, but his opposition to women singing was of a piece with his own, localised Taliban-like gender code. Women were barred from taking taxis alone or learning to drive. There were also restrictions on their access to education, and they had to wear body-covering chaddaris[4] or burqas outside their homes. These rules were enforced not only by local police but by Khan's militia, acting much like the Taliban's religious patrols.

On his watch, the province became known for young women setting themselves on fire in response to abusive forced marriages. I covered several such cases at the time, and hundreds of similar incidents were reported during the early 2000s in what became an outbreak of copycat, self-harming rebellion. The governor's response was to go on the attack, saying, 'They were not good women,' and that they lacked the courage to address the problems in their marriages.[5]

Khan's treatment of women garnered the attention of human rights activists, but among the men of Afghanistan's newly empowered political class, his views on the status of the other half of the population were far from unusual. The Taliban had no monopoly on misogyny.

If you were in Kabul, tuning in to one of the new commercial stations, it was easy to believe that changes were taking root everywhere. Arman and then later, Tolo TV, were soon available nationwide, but the new Generation Z audience they built up was predominantly urban – helped by the fact that there were more televisions in the cities, and a stronger signal.

The country's population may have been young, but the majority of Afghans also lived in the countryside where patriarchal tribal codes prevailed, and purdah and polygamy remained entrenched,

---

[4] Long black cloaks, like those worn by some women in Iran.
[5] Human Rights Watch report on Herat. https://www.hrw.org/reports/2002/afghnwmn1202/Afghnwmn1202-04.htm#P302_54913

especially in the Pashtun belt. Few girls or women there even learned to read or write; education was considered unnecessary for their role of marrying and having children. Narrowing the divides between city and countryside, and between the rights of men and women, would be the true test of the new Afghan government and its Western partners.

* * *

A cluster of men with sun-dried faces, dressed in turbans, long, flowing shirts and loose trousers, looked on warily as the American soldiers stepped out of their vehicles. The dust they had spun up with their arrival drifted over the village's mud-and-straw houses. A few children, young girls among them, peeked out from the spaces in between. Of women, there was no sign.

The lieutenant, two subordinates and their interpreter had removed their body armour, helmets and sunglasses as they walked over, seeking to appear less threatening. But the other soldiers in the unit stayed in the vehicles in full battle gear, rigid behind their mounted machine guns, guarding both entrances to the village.

The border with Pakistan was close by, and this was one of many areas where Taliban fighters were known to be coming across from safe havens on the other side. Some of the soldiers in the unit were on edge because they had been ambushed the day before.

Officially, this was a hearts and minds exercise, to build bridges with people living near a new airstrip that the US military was carving out of an isolated desert plateau nearby. At the same time, the soldiers were gathering intelligence about their new neighbours, to try to find out how much of a presence the Taliban had built up.

En route to the village, the young soldier manning the heavy-calibre weapon had told me to be ready to grab his personal rifle, which was on the vehicle floor just beside me. 'I can't believe you media people travel without weapons,' he shouted down at me.

I was spending a few days with them as part of a report I was doing on US military operations in the border region.

The lieutenant told the Pashto-speaking interpreter to ask if the Taliban ever came into the village. 'We've never seen them,' said a thickset man to whom everyone else deferred. He fixed his Afghan compatriot with a look that made clear he wouldn't answer any more questions on the subject.

'Go get the school bags,' said the officer to one of his subordinates.

The village was called Marana, and it was in Paktika, one of the poorest and most under-developed parts of the country. It was home to some 20 families, the elder said, who lived off their herds of sheep and goats. Looking at the sandpaper landscape, it was hard to believe anyone managed to live there. It was in places like this that the new Afghan government and its US backers had the most to prove.

There could be few clearer demonstrations of the kind of resources the United States could draw on than this project to build an airport in the middle of nowhere. The US command had flown all the necessary bulldozers and excavators from Germany in a fleet of giant transport aircraft, dropping everything in by parachute. The area was too remote and the journey too risky, they had decided, to bring the loads in overland.

I'd watched the soldiers coordinating with the aircraft above, as hundreds of tonnes of expensive machinery fell through the night sky above the Afghan–Pakistan border and landed exactly on target. As soon as they had pulled off whatever the equivalent of bubble wrap is for bulldozers, the soldiers got to work clearing the desert, using night-vision goggles to see their way. It was a stunning display of high-tech might.

Building bridges with local people would prove more complex. The soldier returned with a box of blue backpacks adorned with the Afghan and US flags and a white dove. 'For the children to go to school,' the officer said to the elder, through the interpreter.

'There is no school here.'

The lieutenant added another note in his book: 'No school.' Looking up again, he asked the elder what he thought of the new government in Kabul. The man examined his visitor from the other side of the world and said: 'You're the first person we've seen from the government in 40 years.'

* * *

The divide between city and village life, between tradition and change, became clear to Farzana in her early teens. During school breaks and the two Eid holidays, she travelled down to see her family in Ghazni province, usually taking a minibus with her male cousin.

Rural Afghanistan reasserts itself as soon as you leave Kabul on the south-western road leading to Kandahar. Gnarly peaks and ridges loom above, with little villages hugging the dry slopes below. On each journey she made into the countryside, the aisle usually crammed with bags and boxes, Farzana felt the press of entrenched custom and behaviour.

Her cousin, who was about 18 at the time, tended to mansplain as he assumed the role of being her guardian. 'Because he was the man, he felt he should decide where we sat when the bus stopped for a break and what we should eat. He had a younger sister who used to clean his shoes and he tried to treat me the same way, controlling everything,' she said. One time, as they were getting back on the minibus after a rest stop, the tension boiled over.

'I have to act as your mahram [chaperone] as long as we travel together,' he said. 'I'm the one who decides everything.'

'I'm not your sister,' Farzana exploded. 'You cannot treat me the way you treat your sister.'

They started cursing each other, until fellow passengers intervened.

Inside the bus, Farzana was dismayed by the way passengers were automatically separated by gender: 'No one said anything. There was just an unwritten rule that women always sat at the back.' While fathers slept up front, where the ventilation was better, mothers were expected to look after their noisy kids in the back, the teenage Farzana noted. 'The women were always in hijab and some had burqas, even in the hot weather. I rarely saw any sympathy from their husbands. If their kid was crying, they would never come and take the kid.'

A few hours on, after Wardak province, the mountains descend to a semi-arid plain where crosswinds scoop up the desert and dump it on the road and blow it over the traffic. The first thing Farzana always did when she reached Ghazni was take a shower.

Centuries ago, camel trains passed back and forth this way when it was a branch of the Silk Road. In 1839, the British invasion force took this route, bringing with them their chosen Pashtun strongman, Shah Shuja Durrani, at the start of the first Anglo-Afghan War. They took the southern route into Afghanistan after crossing over from what is today Pakistan's Baluchistan.

The road snakes across the plain until you see the bulk of an old fortress rising out of the haze, announcing Ghazni. The citadel is a legacy of the city's past as the capital of a 10th- and 11th-century empire that encompassed northern India and most of contemporary Iran.

History had also influenced the way Farzana's extended family lived in the early 2000s, in a village of cob-brick houses just outside Ghazni. Almost all their fellow residents were fellow Hazaras. Their persecution hadn't ended with the Iron Amir's ethnic cleansing. Surviving communities concentrated in particular places for safety. One of them was Ghazni province, which had several districts where Hazaras were in the majority.

It was an environment that helped to shore up traditional views about the respective roles of men and women. 'My village was a very insular place,' said Farzana. 'You'd hardly see any women outside. So I could clearly see the shift in those four hours from Kabul.' But, having got used to the relative freedoms of life in Kabul, she saw no reason why she should make concessions to such attitudes when she was back in Ghazni. Her approach didn't go down well.

Via her mother, her older relatives delivered an injunction. Now she was 13, Farzana needed to wear a headscarf. 'But I said what does that mean, to say "need"?

'The only thing I knew at that time was that if I don't want to wear a headscarf, I shouldn't be wearing one.' Her relatives also objected to her going outside in jeans and T-shirt, and to her purple sunglasses. It was the start of a battle that escalated with each visit.

When Farzana was around 14, her father gave her a radio to listen to music and news. Television reception in their area was still patchy. Her favourite station was Arman FM, where she liked to listen to their playlists of Afghan vocalists. They included female singers such as Parasto; the wildly popular Ahmad Zahir, often dubbed the 'Elvis of Afghanistan'; and older crooners like Nashenas, who first became known in the 1950s, around the same time as Mirmen Parveen. Sometimes, she tuned into *New Home, New Life*, comparing her own experiences with those in the fictional village of Bar Killi.

But when her grandmother saw her listening to the radio, she erupted, saying that Farzana's cousin, a boy of around the same age, needed the radio more than her. A family row broke out, with each side advocating for the opposite gender; her father pushed back by arguing that it was important for his daughter's education that she keep abreast of events.

'Nonsense!' replied his mother. 'She's a girl, and she's not ours.'

It was a chilling moment that became a lifelong memory.

Her mother may have done everything she could to ensure her daughter had access to learning when she was younger and they were in Tehran, but as Farzana approached marriageable age, everything was changing. What was important now was the traditional role ordained for her by society and custom. Farzana was to get married and leave home.

'It didn't matter to her if I am educated or not,' she realised. 'It didn't matter if I am strong. I cried about it for the rest of the day.'

Farzana's grandmother was unmoved: 'We need to invest in our boys.' The subtext was clear: Farzana was not the priority and her father would not gain the full respect of the village until he had a son.

* * *

The rat-a-tat-tat of automatic gunfire crackled in the air, followed by the tell-tale zip and whine of ricocheting bullets. I ducked behind a wall. Across the street near the governor's compound, Afghan soldiers took cover behind their US Humvees, their weapons trained in the direction of the firing. An American helicopter looped above the centre of Herat, watching events below.

It was September 2004, and a joint US and Afghan government operation was under way to install a new governor and remove Ismail Khan. I had just left the ornate marble hall in the provincial government compound where the man tapped to replace him had arrived to take over, flanked by bodyguards. He had been hastily recalled from his post as Afghan ambassador to Ukraine.

This was a significant moment. The Americans were moving against one of their most prominent anti-Taliban allies, as part of a broader effort to boost President Karzai's authority ahead of the elections the following month. But the 'Amir of Herat' was refusing to go.

He had barricaded himself inside his villa, and his supporters were demonstrating his capacity to create trouble. They had torched the local United Nations office and several other organisations associated with the Western-backed government. Ten people had been killed and dozens more injured in clashes with Afghan and US troops. A small hospital I visited was overwhelmed with casualties, leaving the corridors covered with pools of blood.

I had got a seat on the plane that brought the replacement governor in from Kabul, and I was working with a local Herati journalist Bilal had put me in touch with. When we caught up with the new governor again, he was sheltering in a hilltop guest house ringed by US and Afghan soldiers. He looked as if he was missing Kyiv.

The plan to unseat Ismail Khan had been spearheaded by Zalmay Khalilzad, now based in Afghanistan full-time as the US ambassador. He had persuaded his superiors in Washington to drop their resistance to 'nation building', arguing that without a more interventionist approach, the whole project of stabilising Afghanistan would be put at risk. In his view, that meant creating a new police force and army, and reining in warlord figures such as Khan who were challenging the central government in Kabul.

Khalilzad had been involved in shaping American policy since the Soviet invasion. Born in Afghanistan, he had first come to the United States in the 1960s on a US-funded high-school exchange programme before later becoming an American citizen and foreign policy academic. With his title of special presidential envoy, Khalilzad had been empowered by the Bush administration to act as America's de facto viceroy, intricately involved in the day-to-day running of the Afghan government.

At his news conferences at the US embassy, he sometimes announced new policy initiatives before Karzai did. Tall, and with an engaging, garrulous manner, he had become a local celebrity. Joking and bantering with Afghan journalists in Pashto and Dari, prayer beads clicking through his hand, he could seem to observers like Kabul's man in Washington, rather than the other way round. He didn't always disabuse them.

'Some people say I should run,' he joked during one pre-election media gathering I attended, as he discussed Karzai's likely opponents. 'Maybe I could beat him.' The more conventional US embassy press officers present at the time blanched. Years later, Khalilzad did briefly weigh an Afghan presidential run.

In negotiations, he sometimes offered the equivalent of a drinking contest. 'If we need to sit down for six hours and drink tea, we'll do that,' he said in the midst of trying to resolve one political dispute. 'I can drink as much tea as the next person.' His Afghan origins meant that there was a weight of expectation on his shoulders inside Afghanistan that didn't apply to any other US diplomats.

Khalilzad's first move to crimp the warlords was directed against Abdul Rashid Dostum after he tried to block Karzai's candidate for governor from taking office in one of the northern provinces under the Uzbek warlord's sway. Working with his US military counterpart, Lt Gen. David Barno, Khalilzad came up with a plan to fly an American B-1 bomber low and sound-barrier-breakingly fast over Dostum's home.[6] The show of strength worked. After the sonic boom, he backed down.

Following the initial burst of violence, so, too, did Ismail Khan, in return for a post in Karzai's cabinet. That allowed the central government to gain a greater degree of control over the lucrative border customs revenues and take charge of Khan's arsenal of heavy weapons. Significantly, it was Khalilzad who did the deal, not the Afghan leader, when he flew to meet the Herat strongman in person.

Khan's resignation had something of a domino effect, with his local rival then surrendering to the government.[7] It also set the scene for a third move by Khalilzad and Karzai, designed to reduce the influence of the most powerful warlord figure, Mohammad Fahim, the defence minister and commander of the Panjshiri-led Northern Alliance.

This time, it was Barno who took on the role of messenger, speaking soldier to soldier and asking Fahim to step down as Karzai's running mate. The veteran commander was well looked after and promised the honorary title of 'Marshal'. And when Barno arrived,

---

[6] Interview with the author.
[7] This was Amanullah Khan, who had launched an armed attack on Ismail Khan's militia in August 2004.

he found him in emollient mood. 'I understand this is how democracy is supposed to work,' he said, telling his American visitor that he had been reading the American Constitution.[8]

It was an illuminating demonstration of how the US government was driving day-to-day politics. And right then, many Afghans were applauding. 'I hope this is the start of removing all the warlords,' said Abdul when I got back from Herat. Yet some critics saw it as window dressing, because all three men still retained considerable influence.

Khalilzad's retort was that while warlord figures had to be contained, they needed to be treated with respect and dealt with case by case, in recognition that they had a constituency and some support. Trying to sideline them entirely risked triggering what he called a 'vendetta process'.[9]

Different rules applied in the south and east, where the US military and the CIA continued to pay an array of controversial local strongmen for their help in pursuing the Taliban and Al Qaeda. US strategy may have shifted to include nation building, but in the Pashtun belt its counter-terrorism campaign took precedence – even if that conflicted with efforts to build up the Afghan government's legitimacy.

It meant that while one US mission was working to build up the Afghan state, another was helping to undermine it by sustaining the old guard, accentuating the divide with Kabul in the process. Yet the violence Ismail Khan had triggered when Khalilzad first put into effect the plan to remove him was a warning that these strongman figures had to be handled with care. Ultimately, it was a lesson about the risks of foreign powers interfering in local politics and trying to mould them according to their own interests. Britain had learned that lesson in the past, but it would be forced to learn it again.

* * *

---

[8] Interview with the author.
[9] Interview with the author.

Election rally in Ghazni, 2004.

The two helicopter gunships looked like mosquitoes on steroids from below, the growl from their engines waxing and waning as they circled around Ghazni, Farzana's home city. A pair of ground attack aircraft were on standby several layers of air higher. And it was the thundering noise of two Chinook troop-carrying helicopters that announced President Karzai had arrived for his election rally in Ghazni.

There could be no clearer demonstration of who the Americans wanted to win Afghanistan's first post-Taliban election. No other candidate got a superpower protection detail. But no one else on the slate had survived as many assassination attempts, either.

This military operation had been launched to allow Karzai to make a campaign stop outside Kabul and rally his base in the Pashtun south, just a day before the vote. He had abandoned his previous attempt after his helicopter came under fire. Some jibed that Karzai was no more than 'the mayor of Kabul'. Therefore, even if the trip didn't garner many votes, it was important symbolically that he showed up, in what was also the Taliban's turf.

A carpet had been draped over some steps in a run-down park on the edge of Ghazni to create a stage, with a canopy above strung with Afghan flags. More flags had been erected around the venue. Pictures of candidate Karzai smiled from posters urging Afghans to hold their heads high and vote for the man who stood for prosperity and unity. Ethnic division, warned one banner, led to Afghanistan's destruction.

Seats had been reserved for local dignitaries and elders in front of the makeshift stage, with a crowd of several hundred people standing behind, held back by a cordon of Afghan police and soldiers. They had tough, rural faces, scorched by daily work outside. If there were any women there, we didn't see them. Bilal, Abdul and I had driven down on the same road through the mountains of Wardak that Farzana took from Kabul.

'He's an honest man,' said one elderly man in the standing crowd when we asked for his thoughts about Karzai. 'We hope he will bring peace and jobs,' said another. Some admitted the main attraction of being there was the after-rally meal.

The brooding mass of Ghazni's old fortress looked down on the rally, from behind the crowd, providing a reminder of the past. In a pivotal moment during the first Anglo-Afghan War, the British colonial army took the city without firing a shot, after taking the citadel's defenders by surprise. Weeks later, the British marched into Kabul and installed Shah Shuja Durrani as Amir, setting in train the pattern of Afghanistan's rulers being chosen by foreign powers. Safeguarded by America's high-tech might, the latest example was Hamid Karzai. As it happened, he was from the same Pashtun clan as Shah Shuja.

Karzai's dependence on the West was almost total. Four-fifths of the national budget was funded by overseas donors, including the entire cost of the emerging Afghan police and army. What revenues the Karzai government had of its own – such as import duties – were considerably reduced by corruption.

'Brothers and sisters,' implored President Karzai, his voice pulsing through loudspeakers, 'I ask you to vote for me freely, with no pressure. We want a proud Afghanistan, a stable Afghanistan, a peaceful Afghanistan.' Energised, he stepped down into the crowd after delivering his speech to press the flesh, like any good retail politician.

Behind their wrap-around shades, his American bodyguards grimaced as they closed in to protect their principal. 'Don't push him!' shouted Karzai, as he reached to shake one man's hand. 'This is democracy.'

Thirty minutes later he was gone, in a spiral of helicopter dust.

* * *

It was hardly surprising that the elder in Marana hadn't seen anyone from the government for 40 years. It's unlikely anyone had come in the two decades before that. It was an old story.

In so many countries, industrialisation had drawn more people out of the countryside, blurring divisions, diluting social barriers and ultimately flipping the population distribution so that city dwellers became the majority. But there was little industrialisation in Afghanistan before it became embroiled in war.

Conflict provoked plenty of migration, but going the wrong way, out of the country, and so often depleting Afghanistan of its best and brightest. And when refugees returned, as Farzana found, they typically restored their old social formations. Many hoped that the 2004 election would offer a chance to start breaking some of these barriers down.

That election also gave Farzana, still just into her teens, her first taste of politics. Through a family connection, she was asked to help distribute flyers for one of the candidates, before graduating to the job of being the voice on a megaphone, touring neighbourhoods by car and calling for people's support. 'I even came up with my own speeches,' she said. 'I'm embarrassed when I think about it now, but I had opinions, and a very loud voice.'

I made trips all over the country at that time, covering the run-up to the vote. I will never forget election day on 7 October 2004. As Bilal and I toured Kabul and nearby districts, the lines of people waiting to cast their ballots stretched for blocks. Trying to stop the process, the Taliban had threatened violence nationwide. Many voters responded by writing their wills, and then going to their polling station. It was the biggest exercise in democracy in the country's history,[10] and the turnout reached 84 per cent.

There was violence: around 30 people were killed nationwide during the election process, including soldiers and polling workers. Yet there had been expectations of far worse. For General Barno, the Taliban's failure to stop the election represented their second defeat. The question was whether this represented lasting change.

One concern was that the candidates had simply shored up Afghanistan's traditional divisions, using an ethnic and tribal lens to target their campaign efforts. This was vote bank politics, with areas defined by clan and identity rather than as communities of individuals who could be won over with policies and ideas.

When Karzai invoked the need for peace and prosperity, that was about as close as he got to a policy programme. His posters may have highlighted the risks of ethnic division, but his campaign team focused their outreach on his natural vote banks in the Pashtun south and east, giving much less attention to regions with different identities. And although it may not have changed the overall result, given Karzai's profile, there was also widespread fraud.

By coincidence, Mirmen Parveen died the day after President Karzai was inaugurated in December 2004. Her singing had represented a

---

[10] There were various elections between the late 1940s and early 1990s, but limits on the voter franchise or security conditions and boycotts resulted in much lower turnouts than in 2004.

note of hope from a past era for the next. 'Parveen was more than just a singer,' said one fan paying tribute online.[11] 'She was a symbol of resistance against ignorance, bigotry and blind tradition, using her voice to stand up for love, friendship and honesty.' They were words so many Afghans wanted to believe in.

---

[11] See https://www.bbc.com/persian/afghanistan/story/2004/12/041209_v-afghan-parvin

Chapter 6

The Taboo of Love and the Seeds of Failure

Farzana's father didn't want a second wife.

He respected the codes of Afghan society. But there were limits. He and his wife were happy to have their two children, without plans for more.

From a traditional Afghan standpoint, though, their family was not only small but incomplete. There was no male heir. Her grandmother and uncles never missed a chance to point this out, using the bleak refrain Farzana had heard before: 'These girls will go away. They are not ours,' they said. 'You need to have a boy, so there is someone who can inherit.'

Her uncle in Kabul gave her the same message. 'You don't have a brother, you're going to go away, and nothing will be left of your father.'

The pressure built up. Family honour was at stake. Farzana's grandfather was a respected elder in their village outside Ghazni. And the family consensus was that her mother could no longer bear children. It was 10 years since she had given birth to Shireen, her sister. Just when their father was about to give in to the arm-twisting of his mother and brothers and accept a second wife, Farzana's mother announced she was pregnant.

There were huge family celebrations when she gave birth in late 2005, especially among their relatives in the village. The two sisters now had a brother, and it was Farzana who came up with his name, Sherzad – inspired by a character in one of her favourite stories. It was a choice that connected her brother to the family's Farsi-speaking, Persian heritage and also exemplified her love of stories and reading. One result of her topsy-turvy schooling in Tehran was that she had turned into a voracious reader.

By the time Sherzad was born, she had moved back to Ghazni to live with her parents again. 'My uncle had complained to my dad, saying he couldn't tolerate me any more,' she smiled. After their regular clashes on the minibus from Kabul, his son had also had enough.

Her father had joined the expanding Afghan national police force and was rising through the ranks. Her mother had a job as a teacher with a charity that ran catch-up literacy courses for older women who had been barred from going to school during the first Taliban regime. And they now lived in a rented house in the centre of the provincial capital. Ghazni City is not a big place, with a population then of around 140,000. But socially, there was more breathing room than in the family village. Farzana also had her books.

'I often skipped meals and kept reading at night,' she said. There was rarely any electricity in Ghazni then, so she used torches to read. She carried on dressing much as she had in Kabul, in jeans and T-shirt – sometimes tying her hair up and wearing a hat along with her sunglasses, 'so I looked like a boy'. Predictably, this generated more static with her relatives.

In addition to her treasured purple shades, Farzana had a new favourite garment – a Western-style orange jacket that her father had bought for her. 'Orange was definitely not a colour he would buy for himself, but he had a distinct taste,' she said. 'I loved it.'

Like a magic wardrobe, novels were an escape from the real world of fights with her parents, to places where people were freer and rebellion succeeded. 'I was very idealistic, revolutionary even. Every book I read, I put myself into, so I was the hero character.' She laughed at the memory. 'But those dreams kept me going.'

Farzana read quickly, a legacy of her schooling in Tehran, where she was taught to scan and speed read. So fast that she ran out of books, and her parents couldn't afford to buy more. The librarian running a small public collection near one of the city's mosques provided a solution. He offered Farzana a bartering deal, using her old school textbooks as the currency.

'We had 12 or 13 subjects then. And when I was done with my school books, I took them to the librarian and he gave me six novels,' Farzana said. School textbooks were scarce, and expensive if you bought them new from the Education Ministry. That's why the textbooks you see in Afghan public schools often look like ancient scrolls. They are used again and again, passed from one student to another down the years.

The librarian sold Farzana's used textbooks in Ghazni, and she got to keep the novels for as long as she needed. 'It was good for him. He earned some extra money, and after I had read the six novels, I took them back and he would give me three new ones.'

But one day, when she was almost 16, her mother caught sight of the title of her daughter's latest obsession and exploded.

'What is this that you're reading?'

'It's a novel and I like it,' Farzana replied, reaching out to retrieve the paperback, an Iranian romance, from her mother. 'I read a lot of these stories.'

'This is not what you're supposed to be studying,' she snapped, tightening her grip. 'You're too young for these *love* books.'

And then right in front of her, Farzana's mother tore up the book. Its title was *Love in Spring*.

When she told her husband what had happened, he was even angrier, accusing Farzana of putting the family's reputation at risk by reading such literature. 'Why are you into all of this?' he demanded. The 'Love' in the title had crossed a forbidden line. The traditionalists in the family said Farzana should have been married already. But reading about love was taboo.

'So, they took away all my novels,' said Farzana. 'And my dad said I could only read books that were about my school subjects. Of course, I cried a lot, and I stopped eating for a while.' The clashes became routine. She banned her parents from going into her room when she was out. 'Those were the toughest years. I was literally fighting about everything.'

The one activity that provided some relief, and common ground, was work. Even in urban Afghan families with a regular income, it is common for children to do some kind of paid work once they are able and old enough, fitting it around their lessons. Not long before her parents took away her novels, Farzana got a short-term contract with a charity running mine awareness courses, teaching both children and adults about the risks of discarded ordnance and anti-personnel mines that still polluted many areas of the province.

Though still only 15, she secured the job due to her growing proficiency in English, because the charity needed someone who could communicate with its foreign staff. She had started learning English in Kabul at one of the many private tuition colleges that had opened up. Shireen, her sister, had also been studying the language in Ghazni, and they continued to go to lessons together when Farzana moved back.

Farzana sometimes helped her mother with her literacy classes for older women. That led to another part-time job when the mine awareness work ended. Having seen Farzana assisting her mother, the organisers asked her to step in formally when they started another class. Farzana was happy. It felt good to be earning and contributing to the family budget.

Although she couldn't see it then, Farzana acknowledges her parents were on their own journey through Afghanistan's treacherous social currents in a country that was still far from peace. And a lot of the strain fell on her mother. 'She is a very strong person, very assertive, and she was trying to protect me, making decisions for me. But she gave me that personality, too, so I pushed back.'

Educated and earning money for the family, her mother was a role model for that time, Farzana points out. 'But she still was pretty much a housewife. She had to take care of all the chores.' Outside the home, it was her husband who had the power. Yet, he was navigating the same waters, and subject to the censure of the wider community.

Just as he had struggled to resist the family campaign for him to have a second wife, it was hard to fend off pressure for his still-teenage daughter to become one. And after she turned 14, that burden was transferred directly to Farzana. 'My parents would say, "This person is rich," or "This person is educated," and ask me to consider them. I kept saying I wanted to go university and build a life for myself.'

She gives her parents credit for imposing one condition on the suitors they arranged. 'They said: "They have to accept you the way you are,'" and allow her to finish school and work. But it was a concession that she intended to use to avoid marriage at all costs.

'I saw that no matter how open-minded your husband is, you are bound up by cultural norms. I saw my cousins getting married. We were all around the same age, and I could see that marriage in that context was a prison.'

For Farzana, the pressure from her parents to conform seemed cruel and contradictory. 'Once we are in Afghanistan you can make a future for yourself,' her father had told her back in Tehran.

'I was doing that,' she said. Like any teenager, she was trying to shape an identity for herself. But she was up against the forces of tradition.

* * *

US troops in eastern Afghanistan.

One morning, Bilal got a call from the father of Kamal Sadat, our colleague in the eastern province of Khost. We had worked together on several other stories since our trip to meet Naqibullah in Paktia.

But now his father was asking for help. His son had been abducted by American soldiers the night before, in a raid on their home. 'We have no idea where he is,' he said. 'Can you help?'

By this point, Kamal's reporting for the BBC's Pashto service had turned him into a local celebrity. With fewer competitors then, its local language broadcasts were still the go-to source of information in the provinces, and when Kamal came on the radio, people listened. As part of his work, he also had frequent dealings with personnel at the large US base in Khost.

The story that emerged was that a team of US soldiers had broken down the family's door as they slept. Aiming their weapons at him and his terrified parents and siblings, they demanded Kamal identify himself. 'At first, I thought it was the Taliban,' he said. When he realised the intruders were Americans, Kamal showed his press card and another US identity card he had been given to enter the base. He had often been inside for press briefings.

But minutes later, handcuffed and blindfolded, he was being driven away to the base – though with an element of dark comedy. The soldiers got lost and had to ask Kamal for help. 'They took my blindfold off, so I could see where we were, and I directed them,' he told us later.

After passing the news on to me, Bilal started calling contacts he thought could help in the Afghan defence ministry and other security agencies. I called the US military headquarters in Kabul, demanding to know what its forces had done with Kamal. 'I'll look into it and get back to you,' said a spokesperson. I also put in calls to the US and British embassies and contacted my bosses in Delhi and London to get them involved.

Jahan asked if he could do anything to help. He'd met Kamal when he'd visited the bureau. 'He was such a funny guy, always joking. I couldn't understand why the Americans could have taken him,' he said. Everyone in the bureau rallied round. But by the end of the day, we still had no news for Kamal's father. His son had disappeared.

Indirectly, however, we received confirmation that the 'system' was taking notice – via an American officer I had got to know while embedded with US troops earlier that year. He was now based in Tampa, Florida, home to Centcom, the US military command running the wars in Afghanistan and Iraq. Late that evening, I received a curt email from him with the subject line: 'WTFO?' and a message saying: 'Andy. What have you got involved in now?'

The next day, I had a call from the British embassy. 'This is off the record,' said the diplomat, 'but we have been told that Kamal is in Bagram. That's all we know.' That meant he was in the base's prison. When I reached the spokesperson, she refused to confirm this, but said that Kamal had been 'pointed out by others as being a Taliban sympathiser'.

It was a familiar-sounding claim. There was an established pattern by then of the Americans conducting raids or air strikes that later turned out to have been based on bad or skewed intelligence – and Kamal appeared to be the latest victim.

Two days after Kamal's night-time abduction, he was released. The US military spokesperson called to give me the news. 'We truly apologise,' she said, before dictating a prepared statement. 'We have verified his credentials and determined we don't need him any more. The coalition apologises to the reporter and his family for the misunderstanding and the disruption to their lives. Our goal is to rid Afghanistan of criminals and those who use terrorism to further their goals, and sometimes we make mistakes in pursuit of our goal.'

There are several points to this story. First, it was about the power of connections. Kamal was one of so many Afghans who got sucked into the same black hole during the US occupation – boys like Naqibullah among them – and once inside, they were helpless. And, like Naqibullah, Kamal never saw who was holding him because he was always blindfolded outside his cell. The difference was that, like Bilal years earlier, he had contacts who could vouch for him.

Without them, he would almost certainly have been kept in Bagram much longer – and possibly suffered worse treatment.

The second point is related. Kamal's treatment exemplified the arbitrary detentions and aggression that became a hallmark of US tactics. In military jargon, they were known as 'kill-capture' raids, with the emphasis on the first part of the label as time went on. Kamal never found out why the Americans went after him, though he suspects an official unhappy with one of his reports retaliated by spreading rumours that he had Taliban sympathies.

Whatever their reasons, the Americans could have adopted a less confrontational way to react to the information they received, especially as it concerned someone they already knew and whom they had allowed inside their base multiple times. But the US military said criticism of night raids was misplaced. 'They say we should be using police procedures when we carry out arrests, but this is a combat zone,' was how one spokesman I interviewed put it.

As such raids were mostly conducted far from Kabul, they generally escaped the media's gaze. Yet again, it illuminated the urban-rural divide. A colleague being pulled out of his home in a night raid had given us a rare insight into what had become a routine American tactic.

US coalition air strikes were also concentrated in remote rural areas, making it similarly difficult to report on their impact. But enough information trickled out to make clear that large numbers of civilians continued to be killed in aerial attacks. The typical American response – if they accepted that non-combatants were involved – was to pay compensation, the amount dependent on whether it involved death, injury or property damage. Only rarely did they apologise.

The Americans said they were improving their intelligence gathering and verification processes to avoid mistakes. But such statements rang hollow with Afghans, because the 'mistakes' kept happening. The message it sent was that the raids and the air strikes were the priority, not Afghan lives or perceptions. And it was partly to minimise their own losses that the coalition relied so much on air power.

Kamal was fortunate that neither he nor any of his family members were harmed in the raid. And he chose to forgive them for invading their home. 'I understand it was a mistake by the US Army,' he said. But for so many rural Pashtuns, it was US troops busting down their door at night and sometimes killing their relatives that put them on the path to joining the Taliban.

The US military came to Afghanistan to avenge 9/11 and to try to stop Afghan soil from being used as a base from which to attack their country again. But with its own actions, it started a new cycle of revenge and fostered an urge among many Afghans to resist the latest foreign army on their land. And it was rural Afghans who first started calling the Americans' presence an occupation. Yet as the dynamics of the war changed, it also became harder for many American soldiers to understand what they were fighting for – especially for those posted along the frontier with Pakistan.

* * *

The pilots flew so low they almost clipped the treetops, trying to make themselves less of a target to would-be attackers on the ground. It was the summer of 2005 and I was on a US helicopter taking supplies to an isolated base known as Camp Tillman, perched on the Afghan–Pakistani border.

'Jump out as soon as we hit the LZ,' one of the helicopter gunners had shouted over the din of the rotors as I was boarding. 'We get rocketed a lot coming into Tillman.'

The outpost was named after an American footballer who had won headlines at home after he turned down a life-changing multimillion-dollar playing contract to enlist in the US Army in response to the 9/11 attacks. But just two years later, Pat Tillman was killed in Afghanistan, by a fellow US soldier, in a so-called 'friendly fire' incident that American commanders initially tried to cover up.

It was a story that gave his memorialisation on this remote frontier a dark edge. And from the fast-descending helicopter, Camp Tillman had a forgotten, *Apocalypse Now* look to it. Many of the outpost's protective walls, made from 'Hesco' wire-mesh baskets filled with sand, were sagging and punctured.

Tillman was also a place where you could witness up close the growing contradictions in US tactics and strategy, as well as another side to the blowback it was experiencing as a result of arming the mujahideen against the USSR. Beyond a scrub-covered hill above the outpost was the Pakistani tribal region of Waziristan, which had become a sanctuary for a constellation of groups opposed to both the US presence and the Kabul government.

The most effective among them were part of the so-called Haqqani network, led by a hard-line Islamist and former mujahideen commander called Jalaluddin Haqqani. He had been a favourite of the CIA in the 1980s because of his prowess in killing Soviet troops, which showered him with support. But Haqqani subsequently turned against his American patrons, aligning with Al Qaeda and the Taliban.[1]

The region around Camp Tillman was Haqqani's home turf; the British-drawn Durand Line frontier went right through the traditional territory of his Zadran tribe. Although Pakistan always denied it in public, its generals and spies also had close ties with the commander and his network. And right then, in 2005, the Pakistani security establishment was stepping up efforts to bolster its influence

---

[1] Jalaluddin Haqqani offered to work with the new US-backed government after 2001. US actions turned him into an implacable foe. This included airstrikes targeting his followers and the arrest of his brother as he was trying to reconcile with President Hamid Karzai. See Barnett Rubin's chapter 'The Two Trillion Dollar Misunderstanding,' in the 'Scandinavian Journal of Military Studies'.

across the border because it had concluded that the United States was starting to pull back.

David Barno, the US commander at the time, said that after the 'euphoria' around the Afghan presidential elections the year before, his superiors wanted to reduce the American footprint in Afghanistan and hand over to NATO. 'The house was burning in Iraq, and so there was pressure to get troops and resources in there,' said Barno.[2] It was that same pressure that had led to Zalmay Khalilzad being pulled out of Kabul early to take over as US ambassador in Baghdad, to try to calm tensions there.

Pakistan's leader, General Pervez Musharraf, feared this change in US emphasis would lead both to Afghan factions opposed to its interests gaining greater power in Kabul and more Indian influence there. Providing sanctuary for the Taliban and the allied Haqqani network was an insurance policy to keep Pashtuns divided and a Pakistani stake in the Afghan power balance, even as Pakistan officially remained an ally of the United States in its war on terror.

* * *

It was at Camp Tillman that I met Louis Fernandez and his men. He was just 22 at the time, but in command of a platoon of 30 paratroopers as a lieutenant in the US Army's 82nd Airborne Division. He already had one previous tour of duty in Afghanistan under his belt and another in Iraq.

Fernandez had enlisted even more quickly than Pat Tillman – on 14 September 2001, motivated by the same sense of duty. 'To watch those towers falling left us feeling very exposed,' he said. 'We felt at risk in a very real way. Americans needed to get our sense of security back and I felt I had to do something.'[3]

---

[2] Interview with the author.
[3] Follow-up interview with Fernandez in 2021.

But four years later, on this far-flung patch of the Afghan–Pakistan frontier, Fernandez was no longer sure how the war they were fighting helped keep America safe. He was just focusing on keeping his men alive. 'I expected this to be the easiest deployment of the three,' he said, 'But so far, it has been the hardest. We've basically come to a hornets' nest here on the border.'

What made it harder for him and his soldiers to understand was that their adversary seemed to have been given an unmatchable advantage. 'It's easy for the enemy to shoot at us here in Afghanistan and then they just run a couple of hundred metres into Pakistan and we can't do anything,' said another of Fernandez's soldiers. 'They're untouchable.'

The US and Afghan soldiers complained that they were hampered by their 'rules of engagement', which barred them from pursuing assailants over the border or firing on them once they were a certain distance inside Pakistani territory. In many places, it wasn't even clear where the line was. But they could see armed men coming and going in the border region, with no one stopping them on the other side.

In one recent firefight, Fernandez and his US and Afghan comrades had almost been surrounded by fighters attacking from Pakistani territory. 'They got within 20 or 30 metres. We were hugging the dirt most of the time, just praying to God that He was there for us.'

But when air support arrived – called in by the unit's radio operator – the pilots said they couldn't engage because their attackers were too deep into Pakistan. Fernandez believed they killed several of their attackers, and they eventually made it to higher ground and safety. One American was later hospitalised, but the soldiers said they were lucky not to have sustained more severe casualties.

Bogged down in the border dirt, the soldiers were focused on staying alive and looking after each other. But their battles highlighted the wider issue of the double game that Pakistan was playing and how the United States handled it.

Yet in this relationship, the superpower had become the supplicant. America simply needed Pakistan too much, even as it was giving shelter to Haqqani fighters and other Taliban militants who were attacking its troops. Pakistan provided the main supply route to landlocked Afghanistan, intelligence on Al Qaeda, and secret bases for US drones. In Washington's calculations, there was also the perennial concern about Pakistan's stability and the security of its nuclear arsenal if General Musharraf was toppled.

These were valid concerns, but to troops taking casualties on the frontier, it appeared as if their leaders were giving Pakistan and the militants it was sheltering a free pass. The American soldiers I spoke to at Camp Tillman had been told not to criticise Pakistan. But a towering Afghan army captain working with them felt no such restraint. 'Pakistan is interfering in Afghanistan. They are sending the bad guys here,' the officer said bluntly, in fluent American vernacular. 'They say they are cooperating, but they are not.'

There were also 'some stupid Afghans' among these 'bad guys', the captain added, as he recounted other frontier battles. He also claimed to have seen the corpses of Arabs and other foreigners after some firefights. But most of the fighters he and his men came up against were locally recruited, he said. 'They are all coming from the madrassas in Pakistan.'

This raised the question: how could the United States prevail as long as its opponents had a cross-border sanctuary? And how could the United States hope to stabilise Afghanistan unless it addressed the reasons why its supposed ally, Pakistan, was helping to destabilise it by providing that sanctuary? Back in Kabul, President Karzai had become increasingly vocal about the contradiction.

Before he left for Baghdad, Zalmay Khalilzad had also pressed his superiors to prioritise what he called 'the sanctuary issue', and find ways to address it. Afghan–Pakistan relations had been

'Afghanistan's Achilles heel since the division of the subcontinent [by Britain],' he said.[4]

But just persuading Washington to acknowledge the issue was a struggle. Khalilzad said he got into 'some difficulty with my management' when he kept raising concerns about Pakistan's actions. 'Colin Powell [the US Secretary of State] was the most upset because he had developed a personal relationship with Musharraf.'[5]

It wasn't easy to report on the border war. I had asked to visit one of these bases before, but received no response. The military's media relations people in Kabul and Bagram preferred to keep journalists away from this controversial and hard to explain front line. But on a trip to the nearby regional base of Salerno, the same one that Kamal Sadat had been taken to the year before, I mentioned my interest in the border to its press officer and he offered to find me a space on any helicopters going that way.

Camp Tillman may have looked like a forlorn and neglected place from a helicopter. But under layers of defensive sandbags and blast shelters, the soldiers had some comforts: air conditioning for the summer heat, satellite TV, internet access and two hot meals a day. Everything ran on generators, powered by gallons of fuel shipped in at great expense.

The US base stood in awkward contrast to an Afghan settlement down the slope, which was coated anew in dust each time helicopters took off or landed. There was no AC or internet in Lwara, and not much contact with their heavily armed neighbours, either. Being seen with the Americans was risky. Informers were everywhere.

From one of the base machine-gun posts, I watched a man herd his goats past. He clipped the stragglers with a long sapling, ignoring the alien structure above him. It was an odd and uneasy co-existence: the hyperpower and the hamlet, brought together on an unmarked frontier by events far away, invisible forces still keeping them worlds apart.

---

[4] Interview with the author.
[5] Ibid.

There was a roughly painted wooden sign just inside the base, announcing its name in capital letters. The date Pat Tillman died had been added below, though not the cause. But the 'N' in his last name was missing. The right-hand end of the sign had snapped off. The snap of flying rounds on the border was the sound of America's strategy cracking as well.

* * *

The majestic northern flanks of the Hindu Kush rose above us, the upper reaches covered with snow. But the slopes below were covered with screes of rubble and shattered beams. All the houses in the lower section of Bajgah village had been flattened.

Fragments of people's lives were mixed up in the debris – a metal bowl, a broken tea flask and a shredded floor cushion. Several children were among the 28 people who had been killed. Dozens of others were injured. It looked like the aftermath of an air strike, I thought to myself, as I walked around the ruins with Bilal and Abdul. 'Look at this,' said Abdul, pointing with his foot at a small heap of school exercise books. 'This must have been a classroom.'

We had come to investigate a story that pulled together many of Afghanistan's threads, and showed why it was so hard to disentangle them. The isolated mountainside hamlet was in the north, far from the Pashtun-majority provinces where Taliban resistance to the US-backed government was then centred.

It was not an air strike that had caused the destruction, but the accidental detonation of a stockpile of dynamite and Soviet-era tank and artillery rounds[6] hidden in the village by a former mujahideen commander called Jalal Bajgah.

---

[6] There were caches like this all over the country, consisting of weapons and ammunition captured from Soviet forces, left behind when their allied government collapsed in 1992, or donated to the mujahideen as part of the CIA's 'Operation Cyclone' support program.

As his name suggested, he was from there, and all those who died were members of his extended family. They included Bajgah's brother, as the ammunition had been stored under his house. It was a close-knit place and, there, the former commander was the boss.

All the dead had been buried by the time we arrived, in accordance with Islamic tradition. Among the survivors there was a mood of quiet fury. 'We knew the weapons were there, but we couldn't say anything,' said one man with a bloodied bandage around his head. He wouldn't give his name, fearing Bajgah's retribution. This was Afghan blowback, deep inside Afghanistan, half a day's drive from Kabul.

What added an extra edge to the disaster was that the commander had been certified as 'disarmed' under a United Nations-led programme to demobilise Afghan militia forces. Some 50,000 former mujahideen fighters had passed through the programme by that point. Under the scheme, Bajgah had supposedly disbanded his local force and turned over his entire arsenal in return for substantial compensation. That also meant he was entitled to stand as a candidate in the upcoming parliamentary elections, due to take place later that year.

Our visit to his village made clear that he had lost none of his influence. And he'd been in no danger when his ammunition store exploded because he had built a new house for himself in a nearby town since receiving his disarmament compensation payments.

He was on his mobile when we were shown into his reception room, reclining against the wall with a plump cushion to support his back. A servant brought in green tea and little dishes of dried chickpeas, almonds and raisins, the tea glasses clinking gently as he set the tray down between us on the carpet.

In profile, with his neatly trimmed beard and pakol hat, he bore a passing resemblance to Ahmad Shah Massoud. He had indeed once fought with the Northern Alliance. In between sips of tea, Bajgah claimed 'the Taliban' were responsible for the blast, though without much conviction. They had no known presence in the region at the time.

He said that accusations from the government that he had secretly retained some weapons were 'unfair', claiming that he had been trying to enlist the help of the local NATO peacekeeping detachment to dispose of his ammunition. The shocking loss of life in this mountain village did raise hard questions for those running the disarmament programme.

Large quantities of heavy weapons had been collected, among them the tanks, artillery pieces and other equipment I'd seen Afghan soldiers taking over from Ismail Khan in Herat the previous year. But some of the handover ceremonies the UN and Afghan authorities organised looked more like flea markets for weapons collectors.

At one event I travelled to in the Panjshir Valley, rows of dented and rusting Soviet tanks and artillery pieces, some of Second World War vintage, were lined up. You didn't need to be an arms control expert to see that much of the hardware being turned in was of more value to a scrap dealer than a warlord.

It was fair to assume that in many cases more serviceable equipment was being held back as an insurance policy. Bajgah was just one who got caught. Commanders could additionally siphon off cash earmarked to demobilise their militias by inflating the number of men in their ranks and controlling the disbursement of the funds. And it provided an early example of how such reform efforts could be corrupted and even bolster the very people they were supposed to squeeze.

After Commander Bajgah's own insurance policy exploded, it seemed he wanted to be more transparent. He told Bilal he had another weapons cache. He also mentioned that he was considering running for parliament. 'All the elders have asked me to stand,' he claimed.

His other arms store was on the edge of the town, with several families living nearby. Inside an unguarded outhouse we saw stacks of tank and artillery rounds, along with Russian-labelled boxes of rocket-propelled grenades and mortars. Many of the projectiles were covered with mould and oozing fluid, and there was an ominous chemical stench. We left quickly.

* * *

To reach Bajgah village from Kabul, we had travelled over the Salang Pass through the heart of the Hindu Kush range, on a road built by Soviet engineers in the early 1960s. It culminates in a nearly two-mile tunnel, one of the highest in the world. This is another of Afghanistan's unforgettable journeys. Before reaching the tunnel, the Salang Highway twists and turns beneath peaks capped with snow all year round and you feel your lungs tug on the thin air as you climb.

The road that the Soviet Union built was also the route of its retreat in February 1989, the last columns of Red Army troops crawling up the switchbacks. Of all the USSR's bequests to its neighbour, the Salang Highway was the least controversial and arguably the most significant as it properly joined up the country's northern and southern halves.

Once the road opened, the journey time between Kabul and major northern cities like Mazar-i-Sharif and Kunduz was cut from a minimum of three days to 10 to 12 hours. Following his own retreat from the capital after the Taliban takeover in 1996, Ahmad Shah Massoud blew up the tunnel to stop their pursuit. After the American invasion, Russian engineers were brought in to repair the route.

But there had been little maintenance after that, and large portions of the road had turned into a broken track, rutted by the weight of the trucks, buses and cars using it each day. It was a drive that required Abdul's maximum focus, especially once we got into the unlit tunnel. Many vehicles had broken headlights, or none at all.

Conditions were made more hazardous by the fog-like dust cloud stirred up by the traffic. Abdul often had to brake suddenly for a giant truck appearing without warning out of the haze around us. There were frequent collisions. Even if you weren't injured, you could be asphyxiated by the exhaust fumes trapped inside the ill-ventilated tunnel. It was a relief to reach the light on the other side.

Always focused when he was driving, Abdul would lean in closer to the wheel and edge sideways towards his door when there was a tougher obstacle to negotiate. His body moved with the contours as he steered his way through. I still subconsciously mimic his movements when I'm behind the wheel myself. But there is another reason why Abdul's driving has always stayed in my mind.

One night, back in Kabul, he picked me up after dinner at a restaurant in the Qalai Fatullah neighbourhood, just beyond the city centre. We offered a lift home to two colleagues I had been eating with as they lived nearby.

A minute or two later, we were talking and not paying much attention when Abdul braked hard. Looking out, we could see a man who appeared to be a police officer flagging us down. He wore the peaked, French-style cap of the Afghan police that was standard issue at the time. A vehicle beside him flashed its headlights.

Abdul switched on the interior light so we could be seen – as we would approaching any night-time checkpoint. Sitting beside him, I heard a clunk as he engaged the central locking. But as we drew closer, the man in the police cap stayed in the road and raised his Kalashnikov, pointing it straight at Abdul. Then a second man jumped out of the darkness on my side of the car, aiming a Kalashnikov at me. He was not wearing a uniform.

A third gunman then appeared from the shadows, on Abdul's side. All three were now shouting: 'Get out of the car.' Eyes fierce, the gunman on my side banged the barrel of his weapon hard on my window. But when I said to Abdul that we should open the door, he quietly hissed: 'No!'

Everything happened in seconds. Abdul had his window open a fraction and he called out to the man in the police cap, telling him, 'I'm going to pull in.' As the man stepped aside, Abdul floored the accelerator. Instinctively, I crouched down in my seat, expecting the gunmen to open fire, before I had fully realised what Abdul had done.

When we were safely out of sight past a bend, he doubled back via a cross street so we could drop my two friends at their doors. Local knowledge and years of surviving in Kabul had been distilled into his split-second calculation.

'I knew they weren't real police,' Abdul explained later. 'Their uniforms didn't look right, and I was sure they wouldn't fire.' There was a real police checkpoint nearby, he added. 'They would have heard if they started firing.' There was a quiet confidence to the way he explained his decision, but I was still astonished we had got away with it.

We told Bilal what had happened and spread word of our near miss through our contact networks. Afghans had always been the main victims of kidnap gangs, but abducting foreigners got more publicity and ransom money. And we had no doubt that this was the goal of the group who stopped us.

A day later, we heard news that an Italian aid worker had been kidnapped in the same part of Kabul, by gunmen who appeared to be police officers. Fortunately, Clementina Cantoni was released unharmed around a month later. Across Afghanistan, the number of violent incidents was climbing.

Chapter 7

Lost in Translation and the Shadow of Iraq

Sentences/جملات
I am going to the market
بازار می روم
I bought fruit in the market
من از بازار میوه خریدم

'Sherzad English Courses' in Ghazni.

In early 2007, Farzana's mother lost her job. The aid organisation employing her was forced to make savings and cut back the catch-up educational classes she had been teaching for women in rural Ghazni. It meant a budget crisis for Farzana's family, too.

Her father was now deputy commander of one of Ghazni's police districts. He had his own protective detail because of the growing number of Taliban attacks in the province. Even so, his salary of around $150 a month was not enough on its own for the family to live on.

Farzana and Shireen said they could fill the gap. They had carried on with their English lessons and told their parents they would offer their own private language classes. Though Farzana could boast some teaching experience from her part-time work on the mine awareness project and in assisting her mother, it is hardly surprising that her parents did not take the idea seriously, especially as Shireen was then around 12. But the two sisters were not put off.

Next morning, they hung a big paper sign outside advertising their classes, with a message saying 'registration open'. They named their home school after their brother, calling it 'Sherzad English Courses'. By the end of the day, they had signed up enough students to start a regular class in the guest room. None of them seemed concerned whether the two sisters had any teaching credentials. 'They just wanted to learn,' said Farzana.

To start their classes, she repurposed a whiteboard that she had been given to run her mine awareness courses. Within a couple of weeks, 'Sherzad English' was running a programme of four classes a day, in the early morning and late afternoon, the sisters scheduling them around their own school lessons and extra English tuition, as well as the commitments of their students. They sometimes started at 5:00am.

'Between going to school and running our course, that became our lives,' Farzana said. Wearing her orange jacket against the morning cold, purple sunglasses sometimes propped on her head, she didn't look like any other teacher.

Shireen started a separate class for children, but most of their students were older boys or young men who couldn't afford the price of tuition elsewhere in Ghazni. Their fees of roughly $10 per three-month course undercut the market price by a sizeable margin. But with dozens of students signing up, they were earning as much and sometimes more than their father, even after deducting the cost of buying course books.

They also cut their own overheads, deciding that just Shireen would carry on learning English. 'She came back and then taught me,' Farzana explained. Their mother eventually got a new job with another humanitarian agency, but even then, Sherzad English Courses remained a mainstay of the family income.

Their success was testament to the hunger among Afghans to better their lives. Learning English was seen as a gateway to new and better opportunities. In their own way, the two sisters were helping to close the gap between their provincial home and the big city.

* * *

I was based in Baghdad by then, reporting from a country in the midst of its own civil war. It was a conflict both totally different to Afghanistan's and forever linked. That was not just because the 9/11 attacks had led the United States to invade Iraq, but also because the progression and dynamics of the two wars so closely influenced each other.

From suicide car bombs and jihadi recruitment videos, to troop surges and tribal militias, tactics first used between the Euphrates and Tigris were then transplanted to the Hindu Kush. Because of the way the US military carves up its operations geographically, the Afghan and Iraq wars were also under the command of the same general back at Centcom in Florida.

Zalmay Khalilzad had been part of the diplomatic crossover from Afghanistan to Iraq when he was sent to take over as ambassador there, the Bush administration hoping his knowledge and prayer beads would repair the damage caused by his predecessors. One result of his move was a certain amount of copying and pasting of the language defining citizens' rights from the Afghan to the Iraqi constitution, as Khalilzad was involved in drawing up both.

Like Kabul just over a decade earlier, Baghdad had become a patchwork of militia fiefdoms. Living and working in the middle of it was all-consuming and soul-sapping. In our fortified Baghdad office compound near the banks of the Tigris, we woke to the sounds of mortars and car bombs and went to bed to the rattle of gunfire. I remembered the stories that Bilal, Abdul and Jahan had told me of surviving Kabul's bloodletting. It helped put things in perspective when my phone rang with a +93 Afghan number and one of them was on the line.

Bilal and Jahan often texted, or rang for a chat, after seeing me broadcasting live from Baghdad, asking how I was and filling me in on the latest news from Afghanistan. At the time, Bilal was counting down to leaving. After deciding he wanted to make up for his disrupted education, he had won a scholarship to study international relations in the United States. He credited his success to his grasp of English, 'But I did so badly when I was at school. They just put you in exams and it didn't really matter if you failed.'

I was still in Kabul when he had started the application process. As he followed up his applications with calls to professors and admissions staff, he provided a masterclass in how to sell yourself. 'You won't have any students like me,' he said, meaningfully.

Sometimes, I received messages from Afghan politicians and other contacts, including the occasional barbed comment about how much more often I appeared on television now I was in Baghdad. 'It seems the BBC cares more about Iraq than Afghanistan,' said one lawmaker. Yet even as the carnage in Iraq was dominating the airwaves, the 'other' war to the east was reaching a tipping point.

One day in the spring of 2006, I came into our sandbagged Baghdad newsroom to see reports on television that anti-American riots had broken out in Kabul. The footage looping on the screen showed men pelting stones at US and Afghan troops, and buildings on fire. I texted Abdul, Bilal and Jahan to check they were OK. 'Salam, Andrew jan,'[1] Jahan replied, in between his news-gathering duties. They were fine, he said, but confined to the office.

The bureau and the surrounding neighbourhood had gone into lockdown as any location associated with the government and its foreign backers came under attack. Hotels and banks were looted and torched as the violence spread like a bushfire. By the time Afghan security forces had restored order with a curfew, 20 people had been killed and hundreds injured.

The spark for the riot was an accident involving a US military supply convoy. The lead driver had lost control, killing someone when he ploughed into a Kabul junction. An angry crowd started throwing stones and soldiers opened fire. The mass riot that followed was fed by smouldering resentment towards Afghanistan's US-sponsored order, now five years old.

The billions of dollars pumped into the country had brought some changes, but people could see that most of the benefits had gone to a select few, including the old commanders and their associates. It was hard for anyone to understand why basic services like electricity were no more reliable than they had been just after the fall of the Taliban. And to many Afghans, the Americans came across as arrogant and careless of Afghan lives.

The week before the riot, there had been another US air strike that had killed dozens of civilians. President Karzai had criticised the Americans publicly for such incidents, but his inability to prevent them made him look impotent. Protesters denounced him as America's puppet.

The only dealings most Kabulis had with Americans were encounters with military convoys. To protect themselves against attack, US soldiers forced other drivers to keep their distance, their

---

[1] 'jan': literally 'soul' but commonly used in Farsi/Dari as a term of endearment.

vehicle turret gunners barking warnings through megaphones. If their signals were misunderstood – which happened often – they fired warning shots. I'd been in one of those cars scuttling to the kerb plenty of times, witnessing passengers in other vehicles cursing as the US convoy roared past. For older residents, it conjured up memories of the Soviet occupation.

Yet even as they were losing friends in some places, the Americans were collecting them in classrooms. It may not have been one of the goals of the invasion, but one demonstrable effect was the increase in the number of Afghans in education, girls and women in particular.

Just weeks before the riot flared, the recently completed American University of Afghanistan had begun enrolling its first students at its campus in west Kabul. And Bilal was the latest to join a growing number of Afghans winning places to study abroad. His last act before leaving Afghanistan was to hand over his phones. 'It was my peaceful disarmament process,' he joked. 'The warlords had their guns and tanks and rockets. My weapons were my phones.'

Their recipient was Jahan. He was still only around 18, but on course to become the Kabul bureau producer. His childhood spent shining shoes on the streets seemed far away.

But Abdul had reluctantly decided to give up on his dream of becoming a doctor. Ten years Bilal's senior, he felt it was too late for him to catch up after all the false starts caused by war. 'My family put a lot of pressure on me to stop studying,' he said. Between going to college and driving, he hardly had any hours left for them. His goal now was to make sure his children had the chances that he had not.

* * *

When I first reported from Iraq in the years before the US-British invasion, Fallujah was just a town on the road to Baghdad. Wars give seemingly random places global fame: the Somme, Stalingrad, Srebrenica. So it was with Helmand.

When reports first started circulating in Kabul that Britain was preparing to send troops to this desert province in the Pashtun south, many people had to look up where it was. A day's drive from the capital, none of my Afghan colleagues had ever been there. A British colonial army was defeated in the region in 1880. More than 120 years later, few officials in London knew anything about that history, or that of southern Afghanistan. Why was Britain going back?

The simple answer was a commitment made by Prime Minister Tony Blair to contribute to NATO's expansion across the south, to bolster the Afghan government. As different provinces were divvied up between alliance members, with colonial overtones, the UK opted for Helmand. It was also about narcotics. Britain was the so-called 'lead nation' tackling the Afghan drugs trade, and Helmand was the lead opium-growing province. The idea was to bring in development specialists as well as soldiers, to build up the government's capacity. But there was also a big geopolitical motive driving the mission: the UK's relationship with the United States.

Britain's occupation of southern Iraq had not gone well. Its troops had started off in 2003 patrolling in berets, their commanders confident that they could apply their experience of counter-insurgency warfare in Northern Ireland, where they spoke the language, to the sun-roasted streets of Basra, where they didn't. They rolled their eyes at the difficulties the Americans were having in Baghdad. 'We've got a better feel for it here,' one officer said to me on a reporting trip I made to Basra in 2004. But, even then, the cracks were showing.

On return visits to British troops in Basra, I ran for cover as barrages of mortars landed on their bases. As local resistance in southern Iraq grew, helmets were back on and British generals felt they needed to prove to the United States that the UK could still be an effective ally. Helmand offered that opportunity.

In late 2005, I travelled there to see it for myself. It was a snapshot of a visit, but still a revealing voyage into Afghanistan's tricky local politics and the dangers of outsiders interfering. And as reports began to appear on our Baghdad television from the summer of 2006 of British troops under attack in Helmand, that trip gave me some insights into the trouble they had fired up.

I stayed at the small American base in Lashkar Gah, the low-rise provincial capital, partly because there was already an advance British team there and I was hoping to find out more about their plans. They included soldiers, diplomats and intelligence officers.

Some of the Britons were polling experts who had come in to run focus groups. There was definitely a whiff of the Great Game about them, though with a modern touch.

However, I failed spectacularly to glean anything useful from my compatriots, on or off the record, because they had been told not to talk to me, even about the weather. Brigadier Ed Butler, the commander of the military side of the mission, at least managed a cheery handshake when he arrived for a flying visit. But he, too, was bound by this London-imposed omerta. 'I'm sorry I can't say anything,' he said. 'My hands are tied.'

The base was still a useful place to be. The Americans there, as well as their Afghan translators, would talk to me, and I could come and go as I pleased, using a rickshaw or tuk-tuk to get around town. Unlike at other American installations around the country, security was fairly relaxed because there was no significant resistance to the US presence then. 'We haven't been rocketed the whole time I've been here,' said the base commander, looking disappointed at the lack of action.

Pashtun-majority Helmand had been an important source of recruits for the Taliban in the past and it has an even longer history of tribal feuds and land disputes, exacerbated by the communist era and the civil war. But in the early 2000s, the provincial governor appointed by President Karzai was keeping a lid on these tensions.

Sher Mohammad Akhundzada was another warlord figure with a predatory reputation and a puppeteer's command over tribal politics. His father had been governor before him; his uncle was a celebrated mujahideen commander. Like Ismail Khan in Herat,

Sher Mohammad ran Helmand as his own fiefdom, employing patronage and violence, underwritten by government funds, but also – it was widely reported – by profits from the local drugs trade.

One afternoon, I watched as Sher Mohammad lectured a gathering of tribal elders about the evils of cultivating opium. He was going through the motions of rallying support for a Western-funded initiative to encourage farmers to grow more wheat and other legal crops instead of opium poppy. 'It's against the law and we need to stop doing this,' the governor said, using an old Afghan proverb to make his point: 'We can't hold two watermelons in one hand. If we want to have a better country, we have to change.'

Seated under a colourful sun awning strung over the yard of Sher Mohammad's compound, the elders looked bored. Some were dozing. One stood up to offer an old excuse for farming poppies. 'Opium is not outlawed in the Qur'an,' he said. 'But alcohol and prostitution are, and the government is doing nothing to stop this.' The governor smiled, but didn't engage.

Sher Mohammad had quick, darting eyes, on constant alert. The smart, crisply pressed turban he wore made him look older, but he was only in his thirties at the time. 'It's good to see you here,' he said, unconvincingly, when I was introduced, but he talked the talk on drugs. British forces needed 'to stop smuggling across the border with Pakistan,' he said. What I didn't know then was that the Americans had searched his compound around that time and found a substantial cache of opium there – enough to make several million dollars' worth of heroin. He later claimed it was a store of confiscated drugs that was due to be destroyed.

Privately, US officers described the governor as 'totally corrupt'. But one said, 'We need him right now.' Helmand was a backwater for the Americans then, and they were content to have him keep the peace in his own rough-handed way. The governor was no model of governance, but he wasn't challenging Karzai's authority like Ismail Khan had been.

Ironically, it was a 1950s American aid programme that had helped boost local opium production. As part of their Cold War battle for influence with the Soviet Union, the US built a network of dams and canals along the Helmand river valley, opening up more land to irrigation. Much of this was later planted with opium poppies. The regular, US-style street grid of central Lashkar Gah is another legacy of that period, and so was the governor's compound.

As it geared up for its expedition to Helmand, the Blair government saw the situation through a London lens. It could not have its soldiers working with a suspected narco baron, especially as it was also supposed to be fighting the drugs trade. Sher Mohammad had picked up the signals. 'Don't say bad things about me,' he warned me after we spoke.

Locals who had heard the British were coming had their own lens, tinted by the past. 'Why are the Angrez coming?' several people asked me when I visited Lashkar Gah's main bazaar with a translator. Angrez is the Pashto word for the English. I tried to explain the goals of the British as best as I understood them, but I had no idea how my answers sounded when they were passed on in Pashto. It was easy for misunderstandings to take root.

'If they bring jobs and security, they are welcome,' said one storekeeper. A cloth merchant, perched on the high step of his one-room store joined in the conversation. 'Some say the Angrez are coming to punish us for Maiwand,' he said, referring to the town nearby where an Afghan army defeated a British and Indian force in 1880, in the second Anglo-Afghan War.

Though Britain's colonial army eventually prevailed, the battle of Maiwand is still a celebrated moment of the Afghan narrative – partly for the legend of Malali, a local woman who is said to have spurred her brethren to keep fighting, using her veil as a battle standard. Rudyard Kipling wrote a poem about the battle too, recording how the Afghans 'cut us up like sheep'.[2]

* * *

A few weeks after my trip to Helmand, I heard that Sher Mohammad Akhundzada, or SMA, as the British called him, had been replaced. But unlike in the deal the Americans did with Ismail Khan, they did not secure the Helmand governor's cooperation. He was left stewing with resentment and a lot of armed men he could no longer afford to pay. This meant that even before the main UK force deployed, an important segment of opinion was against them. It also created a fertile audience for the narrative that the British were invading to take revenge for Maiwand.

Speaking a few years later, Sher Mohammad confirmed that he had subsequently encouraged his men to switch sides. 'The government stopped paying for the people who supported me,' he said. 'I sent 3,000 of them off to the Taliban because I could not afford to support them, but the Taliban was making payments.'[3, 4]

This meant that once in position, the paratroopers of 16 Air Assault Brigade, the teeth of the British force, were soon coming under fire. 'Our assumption was that many of these "Taliban" attacking us were SMA's former forces,' said Brigadier Ed Butler.[5]

Crucially, there had also been a change of strategy, with the 'paras' spread out over a much larger area, in so-called 'platoon-house' outposts, though with no parallel increase in their numbers. British

---

[2] https://www.kiplingsociety.co.uk/poem/poems_thatday.htm

[3] https://www.telegraph.co.uk/news/worldnews/asia/afghanistan/6615329/Afghan-governor-turned-3000-men-over-to-Taliban.html

[4] Akhundzada subsequently denied saying this, claiming his words had been twisted. See *An Intimate War* by Dr Mike Martin, p.140.

[5] Interview with the author.

army insiders have also said that this particular unit was 'itching for a fight', feeling that they had missed out on combat in earlier stages of the post-9/11 wars.[6]

As the fighting intensified, it was portrayed back in the UK as a simple bad guys vs good guys battle between a resurgent Taliban and the legitimate Afghan government. 'Here, in this extraordinary piece of desert, is where the future of the world's security is going to be played out,' said Tony Blair on a visit to the main British base in Helmand.[7]

It was a statement remarkable both for its hyperbole and its hubris. As Ed Butler later acknowledged, the Taliban were no threat to the UK or the West. Blair could hardly admit that his own government's decisions had helped stoke local violence.

Instead of a fight for the world's future, Britain had stumbled into a regional civil war that it didn't understand. That was the conclusion of Mike Martin, a former British officer who served in Helmand and learned good Pashto, allowing him to dissect the intricacies of its parochial power struggles. He saw first-hand how Britain's local allies were manipulating their ignorance.[8]

While some of Sher Mohammad's men took up arms against British troops, others were part of UK-supported police forces who often used their position to muscle in on rivals' drugs income. So-called local 'Taliban' turned out to be militias created by villages 'to keep the [British-backed] district "police" out,' said Martin.[9] British soldiers had to work with 'police officers' credibly accused of raping children. Having blacklisted Sher Mohammad, the British ended up cooperating with people with even darker records.

[6] *The Changing of the Guard: The British Army since 9/11*, Simon Akam, p.213.
[7] https://www.theguardian.com/world/2006/nov/20/1
[8] *An Intimate War: An Oral History of the Helmand Conflict*, Dr Mike Martin, p.16.
[9] Ibid., p.16.

Some British funds went into building up government capacity, but far more went into smashing up Helmand villages with air strikes and artillery, claiming the lives of an untold number of Afghans in the process.[10] Two years into the campaign, around 140 British personnel had died, with the worst casualties still to come as reinforcements were sent in. Among the new troops was a young second lieutenant called Harry Wales, better known as Prince Harry.

By then, the Taliban leadership in Pakistan had seized the opportunity to turn the turmoil into a full-blown resistance struggle against the Afghan government and its British backers. 'We will not let them go back to England and say they have defeated the Afghans,' the Taliban said.[11] Instead of proving their ability to mount a military expedition alone, the British eventually had to turn to the Americans for help.

From late 2006 onwards, Jahan watched things slide on reporting trips to Helmand with other BBC colleagues. A Taliban roadside bomb exploded near him on one visit. On another occasion, in 2008, he witnessed a conversation between an officer and a local elder, mediated by the British unit's translator. They were trying to win the village over.

'We will dig a well and improve the road,' said the British officer.

'We don't want your help,' replied the elder, clearly angry. 'Leave us alone. After you're gone, the Taliban will say we're spying for you. We don't want the Taliban. We don't want you.'

But when the translator turned to the officer, he told him the elder had thanked him for his offer and said: 'We are happy you are here.'

The interpreter was telling his employer what he thought he wanted to hear. Jahan was astonished that the officer did not even seem to realise the elder was angry from his body language, and he decided to tell him what had really happened. He witnessed

---

[10] Evidence later emerged that British special forces may have executed dozens of unarmed civilians in night raids, and that superior officers then tried to cover up their actions. https://www.bbc.com/news/uk-670808.

[11] An Intimate War: An Oral History of the Helmand Conflict, Dr Mike Martin, p.84.

several other similar breakdowns in translation and understanding. It didn't take much imagination to guess how often this occurred in Helmand, and what the consequences were.

Having initially resisted British pressure to dismiss the Helmand governor, President Karzai was furious at the disaster that had ensued. 'We removed Akhundzada [the governor] on the allegation of drug running and delivered the province to drug runners, the Taliban, to terrorists, to a threefold increase of drugs and poppy cultivation,' he told a gathering of Afghan parliamentarians in 2008.[12]

By then, Sher Mohammad was one as well, as Karzai had made him a senator in the upper house. He couldn't resist gloating. 'When I was governor of Helmand for four years, NATO did not drop a single bomb on the province. No civilians were killed and no districts fell to the Taliban,' he said. 'If I were still there, I am sure things would be the same as before.'[13]

* * *

There is a postscript to Britain's ill-fated intervention. In early 2005, just after the Blair government decided to commit troops to NATO's expansion into southern Afghanistan, Britain's military headquarters had sent a special forces team to Helmand to carry out an assessment of the security and political situation.

Their report concluded that Helmand was 'largely at peace' under Sher Mohammad's narcotics-funded regime. They went on to warn their superiors both against removing him and against deploying a large British force, which they said 'would likely cause conflict where none existed'.[14] One of those involved in the review put it

---

[12] https://www.thetimes.co.uk/article/hamid-karzai-blames-britain-for-taliban-resurgence-qckmhpp7fxp

[13] https://iwpr.net/global-voices/helmand-ex-governor-joins-karzai-blame-game

[14] *Unwinnable: Britain's War in Afghanistan, 2001–2014*, Theo Farrell, p.176.

this way: 'There's no insurgency now, but you can have one if you want one.'[15]

But their findings were buried. At the time, Brigadier Ed Butler had already been tapped to lead the first 'Task Force Helmand', and was making his own advance preparations to lead the initial 3,300-strong deployment.[16] Yet neither the report nor its conclusions were shared with him. 'I didn't know about it until after I was back in the UK,' Butler said when we spoke.

He had long retired from the military by then, and admitted he was 'amazed' that he hadn't been made aware of the assessment beforehand, especially as he had spent much of his career in the special forces, including two previous tours in Afghanistan. Butler made the point, however, that it's unlikely the report would have changed anything, because the decision to send British forces had already been made. And in the end, it wasn't even about Afghanistan.

'The train had left the station because of Blair's commitments and [because] NATO was going to prove that it could do out-of-area operations,' he said. Another reason was because 'Iraq had not been a textbook operation, [and] many people thought that Afghanistan was going to be an opportunity for UK PLC and the military to do a better job.'

It was 'farcical' he said, to hope that the combined military and civilian mission could have effected any meaningful transformation on the original three-year timeline and the limited resources they were given – even before they got tangled up in Helmand's local conflicts. 'It took us 30 years to get to a resolution in Northern Ireland.' There was also 'naivety in parts of Whitehall and NATO'

---

[15] *Losing Small Wars: British Military Failure in Iraq and Afghanistan*, Frank Ledwidge, p.61.

[16] Only around 650 were front-line combat soldiers from the paras. The remainder were support troops.

about how British troops were likely to be received. 'I'd fought in Afghanistan twice before. I knew what the reaction was going to be.'

Butler had no involvement in the governor's removal, but he was criticised for the decision to spread his troops more thinly, to try to cover a larger area of territory. He said he was under pressure both from the new governor and President Karzai to bolster the Afghan government's authority: 'We were damned if we did, damned if we didn't.'

In his view, much of the blame for what went wrong lies with senior military leaders who didn't have a clear plan for what they were going to achieve and failed to brief their political masters on the challenges. The outcome, he said, was 'pretty disheartening, to say the least, if you think about the dear old blood and sweat and treasure which we invested in there.'

Helmand may not have started as a battle between the British army and the Taliban, but it ended as one. Ultimately the Taliban could claim success in sending the 'Angrez' back home defeated. They had won the fourth Anglo-Afghan War.

* * *

By 2008, Sherzad English Courses were doing well, while Farzana and Shireen's own English skills were improving too. Their teaching income had helped fund a second floor for their home, giving the sisters more classroom space. 'We hadn't built the walls then,' said Farzana, 'but with that sheltered space we could handle up to 150 students a week in summer.'

Yet even as life was going well at home, they could sense the war closing in. They heard shootings more than before. Her father was often deployed far beyond Ghazni, and was away for weeks at a time: 'My mum was always worrying about him.' One night, a few hours after he said he was on his way, Farzana's mother got a call from one of his fellow officers. Her husband was in hospital.

Close to the city, a bomb buried under the tarmac had detonated under his vehicle, blowing it off the road. Two of his bodyguards had been killed.

The way the bombing had been carried out showed how the Taliban were adapting, often copying techniques perfected by insurgents in Iraq. In the past, they had disguised their bombs as roadside debris, connecting them to pressure plates, timers or command wires.

As the US coalition got wise to such tactics, their enemies buried even larger bombs under the road surface at night, setting them off remotely by sending a text to a mobile phone linked to the detonator. The open plains around Ghazni allowed the Taliban to watch for potential targets from further away with less risk of being spotted. They also had plentiful supplies of explosive material, from old caches of Soviet ammunition, or supplies of ammonium nitrate, which was sold as fertiliser but could be turned into bombs with the right knowledge.[17]

Farzana's father was badly injured and lucky to survive. He was devastated he couldn't make it to the funerals of his bodyguards. When the family went to see him in hospital, Sherzad, her three-year-old brother, seemed even more affected than she had expected. When Farzana asked him why he was so sad, he said, 'Dad has lost his sons.'

Their father did recover, though he was left with permanent pains in his legs. Under pressure from his family, he took a new job with the Afghan defence ministry. 'I didn't believe it, but my uncles thought it would be safer than working for the police,' said Farzana. The job was based at a large army camp near Herat, and so the whole family moved with him.

Starting at high school in the city, Farzana had the kind of reception typical for any 17-year-old arriving from a small town. 'There

---

[17] In 2010, the Afghan government banned imports of ammonium nitrate fertiliser to try to stem its use in roadside bombs.

was this perception in Herat that if you're coming from Ghazni, you're coming from a very backward place,' she said. But there was also an ethnic edge to her classmates' reaction, with some making jibes about her Hazara identity. 'I realised that in their eyes I was a second-class kind of person.'

In Ghazni and Kabul, she had been insulated from this kind of discrimination because she lived in mainly Hazara communities. In Herat, she was the only Hazara in class; most of the students were from the province's Tajik majority, along with a few Pashtuns.

The continued persecution of Afghanistan's Hazaras is partly due to religious differences, as most of them are Shia, living in a mainly Sunni Muslim society. But it's also about appearance. With their blend of Mongol, Persian and Turkic ancestry, Hazaras often look different to the more numerous Pashtuns and Tajiks. Farzana certainly stood out. Many Hazaras try to mask their identity to escape notice. 'For me, that was never an option,' she said, 'because I have a very typical Hazara look.'

In Herat, Farzana's focus was on her studies. She wanted to make good grades and get into university, and signed up for additional classes after school. She also used her English teaching experience to secure a job doing the same thing in a private college, which covered the cost of her own extra tuition as well as contributing to family expenses. And in 2009, she won a place to study law at Herat University.

For her parents, the end of school marked another milestone. They had agreed to shelve the question of marriage until then. One day her mother reminded her of the deal.

'So, you're graduated from school now.'

'So what?' Farzana replied.

'So, this is the time.'

Her mother informed her that two members of their extended family were competing for her hand, one a maternal second cousin, the other a paternal second cousin. While she was studying for her exams there had been phone calls back and forth between Herat and Ghazni.

Farzana erupted. 'I don't want to get married, and I don't want to marry my cousins.'

Enraged, her maternal uncle then came to visit. 'His side of the family were much more conservative, and he just assumed my parents could make it happen.' It was because of her parents that she was under this pressure, but they now came to her aid. Her father told her uncle that Farzana had the final say, using a common phrase to make his point: 'I cannot "put her in a bag" and give it to you. Even if I did, I'm sure she would come back.'

The threat of marriage was put aside temporarily and Farzana began her studies – still living with her family. But university provided little escape from gender-based social codes, at least at first. Herat is a conservative city and Farzana found herself getting into trouble if she was seen chatting to male students after class. College security guards acted as moral police, intervening to separate them and telling them, 'Mixing is not allowed.'

Farzana's attire, sometimes jeans and her orange jacket, sometimes dresses, provoked friction, too. She had a headscarf, but mostly wore it round her neck. Sometimes, female classmates scolded her, telling her what she was wearing was inappropriate. One day, she overheard two of them chatting about their preferred beauticians in the city. 'Don't go to that one,' Farzana heard one say. 'I went there, and they'll make you look as ugly as a Hazara.'

When Farzana protested, her classmate said: 'We don't mean it, it's just the way we talk.'

* * *

By the close of 2008, the two main fronts in America's war on terror had switched places. Since Bush's troop surge, Iraq had become calmer; not by any means settled, but a less pressing

191

concern. But, viewed from Washington, the situation in Afghanistan was getting worse.

The Taliban were gaining ground and deploying more and larger suicide bombs in the cities. Nearly 60 people had died in a suicide attack on the Indian embassy, and both the US and Afghan governments said they had evidence that Pakistan and the Taliban-allied Haqqani network were behind it. Simultaneously, relations between Washington and Kabul were eroding. The Americans said President Karzai didn't care enough about corruption. The Afghan leader said the Americans didn't care enough about Afghan lives.

In August 2008, US forces killed more than 90 Afghan villagers, including at least 60 children, in a night-time air raid on Azizabad in Herat province, claiming a Taliban leader was sheltering there.[18] It was never clear whether the man was there. Even if he was, the violence unleashed by the units involved was wildly disproportionate. It was the worst such incident of the war, and when Karzai went to the village to meet grieving relatives, he said the Americans had 'bathed them in blood'.

A new approach was needed, argued retired Lt Gen David Barno, which made 'the Afghan people the centre of gravity'.[19] He was speaking at a US Senate hearing on the conflict in his new role as a defence academic. Barno had been back in Afghanistan a few weeks before, and in his testimony to John McCain and other senators, he said that the US-led campaign was 'drifting towards failure'. It was February 2009, and the nearly eight-year-old war had just become the responsibility of President Barack Obama.

In diplomatic language, Barno took aim at the over-reliance of his successors on air strikes and night raids, arguing that operations

---

[18] Human Rights Watch report: https://www.hrw.org/news/2009/01/15/afghanistan-us-investigation-airstrike-deaths-deeply-flawed

[19] US Senate hearing transcript: https://www.govinfo.gov/content/pkg/CHRG-111shrg53725/html/CHRG-111shrg53725.htm

'that alienate the Afghan people, that offend their cultural sensibilities, or further separate them from their government, are doomed to fail.' He also said that the United States had to resolve what he called its 'use and abuse relationship' with Pakistan, and demonstrate that it was not looking for a quick exit.

Obama had already ordered in more US troops, with many of them going to Helmand to assist their British allies. Barno's emphasis on winning over the Afghan people would become the guiding mantra of a new 'counter-insurgency' campaign. At the end of that year, Obama took a leaf out of his predecessor's Iraq playbook and ordered a troop surge for Afghanistan.

* * *

The university where Bilal had won a place to study international relations was a liberal arts college in Middlebury,[20] a small town of around 9,000 people in the state of Vermont, in the north-eastern United States. The state is famous for its rolling green hills and its winters, which are cold enough to rival Afghanistan's. On arrival he was struck by the beauty and lushness of the landscape. It reminded him of the lower slopes of the Salang Pass over the Hindu Kush.

When he stepped into a convenience store for a snack, Bilal noticed another, more unlikely, connection with home. The bright blue packets of biscuits on the shelves were strangely familiar. He realised it was the same packaging he'd seen American soldiers use to deliver their dollars to Tora Bora. And once he had tried the real thing, Oreo cookies became a bit of an addiction. He bought packets to eat with a glass of milk when he was up late.

---

[20] The name Middlebury traces to its foundation by New England settlers in the 18th century. In 1778, the town was sacked and burned by British colonial troops during the American War of Independence, so it had a kind of connection with Afghanistan's story as well.

It was Afghanistan, and its eight-and-a-half-hour time difference, that most often kept him up. 'For a while, my father was unwell, and I thought I'd have to go back. And friends and relatives were always calling with news, or just for a chat.' Sitting on the carpet he'd brought with him, Bilal would flip between Skype, news sites and his mobile, his mind still on events back in Afghanistan. His new home in small-town America still seemed very far away. And other anxieties crept up on him.

Though he had wanted a break from his work when he was in Kabul, now he was in Middlebury he worried whether he would be able to return. 'The BBC fascination was still there,' he said. 'I asked myself: "Will they forget me?"' He also wondered how he would be perceived if he did go back, after his closer association with the United States. 'Some of our relatives went to Moscow in the Soviet days, and when they came home, people despised them,' he said. 'I wondered if that would be my fate after being in America.'

Meeting his new professors' demands for long essays was a tough transition for Bilal, too. He was used to doing short exams with a teacher hanging over him for 50 minutes. The new regime felt like 'taking the exam home and then being in the exam for days,' he smiled. 'The first two years were a struggle. I'm not going to lie.'

It helped that the staff were always supportive. Two fellow students he bonded with also helped to turn his American life around, giving him advice about how to handle coursework and introducing him to a wider circle of friends. He started to love college: 'It gave me critical thinking, and a way of seeing that I hadn't had before.'

For one of his assignments he was asked to write an imaginary letter to then US Secretary of State Hillary Clinton about American strategy in Afghanistan and he drew parallels with its war in Vietnam. 'I said the US was relying too much on air strikes, and that so much bombing was counterproductive.'

Bilal couldn't afford to return to Kabul more than a couple of times during his four years at Middlebury, so one of his college friends invited him to live with his family during the holidays. His friend's mother had suggested it after she read an article about Bilal in the college magazine and became interested in his story.

'They were so kind and hospitable. They treated me like I was part of the family,' Bilal said. 'I even had my own bathroom.' But his arrival meant some adjustments for the family's television viewing. They preferred sports channels but, still obsessively following the news, Bilal kept switching to CNN. One day, he came back to the house to find a new television in his room: 'They were telling me in a very nice way, "We don't want to watch CNN."'

His viewing habits and the conversations he had with his host family and fellow students made him realise how little his country featured in America's consciousness by the late 2000s. Memories of 9/11 were fading. 'I hardly ever saw any reports about Afghanistan,' he said. 'People were interested in me, but I'd hear people saying, "Why are we still in Afghanistan? Why do we care about women's rights there?"'

He was the only Afghan at Middlebury at the time, but one of many students from countries in the surrounding region, including Pakistan. Sometimes arguments broke out between them over Pakistan's role in stoking Afghanistan's turmoil, spilling over into student email groups.

Some of the Pakistani students had establishment connections and pushed back at criticism of their military's policies. 'Their argument was that it was our fault that Pakistan had to intervene,' Bilal recalled, due to the series of coups in Afghanistan in the 1970s. That there had been even more coups in Pakistan was beside the point for them. It was a useful insight for Bilal into Pakistani narratives about themselves.

One day, he was working in the library on an essay assignment about Afghan-Pakistan relations when he got a call from the college dean, with whom he got on well. 'Should I be worried?' she said. 'I've got two FBI agents in my office and they want to see you.'

The day before, Bilal had been to a Western Union office to collect some money sent from home. He was going to use it to buy a ticket back to Kabul that summer. But the employee he dealt with became suspicious and wouldn't give him the money. He had left his card and asked her to get in touch.

With his dean present, the FBI agents interrogated Bilal for several hours. Some of their questions about why he was in America surprised him. He assumed he had already been thoroughly checked to obtain his visa. His answers seemed to satisfy them though, and their interest broadened into conversation about the situation back in Afghanistan and what had happened to Osama bin Laden.

'Where do you think he is?' one of the agents asked.

'Pakistan,' Bilal said. 'And definitely not Afghanistan.'

Having answered their questions about the whereabouts of Al Qaeda's leader, he headed back to the library to finish writing about the two neighbours and why it was so difficult for them to get along.

Chapter 8

The End of bin Laden and the Start of the Book Club

War and Peace by Leo Tolstoy.

People were giving strangers hugs. Some were perched on the shoulders of partners and friends waving large American flags. Others had climbed into trees on the edge of the park and strung the Stars and Stripes between the branches. Nearly 10 years after 9/11, the chant 'U-S-A! U-S-A! U-S-A!' once more rang out.

It was late on 2 May 2011, and outside the White House in Washington a large and still-swelling crowd was celebrating the news that Osama bin Laden had been killed in a US raid on his safe house in Pakistan earlier that day. Most of them were young, in their late teens or early twenties, and would have been children at the time of the attack.

Even larger crowds had turned out in New York's Times Square and at Ground Zero. President Obama had stamped his name on the war he had inherited, by killing the man who had started it. As he paid tribute to bin Laden's victims in a live address from the White House, his words had a poignant ring.

'The worst images are those that were unseen to the world,' Obama said.[1] 'The empty seat at the dinner table. Children who were forced to grow up without their mother or their father. Parents who would never know the feeling of their child's embrace. Nearly 3,000 citizens taken from us, leaving a gaping hole in our hearts.'

Watching the throng outside the White House that night took me back to the sombre, fearful gathering I had witnessed around the civil war monument in Peabody, Massachusetts, in September 2001. It was as if the war was over. 'It's like it's VE Day,'[2] commented an American officer I spoke to.

It was understandable if many thought that way. Capturing or killing bin Laden had been the objective when the war began. A decade later, polls showed that around three-quarters of Americans wanted their troops home. With the economy still in recession after the 2008 financial collapse and unemployment above 9 per cent, the war in Afghanistan was far down the list of priorities for Americans,

---

[1] https://obamawhitehouse.archives.gov/blog/2011/05/02/osama-bin-laden-dead

[2] 'Victory in Europe Day', on 8 May 1945, when the allies accepted Nazi Germany's surrender, marking the end of the Second World War in Europe.

if it even featured at all. Several lawmakers echoed the polls, urging a rethink in US strategy.

President Karzai said bin Laden's discovery in Pakistan underlined his belief that the Americans should switch their focus there. Their conflict, he said, 'is not in the houses of innocent Afghan civilians'. But while the United States had achieved its original goal, it was no longer the same war. After Obama's troop surge, the light footprint of the 2001 invasion had grown into a 100,000-strong army spread across 800 bases. They were supported by an army of contractors almost as large, and another 30,000 NATO and other allied troops.

Over time, the list of Western goals in Afghanistan had grown longer and more diffuse – defending democracy and the rights of women and girls, as well as preventing a Taliban and Al Qaeda comeback. Western leaders sometimes reworked a slogan coined by President Bush, arguing that fighting militants 'over there' meant 'we do not need to face them in the United States'.[3] As the Taliban had never threatened to carry out attacks outside Afghanistan, that reasoning began to sound increasingly hollow.

Behind the scenes, small groups of US and European officials were making tentative efforts to start negotiations with the Taliban for a political settlement. But the Americans involved often had to contend with leaks from their own side trying to undermine them, particularly from the Pentagon and the CIA. 'Peace was not the priority,' said Barnett Rubin, a veteran US expert on Afghanistan and one of those involved in these early initiatives.[4] The US military remained the main driver of the mission, and the generals still hoped they could find a way to defeat the Taliban on the battlefield.

---

[3] https://georgewbush-whitehouse.archives.gov/news/releases/2007/08/20070828-2.html

[4] Interview with Barnett Rubin for Foreign Policy podcast series *The Afghan Impasse*.

Right then, for the first time in years, US and NATO commanders were having some success. The extra surge troops had helped them push the Taliban back in parts of the south, including Kandahar and Helmand. It had come at a heavy cost in lives, but it also changed attitudes when people saw the Taliban's momentum ebbing away.

But these gains were fragile and would have little prospect of lasting. When he announced the surge, President Obama also put a date on when the reinforcements would start to come home – July 2011. Over the next three years, Afghan security forces were due to take over the lead, with Western forces falling back into a support role. But naming a withdrawal date sent a message to the Taliban and Pakistan. They now knew they could wait out the clock, because the West was not going to stay.

Obama's vice president – who had opposed the surge in the first place – had made it clear there was no chance of the drawdown being postponed. 'We're starting it in July of 2011,' said Joe Biden, 'and we're going to be totally out of there, come hell or high water, by 2014.'[5]

* * *

Something was bothering Farzana, and it was fundamental.

'It was funny,' she said, laughing. 'I was seriously asking myself, "Do I exist or not?"' In her first year at university, Farzana had continued reading as voraciously as ever, and had begun to explore the works of different philosophers. When she reached Descartes, his famous question vexed her, too.

His conclusion, 'I think, therefore I am,' provided an answer. But Farzana found herself doubting other aspects of her life. 'Why am I reading? Why am I bothering with law school? Who am I?

---

[5] https://nypost.com/2010/12/19/biden-us-out-of-afghanistan-in-14-come-hell-or-high-water/

What lies at the end of this?' Herat's rigid social codes and expectations were stifling for a 19-year-old with a curious, probing mind. She was getting a bit depressed. But from talking with her fellow students, she began to find that she wasn't alone: she had soulmates among both her male and female classmates who were just as intrigued by life's big questions. Together, they decided to set up a book club to tackle them.

Their choices were eclectic and challenging. They started with the writings of Islamic thinkers, discussing the comparative rights and status of women and men in Islamic and Christian societies. One name on their early reading list was Ali Shariati, a prominent 1960s and 1970s Iranian intellectual and revolutionary who argued that women in the West had only gained sexual liberation, not true freedom. But his model of society, run according to orthodox Shia Islamic values and traditions,[6] didn't offer much hope for improvements in women's rights either.

They moved on to works by the father of existentialism, Jean-Paul Sartre. A favourite was his play, *The Devil and the Good Lord*, which ultimately concludes that there is no heaven or hell, just humans and their own personal choice to do good or evil. One of her male classmates became fascinated with Friedrich Nietzsche, which led to weeks of earnest argument about nihilism and what it meant for the world they were living in.

It wasn't only their reading which was pushing boundaries. Just getting together to talk was difficult for a group of unrelated young women and men in Herat. Even with books on the table, the college cafeteria was off limits; security guards broke up an early gathering there. Other classmates sometimes acted as social police too, focusing on the women in the group and telling them it was inappropriate

---

[6] Ali Shariati is regarded as one of the ideological inspirations for the 1979 Iranian revolution, which occurred two years after his death.

to be with their male classmates 'sharing books, or whatever you're doing'. Sometimes, the reading group had to be semi-virtual, the men in one place, the women in another, discussing their latest read over a mobile phone on speaker.

Most of the group's 10 members were, like Farzana, from the provinces, not Herat or Kabul. They became close friends, with their informal club providing a mental oasis in a real world that often felt arid. 'It was a huge thing,' she said. 'Our book club really meant a lot to us.'

It also turned into an intellectual networking opportunity as the group's members tapped their contacts to find other people they could learn from, some of whom could also give them a space to meet without being harassed. 'There was a guy someone knew who'd read a lot of different philosophy. So, we used to go to his house every Wednesday to listen to his theories about life.' The man had learned Arabic, and for a while he also taught them the language.

At first, everything they read was in Farsi, because most books on sale were printed in that language. But English versions were becoming more available. They started on the work of the novelist Paulo Coelho. They read *The Alchemist*, but Farzana's favourite was *Eleven Minutes*, telling the story of a young village girl's suffering in pursuit of love: 'The way Coelho portrayed her, as such a strong personality who decides her life, was inspiring for me.' Next, they decided to tackle Tolstoy's *War and Peace* in Farsi.

'It was hard to get into at first,' Farzana said. 'But I found it resonated with everything that was happening in Afghanistan. My world was very small, so this and other books we read were a gateway to a bigger world. They told me how so many other places had had wars, that life still went on, and that it was possible for these wars to end.'

* * *

Another feature of America's war in Iraq had been transplanted to Afghanistan by 2011. Kabul had its own 'Green Zone', modelled on the fortified government and diplomatic quarter in Baghdad. The Kabul version was defended by a similar 'ring of steel', comprising blast walls, gun towers and checkpoints equipped with vehicle scanners and sniffer dogs. A tethered surveillance blimp kept watch on the Green Zone and the city from far above.

But two days after the 10th anniversary of the 9/11 attacks, a large group of Taliban fighters penetrated the ring of steel with a carefully planned assault. After a suicide bomber detonated at one of the gates, a second group ran inside and took over a half-built multistorey tower, from where they directed a hail of rocket-propelled grenades and machine-gun fire down on to the US embassy and other compounds in the Green Zone. The city centre became a battleground, and it took Afghan and NATO troops until the next day to regain control.

One of the reporters covering the siege was Bilal. He had completed his degree the year before and decided that he had to return home. 'Like many of my friends, I had these grand ideas of helping to rebuild my country,' he said with a weary chuckle. 'You know JFK's famous line, about being an idealist without illusions? Well, our problem was that we were idealists with illusions.'

He had got straight back into his reporting work, tapping contacts who were now rising up the Afghan government. They gave him an inside view of the Taliban's patience and sophistication. He learned that their fighters had evaded the Green Zone's defences by getting jobs on the construction site months earlier and then smuggling weapons in piece by piece. They had also prepared by leaving themselves a cache of food and energy drinks.

The Taliban were still under pressure in the south. But their losses there were offset by these 'information war' successes in the capital, which dented the Afghan government's authority and generated dispiriting headlines around the world. The Taliban had mounted several other high-profile attacks that summer, including a mass suicide assault on the Intercontinental hotel.

A week after the Green Zone attack, the Taliban delivered a ruthless follow-up, blowing up a former Afghan president named Burhanuddin Rabbani who was trying to initiate peace talks.[7] There was a *Godfather*-style twist to this suicide plot, as the former president knew his assassin, and so the man wasn't searched when he arrived for a meeting. His explosive device was inside his turban.

Washington again linked the Taliban's Haqqani faction and the ISI to these attacks, with the United States' most senior military officer saying so publicly. 'The Haqqani Network acts as a veritable arm of Pakistan's Inter-Services Intelligence [ISI] Agency,' said Admiral Mike Mullen. 'They may believe that by using these proxies they are hedging their bets or redressing what they feel is an imbalance of regional power. But in reality, they have already lost that bet.'

Viewed from the ISI's headquarters on the edge of Islamabad, the bet had never stopped paying off. Washington had exacted no price after accusing it of orchestrating the bombing of the Indian embassy in Kabul in 2008, nor even after bin Laden was found to be hiding out in a house near Pakistan's military academy. And Pakistan, for its part, had a host of its own unresolved grievances and anxieties.

There was Afghanistan's refusal to recognise the British-drawn 'Durand Line' frontier as the settled border, which encouraged its fears that Pashtuns on either side could unite to dismember Pakistan. There was also its frozen conflict with India over Kashmir. Having fought four wars rooted in the issue, the Pakistani military had turned Kashmir into a cornerstone of the national narrative, making it even harder to resolve. It meant that many believed the road to peace in Kabul had to run through Islamabad and Delhi first. If they could

---

[7] Burhanuddin Rabbani was one of the leaders of the Northern Alliance and Afghan president from 1992–96 during mujahideen rule and the civil war.

settle their differences, went the thinking, there would be less incentive for them to face off in Afghanistan.

In the meantime, the US and NATO's dependence on Pakistan grew with their Afghan footprint. By 2011, they required a baggage train of some 50,000 trucks a year from Karachi port to sustain their operations. After a deadly clash with US forces along the border in the months after the bin Laden raid, Islamabad shut down the supply lines entirely. It took more than six months, millions of dollars and an American apology to get the trucks moving again. Always in the background for Washington was the nagging fear of Pakistan losing control of its nuclear weapons. Officials likened the relationship to a bad marriage, with the kicker that divorce was impossible.

It was Washington and Islamabad's partnership in the war against Moscow that had institutionalised this toxic marriage. General Hamid Gul, one of the ISI chiefs during that period, even boasted about the agency's success in gaming the relationship. 'When history is written, it will be stated that the ISI defeated the Soviet Union in Afghanistan with the help of America,' said Gul, in a 2014 television interview. 'Then there will be another sentence. The ISI, with the help of America, defeated America.'

Yet even before that provocative statement, the Afghan government had realised that US policy towards Pakistan was unlikely to change, even though it was costing American lives.

After his inauguration for a second term in late 2009, President Karzai hosted a dinner for then Vice President Joe Biden at the Arg palace in Kabul. Ten other people were present, including the Afghan defence and foreign ministers. At one point in the conversation, two of those at the table told me, Karzai turned to Biden to reiterate what was already an old request – for the United States to focus its attention on Pakistan.

The two men had a testy history. On one of his previous visits, as a US Senator, Biden had walked out on Karzai after he denied that his government had a problem with corruption. And their meeting in 2009 followed widespread reports of fraud during the Afghan leader's recent re-election. But the aggression of Biden's response still stunned everyone there. 'Mr President,' he said to his host. 'Pakistan is 50 times more important for us than Afghanistan.'

'Everybody heard it,' said one of those present. 'It was like a cold shower. The table went quiet. No one knew what to say.'

'Why did he say, "50 times"?' said someone after Vice President Biden was gone. Nobody could say. Neither could anyone imagine then how much his position would matter.

* * *

'For you,' said Abdul, indicating skewers with small chunks of lamb meat and tail fat, sprinkled with a seasoning made of dried grapes. Known as 'chopan' kebabs, I loved the combination of the sour spice and rich meat. Accompanied by pieces of hot flat bread, it was our favourite meal at roadside grill shops around the country. Abdul and I had eaten it together time and time again over the years we had regularly travelled across the country.

But this was a different occasion: now Abdul was the host. It was early autumn in 2012 and we were eating in a restaurant he had opened with his brother at Qargha Lake, a popular weekend retreat on the edge of Kabul.

His waiter set down plates of spiced meat 'chapli' kebabs next, along with bowls of 'sabzi' – spinach fried with onion and coriander in clarified butter – and roughly sliced pieces of white and red radish. A tantalising aroma rose from the spread. Then came two kinds of dumplings, whose origin you could trace back to the Mongol invasions. The 'mantu' were filled with ground meat and steamed, with a garlic-flavoured yogurt sauce. The 'aushak' were the reverse, dough cases filled with chopped leeks and boiled, served with a meat and grilled-tomato sauce, then topped with yogurt and coriander.

Abdul had taken a loan to start the business the year before, and it was doing well. He had traded long hours of driving for a better paid administrative job, but by starting the restaurant he was thinking ahead, ensuring another income for his family.

For months, Abdul had been pressing me to come and have a meal. Finally, on what seemed like a quiet Friday – the Afghan weekend – I'd made it up there, along with Bilal, Jahan and some local friends Abdul had invited.

It was from this area that he had fled with his family when he was six, during the first year of the Soviet invasion. Now he had moved his own family back, after buying a plot of land and building a house stage by stage over several years. I was based in India at the time, but still reporting on Afghanistan and making regular trips back.

Another waiter passed around glasses of a tangy yogurt drink known as 'doogh' as we chatted, leaning on cushions around the eating mat. Last to be served was a dome of white and yellow rice, laced with tender chunks of beef and strips of carrot and plump raisins, preceded by a wonderful cloud of flavour-filled steam. It was the Qabeli pulao, the national dish and centrepiece of any Afghan feast.

The scene below us on the water was just as relaxed and peaceful. Couples floated lazily past in coloured pedal boats. Children were paddling at the water's edge, watched by their parents.

When Abdul said, 'Nosh-e jan,' the Farsi equivalent of 'Bon appetit', everyone reached out to scoop up a morsel of the pulao in their right hand before popping it neatly into their mouths. I always made a mess when I tried to eat that way, so I used a strip of bread to press the rice and meat together. There were murmurs of approval from around the mat. But despite the delicious food and idyllic setting, the mood at the meal was flat.

Abdul had hoped that exchanging Kabul and its Taliban attacks for living up in the hills would be safer. His children were going to local schools. But just months before our lunch, the Taliban had struck there as well. They had launched a daytime assault on an adjacent restaurant complex when it was full of families escaping the summer heat, killing nearly 30 people, including many children. The Taliban justified their attack by falsely claiming that foreigners were using the restaurant. All the casualties were Afghan.

Learning I was British, one of Abdul's friends asked me: 'Why are the British troops going home? What about us?' The British Prime Minister, David Cameron, had announced that 500 soldiers were due to leave Helmand by the end of the year and there were rumours of larger reductions to come. His questions encapsulated the conflicted perspectives of many Afghans.

A growing number of Afghans wanted Western troops to leave, but they didn't believe the new army and police force could stand on its own. The post-surge plan that President Obama had announced meant Afghan security forces needed to take over the job of fighting the Taliban after 2014. But to many urbanites, that sounded like the United States and its allies were leaving before the new Afghan state they had created was ready.

Abdul said that he had been looking into how to get his family out of the country. This was coming from someone who never left throughout the civil war and the first Taliban. The signs of peaceful change around the lake looked promising, but without lasting security they were little more than a mirage.

Corruption had also undermined confidence, corroding day-to-day life like rust on an old metal beam. Soon after the brothers opened their restaurant, local officials appeared, accusing them of failing to file the requisite paperwork. Abdul wasn't there at the time and his brother called him saying they wanted $200 to make the problem go away: 'I told him to negotiate.'

The final bribe price they agreed was $100 up front, with free meals for the officials and their families whenever they came. 'What can we do?' Abdul said, with a shrug. He made sure not to serve them his best food.

* * *

In Herat, Farzana and her friends were still expanding their horizons through their book club. Books were changing many other lives, as more Afghans went to school and university. But they could also be dangerous.

In early 2012, Afghan workers at Bagram airbase complained to their superiors after spotting US soldiers dumping old copies of the Qur'an in the base's giant trash incinerator. When the news reached Kabul, it landed like a match on petrol.

Anti-American riots erupted across the capital before spreading nationwide. For the Taliban, it was a gift, allowing their leaders to amplify their message that the Americans were waging war on Islam. The US commander immediately apologised, but the protests raged for four days, claiming 30 lives. Most of them were Afghans, but four Americans died as well. Like the rioting in 2006, the unrest had been an opportunity to vent wider discontent.

The Qur'ans had reportedly been confiscated from prisoners at the base because guards believed they were using the books to pass messages between each other. The books were all in Arabic, and the American soldiers on the waste detail did not know what they were throwing out – in itself a damning admission after more than 10 years of US military presence in Islamic Afghanistan.

I was in Kabul at the time, keeping a low profile as we reported on the disturbances. The Americans were making the same mistakes as the Russians, an Afghan official told me, recalling how the Soviets had gone up against Islam in a losing battle. When Jahan and I visited a hospital treating some of the casualties for a television report, we had to make an early exit. Enraged by the sight of an obvious foreigner, some patients tried to attack us, lashing out from their beds. 'Get this infidel out of here,' one shouted.

A couple of weeks later I was back in Delhi when news came that a US soldier called Robert Bales had stolen away from his base in Kandahar province in the middle of the night and fatally shot and stabbed 16 Afghans in their homes. Nine of the victims were children.

Bales's motive remains unclear. He had previously complained that soldiers he served with were, in his view, too passive. He may also have been suffering the effects of traumatic brain injuries sustained during previous tours of duty in Iraq, and on the night he carried out his mass murder, he had been drinking, in violation of US military rules. Whatever the explanation, the massacre became a grisly symbol of the toxifying effects of an indefinite occupation, which had encouraged soldiers to dehumanise their opponents and forget that they themselves were the outsiders. Bales's killing spree was also, inevitably, a gift for Taliban recruiters.

The increasingly polarised atmosphere was squeezing out moderate voices, and anyone trying to bridge different factions and faiths. One such person was John Butt, the co-founder of *New Home, New Life*. I had fairly frequent contact with him around that time, because he, too, was living in Delhi, and going backwards and forwards to Afghanistan. Since leaving the BBC back in the late 1990s, he had established his own radio station and a small madrassa, both of them espousing his ideals of peace, reconciliation and a more inclusive brand of Islam.

Initially, Butt had set up his radio station in Pakistan's Swat Valley, his first home when he arrived in the region in the 1970s. Following the success of *New Home, New Life*, he began producing a radio soap opera for Pashtun communities on both sides of the frontier. It was called *Da Pulay Poray* or *Across the Border*. But from 2008 onwards, he began to face a direct challenge from Pakistan's own emerging Taliban movement, the Tehreek-e Taliban Pakistan, or TTP. And they were using the same medium to promote their message.

Mullah Fazlullah, the fearsome leader of the Swat-based Taliban, had his own FM radio operation, and he used it to broadcast tirades against his perceived hates, such as education for girls, the Pakistani government and polio vaccinations.[8] 'Mullah Radio', as he became known, also took aim at Butt's station and its soap opera championing the traditional, moderate Islam that Swat had been known for over generations. When the Pakistani army launched an operation to crush Fazlullah, Butt and his team were forced out of Swat.

They moved to Peshawar, the original home of *New Home, New Life*. The team weren't safe there either, as Butt was warned he was on a TTP hit list. They set up again across the border in Jalalabad, starting a new live radio programme as well as a media training centre linked to his madrassa. But in 2011 the centre was burned down in a suspected arson attack.

When I was passing through Jalalabad the following year, I stopped in to see the team and find out how they were faring. I had to meet them at a new safe house location, because they were no longer giving out their address.

Butt stuck it out, alternating between trips back to Afghanistan and remote teaching his students online from Delhi. 'It was hard for me to admit, but even with my madrassa background, I was perceived as a threat to hardliners on all sides,' he said. 'And my Englishness did not help.'

* * *

When the British prime minister had announced plans in late 2012 to reduce troop numbers – the proposal that Abdul's friend had

---

[8] Mullah Fazlullah would later claim responsibility for ordering the shooting in 2012 of campaigning schoolgirl Malala Yousafzai, who then had to flee Pakistan after winning the Nobel Peace Prize and take refuge in Britain.

raised with me during our lakeside lunch – it was not because of any progress in extending Afghan government control. But Cameron did want to be able to say that the 500 soldiers involved would be with their families by Christmas.

He followed up with a visit to Helmand that December to announce even larger reductions in 2013, claiming 'the Afghan army is doing better than we expected.' But it was clear that what the British government was looking for was a way out of Afghanistan.

There is a small British cemetery in Kabul, first established in the 19th century, which holds the remains of some of the soldiers who served in the first and second Anglo-Afghan Wars, though the original tombstones have long gone.[9] When I first visited in the early 2000s, there were also a few names engraved on a single black marble plaque in the cemetery wall to commemorate soldiers who had given their lives in Britain's fourth campaign in Afghanistan. Back there again in 2012, I saw the wall was covered with plaques, bearing the names of more than 430 British soldiers who had been killed. The vast majority had died in Helmand.

Many other governments contributing forces were looking for an exit as their citizens tired of the Afghan mission. The world had moved on from 9/11. Some 50 countries were providing personnel to the NATO-led force in Afghanistan by then, though most imposed caveats on how they could be used, barring them from actual fighting. In late 2012, France, the third largest contributor[10] to the combat operation, broke ranks.

It had sustained more than 80 fatalities by then. But when an allied Afghan soldier turned his weapon on French troops, killing four, there was outrage in France. Then President Nicolas Sarkozy

---

[9] https://www.bbc.com/news/magazine-18369101

[10] Germany sent more troops but restricted them to stabilisation and reconstruction duties.

called the killings unacceptable and pulled out the country's front-line units. Many more British and US personnel had also died in what had become an epidemic of 'green on blue' insider attacks, sapping morale and trust. During the protests over the desecration of the Qur'an, two US officers had even been shot dead inside the Interior Ministry.

The Taliban recruited government soldiers to carry out some of these attacks, but many 'green on blue' incidents were the result of accumulated resentments. Some of the perpetrators were captured alive and said they wanted to avenge coalition air strikes and night raids. NATO commanders issued new rules requiring Afghan soldiers and police to be disarmed when they were with Western troops, with bodyguards watching over them. Having a double-dealing ally across the border was one challenge; having allies inside the country who you feared could shoot you in the back looked like the precursor to defeat.

It had happened before. Tribesmen hired by British colonial troops in the 19th century sometimes turned on them. Some of the Afghan soldiers trained by the Soviet army did the same. And there was another parallel with Moscow's experience. They, too, had found that controlling Afghanistan's cities was never enough.

'There is no single piece of land in this country which has not been occupied by a Soviet soldier,' said Soviet military commander Marshal Sergei Akhromeyev in a Politburo discussion with President Mikhail Gorbachev in 1986.[11] 'Nonetheless, the majority of the territory remains in the hands of rebels. We control Kabul and the provincial centres, but on occupied territory we cannot establish authority. We have lost the battle for the Afghan people.'

By 2013, the Americans and their allies had already been in Afghanistan two years longer than the Soviet army. And they looked destined to meet the same fate.

---

[11] http://news.bbc.co.uk/1/hi/world/south_asia/8365187.stm

Kareem (r) fought the Russians and then the Taliban.
His eldest son was a soldier and was killed in a Taliban suicide attack.

* * *

The road west out of Gardez is straight and largely flat for miles, following the contour of a high plain overlooked by the mountains that form Paktia province's northern flank. A short drive beyond the city, you come to an area called Chawnai.

By late 2013 and early 2014, that was roughly the outer limit of Afghan government control on the western side of Gardez. Beyond lay the district of Zurmat, where I had travelled to meet Naqibullah and his family a decade earlier. The Taliban's white flag now fluttered from many of the district's high-walled residential compounds.

US troops had steadily pulled back under the plan to hand over to Afghan forces the following year. Across the country, bases were being handed over or closed down. Camp Tillman, on the border with Pakistan, was one of those that had already gone in this eastern region. And as the Americans withdrew, the Taliban had started to push forward.

They couldn't take provincial centres like Gardez, but they had turned many rural districts into no-go areas for the forces of the Kabul government. As they dug in, the Taliban expanded their ranks, attracting new recruits to their cause. Any male could be considered. The prerequisite was to be old enough to grow a beard and to have sufficient references and endorsements from local figures of respect, such as tribal elders and imams.

One of the Taliban fighters then serving near Chawnai had joined a few years earlier when he was still in his late teens. In 2013, he was aged around 22. It was Naqibullah. He now had an impressively full beard, but the same sharp, inquisitive eyes.

When we spoke again years later, he remembered Bilal, Abdul, Kamal and me coming to see him in his village in 2004. He explained that he went back to school after that and studied up to Grade 8, when he would have been around 14 or 15. But then the same economic pressures that affected most rural families put an end to his classroom education.

Naqibullah had more sisters and brothers by then, and the family could no longer get by on the farm produce donations that his father received as the village imam. As the oldest male among his siblings, he had to start working. 'My dream of becoming a doctor vanished,' he said.

They were two men of different generations and backgrounds, but there were similarities between the stories of Naqibullah and Abdul. They were both elder sons whose responsibilities caught up with them before they could complete their education. War had played a part. The biggest difference was that out in rural Zurmat, there were few ways to earn a living. And as the government retreated, the Taliban acquired a monopoly on opportunity.

Naqibullah's association with them had begun with doing odd jobs for local Taliban commanders when he was in his mid-teens, in return for small payments. 'I told them if I saw troops on the roads. Later on, they asked me to hide weapons and ammunition for them,' he said. The Taliban frequently recruited teenagers because they were less likely to fall under suspicion. These local commanders also encouraged Naqibullah to attend a different mosque and study the Qur'an with the imam there, instead of with his father.

It was there that he formally joined the Taliban, after the leader of the local dalgai,[12] the group's main fighting unit, said he was looking for new members. 'The verses I had read in the mosque were clear,' said Naqibullah. 'It was my duty as a Muslim to join.'

The fact that he had been detained and imprisoned by the Americans while he was a boy was not part of his decision, Naqibullah maintained. 'It wasn't about revenge. I had to fulfil my jihadi obligation. The foreigners in our country were infidels and I had to fight them to protect Afghans from their oppression. This was my fate, chosen for me by God.'

The mujahideen in the 1980s had used the same language as they battled the Soviet invasion. As the Taliban saw it, they had inherited their mantle. They also called themselves 'mujahideen', equating their fight against the United States and its Afghan 'puppet' government with the anti-Soviet jihad. It was a powerful message, repeated by imams across the Pashtun areas of both Afghanistan and Pakistan, and it helped ensure a constant flow of recruits, despite the punishing losses inflicted by the US-led coalition.

Afghan and US actions helped drive people towards the Taliban, Naqibullah said. Residents from his Zurmat district were routinely harassed or detained because of the area's historic ties to the Taliban. 'If you had a beard, they stopped you and asked, "Where are you

---

[12] A 'dalgai' is a Taliban fighting unit comprising between 50 and 200 men.

216

from?" If you said "Zurmat" they would beat you or arrest you. Zurmat was like a camel for them,' he said, using a common Afghan analogy for bullying.

After some basic training, he became a member of one of around 12 Taliban cells in the area, carrying out ambushes on Afghan forces, as well as US troops before they pulled back. The Taliban steadily entrenched themselves in Zurmat and other districts by appointing their own government, complete with Sharia courts. Each province had its own shadow governor, representing the Taliban's 'Emirate'.

Their power grew in parallel with their territorial control. Shadow governors generated their own revenue by imposing taxes on everything from mining and forestry to narcotics. The hashish trade in Paktia was an important source of taxation income there. But while girls' schools were closed, government services such as health clinics stayed open, because the Taliban wanted them. And the Western-funded Kabul administration still covered the costs.

Many people in Paktia had historically worked in Arab states like Saudi Arabia and the United Arab Emirates, sending remittances back. That provided another revenue stream for the Taliban to tax, as well as connections to Islamic charities and businessmen in the Gulf who supported their cause.

When signs emerged over the following years that government security forces were pulling back further to defend Gardez, Naqibullah's dalgai commander asked him and his fighters to move into Chawnai. They had a regular combat schedule. Spring and summer were the fighting seasons. In the winter months of rest and study, Naqibullah explained, everyone went to Pakistan.

* * *

When Farzana finished high school, her grades were good enough to apply for medical school. That is what her mother wanted her to do, not law. 'Have you ever heard of a woman getting a job as a lawyer?' she said. 'You'll just end up being a teacher.' But by the second year of her chosen degree, Farzana was even more convinced that law had been the right choice for her, and she was blossoming. As so often happens, one success breeds another.

In 2011, her university began a research project on Afghan women's rights and child education in conjunction with two European universities. Farzana was one of the students invited to join the programme. That led to her and another student being asked to present their findings at these universities in 2012, her first experience of the world beyond her region.

Simultaneously, another opportunity was emerging. Like many law faculties, Herat ran its own 'moot' practice courts and took part in 'moot court' competitions. The Herat team triumphed in the nationwide final in Kabul. That led to a slot in an international 'moot court' competition, taking them to the United States. By then, Farzana no longer had time for the book club.

The United States couldn't stabilise the whole country, but it was still providing a shield that allowed millions of Afghan women and girls in urban centres to change their lives. In America, Farzana's team didn't get past the first round. However, by the time she graduated a few months later, new opportunities had materialised. Farzana's horizons were expanding in ways she had never dreamed of when she was growing up as a refugee in Tehran, and she felt like her journey had just started.

Farzana's story and that of many other young Afghan women like her highlighted another parallel with the period of Moscow-backed communist rule in the 1980s. Though its ideological motivations were the polar opposite, in many cases the Soviet superpower had also opened up undreamt of possibilities for Afghan women. And Farzana wanted to pursue those opportunities at home. 'If there was one place that needed me, I thought, it was Afghanistan.'

Her parents hoped that she was going to stay in Herat. It was one of the best places that they had lived in; affordable, calm and with better electricity than Kabul. And soon after graduating, Farzana was offered a job with the Herat office of a demining agency. They needed an English speaker, and they were offering a salary of around $700 a month.

It was far more than her father was earning. But to her family's dismay, she turned the job down and said she was moving to Kabul. She didn't even stay for her graduation ceremony. 'I wanted to build a life for myself, and I didn't want to delay.'

Farzana had enough savings from her English teaching job in Herat to get started. But even in Kabul, she found that no one would rent to a young woman living by herself. At first she bunked with a friend until a distant male cousin agreed to put his name to a lease. With the résumé she had built up, including her trips to America and Europe, it was not surprising that she secured a job within weeks.

The US government-supported judicial project she joined was paying three times the salary she had been offered in Herat. Farzana had now been admitted to the inner circles of a gilded club – the American-funded aid and reconstruction programme for Afghanistan.

Yet despite her impressive income and outward signs of success, she soon found herself questioning the value of what she was doing. Part of her work involved running training courses for Afghan justice ministry staff, inculcating them in the principles of Western-style rule of law. However, Farzana was dismayed to find that many who came were not directly involved in legal matters and 'not really interested in the training'.

The real attraction for delegates was the expenses they were paid to attend: 'What we gave for a couple of days' transportation and dinner was more than most of them earned in a month.' The funds, already pre-approved, had to be spent. Sometimes, she discovered, the organisation booked a fancy hotel for $50,000 and organised an event just to use up the budget. And the focus of the programme was on Kabul, which did little to tackle the rural-urban divide.

Farzana had been hired as a legal adviser, but what her American managers really wanted, she realised, was her story. As a woman from a Hazara minority background who had undertaken trips to the West and the United States in particular, she made them look good to their superiors. And because Farzana spoke English, she was easily relatable. They were very excited when she was asked to return to America for another moot court competition.

Symbolic actions too often took the place of efforts to effect deeper, structural change. 'Everything was on the surface,' said Farzana. There were other examples of US agencies promoting people who later turned out to have questionable records, including a famously corrupt female prosecutor in Herat.

'It is hard for me to say all this,' said Farzana. 'I had a lot of respect for my supervisors, and this is not a personal criticism of them. It was just how the US system worked in Afghanistan.' A few months into the job, Farzana went to her boss and told him she didn't deserve to be paid so much. She was barely using her legal training, she said. 'He looked at me and smiled and said, "You do." And I said, "I don't."'

Farzana was still only in her early twenties, but she could see what her superiors seemed unable to acknowledge: none of the project's work would last: 'Once the Americans left, everything would be gone.'

Chapter 9

'The Taliban are not Losing'

The piercing light of a big Afghan sky illuminated the mixed hues of pine, oak and walnut trees on the hills; some of their leaves were beginning to turn. The Kunar River was waiting for new rain, but it still ran deep and strong. It was the perfect day for a new politician to sell his vision.

After nearly two decades of being a journalist, observing his country's ills, Bilal had decided he wanted to be involved in trying to cure them. It was the autumn of 2018 and he was standing to be a member of the Afghan parliament.

For the past few years, he had been working as a freelance reporter and commentator, after leaving the BBC. But he had decided to take a break from journalism to run for one of three seats allocated to Kunar, one of which was reserved for a female candidate.

It was the province where his father and grandfather had been born. Part of Bilal's pitch was that he could combine his local roots with his Kabul connections. He wanted to be 'a bridge between the village and the city'.

A few hundred villagers had turned up for his riverside campaign rally, screened from the sun by a large awning strung between the trees. Nearby, a cooking team was stirring the pulao in pots the size of truck tyres.

One of Bilal's policy ideas was to organise accommodation in Kabul for local girls and boys to complete their education, safe from the fighting in Kunar. He also wanted to boost farmers' incomes by streamlining the process for selling their melons, corn and farmed fish in Kabul. Another proposition was to find ways to ensure more revenue for local communities from the province's jade and chromite mines, as well as its forests.

In the context of the time, it was aspirational stuff. But Afghanistan's democracy had become dysfunctional and 'rotten with corruption', Bilal said, with lawmakers treating the system as a money-making machine. In his mid-thirties by then, he said it was time that younger Afghans stepped up to offer an alternative: 'We need a generational transition of power.'

Many of Bilal's friends and relatives saw his parliamentary bid as quixotic at best. On his early exploratory visits to Kunar, he had overheard local elders deriding him for not being married and not having a beard. 'I was clean-shaven at the time. I heard them saying, "He's just a boy."'

Some friends warned that unless he could gather and distribute lots of cash to buy support, he had no chance. 'You will be lucky if you get 100 votes,' said one. They also worried for his safety. Even before the campaign got under way, several prospective candidates had been assassinated. Nationwide, the political and security picture was darkening.

* * *

Since the 2014 election, when Hamid Karzai had stepped down, power had been shared between two leaders, President Ashraf Ghani and Abdullah Abdullah, who had the title of chief executive. The US had brokered the power-sharing deal after months of deadlock, because Abdullah had refused to accept the result, accusing his rival of fraud.

Divided within itself, the Afghan government presided over an ever more divided country, as the Taliban extended their reach into more districts nationwide. And there had been a surge in suicide bombings in Kabul, claiming hundreds of lives.

Afghan opium and heroin production had reached record levels, as narcotics rings profited from the instability. In a high-risk environment, drugs were a low-risk way of making short-term cash. From farming and harvesting the raw ingredients, to cooking up and smuggling the finished products, the narcotics trade was thought to be generating work for as many as 500,000 people, making it the country's largest employer. Children were often among them, hired to harvest the opium resin from the poppies and process it in village labs.

By 2018, drugs producers had expanded into refining methamphetamine, better known as crystal meth, after finding that they could extract its base ingredient from a local plant. Traffickers had also found a local market for a cheap version of the party drug ecstasy, known as 'Tablet K' (pronounced 'Ka'), much of it produced in Pakistan. At least 3 million Afghans were regularly using drugs, often because of trauma and undiagnosed depression.[1]

Since moving into the White House that year, President Donald Trump had escalated US involvement to try to hold the line, ordering a 'mini-surge' and a large increase in air strikes. Although American troops were officially there in a support and training role, their special forces units were still carrying out regular raids.

Trump gave the Pentagon the go-ahead to use the most powerful non-nuclear weapon in its arsenal for the first time, nicknamed the 'Mother of All Bombs', to attack the Afghan offshoot of the Islamic State. For Trump, it had been the mother of all U-turns. Before

---

[1] The Afghan population was estimated at around 35 million people in 2018, but there has been no census there since 1979.

running for office, he had denounced America's continuing presence, tweeting: 'Time to come home!'

True to his maverick style, Trump also upended the establishment US approach to Pakistan, cutting off nearly all American security aid to the country in 2018 in retaliation for what he called its 'lies and deceit' in providing a sanctuary to the Taliban. Yet although the Afghan government welcomed the move, it was little more than a token gesture. And it was not accompanied by any wider US efforts to address the motivations for Pakistan's actions. For Pakistan's generals, the latest American move was déjà vu.

There were many committed people from the US-led coalition serving in military, diplomatic and development roles who saw all too clearly that things had gone wrong and still hoped there was a way to turn the situation round. But, ensconced in the security bubble of the Kabul Green Zone and similar compounds around the country, their capacity to effect change was more limited than ever, however good their intentions.

As US air strikes increased, so did the number of civilian casualties. And for every group of Taliban fighters decimated by a US bomb, there were new recruits ready to take their place.

In the early years of Obama's presidency, Afghanistan had been dubbed the 'good war', as opposed to his description of Iraq as the 'dumb war'. By 2018, it had become the 'long war' or 'forever war'. Although American politicians who used such phrases were rarely referring to the 23 years of conflict that preceded 2001.

With casualties among Afghan civilians and government troops at all-time highs,[2] both politicians and military leaders said there could be 'no military solution' to a conflict that had become a 'stalemate'.

---

[2] In 2018, 3,803 Afghan civilians were killed, according to the UN, most in Taliban or Islamic State attacks, but more than 500 of them died in US air strikes. An estimated 8,000–9,000 Afghan police and soldiers died in fighting that year, but the Afghan government classified the totals.

One American general went further and said, 'The Taliban are not losing,' in a masterpiece of understatement. No US decision-maker wanted to admit defeat.

But by the end of 2018, President Trump had had enough and reverted to his pre-election stance. A few weeks before the official start of the parliamentary election campaign, he had asked the US envoy, Zalmay Khalilzad, to return to government and start talking to the Taliban. The United States was getting out.

* * *

Early that summer, Jahan got a call from the British embassy in Kabul, inviting the BBC to send a representative for a press briefing that evening. The Foreign Secretary, Boris Johnson, was making a short visit to Afghanistan, and after his official meetings, he wanted to talk to journalists who worked for British media outlets. Jahan said he would come.

Johnson's trip had been hastily arranged. He wouldn't even be there a full day, but President Ashraf Ghani and Chief Executive Abdullah Abdullah made time to see him. They didn't get many visits from high-level Western officials any more.

Apart from Jahan, all the journalists at the briefing were foreigners. When Boris Johnson learned that Jahan was Afghan, he turned the questioning around, keen to take advantage of a rare opportunity to talk to someone who was from the country. Running his hand through his hair as he spoke, he asked: 'How is the security situation?'

'It's not good, as you can see,' said Jahan, referring to the heavily fortified embassy complex in which they were meeting.

'What about Afghanistan's free media, girls having more rights and going to school?' Johnson replied. 'Aren't those important?'

'Those are important,' Jahan agreed. 'But security is more important. Mothers and fathers sending their children to school are worried whether they will come back alive or not.'

'Are you serious?'

'Of course I am.'

Jahan was himself a father by then, with a one-year-old daughter, and appreciated Johnson's curiosity about the lives of Afghans. He also felt proud to be the one describing the situation in Afghanistan to the foreign minister of Britain: 'In my past life, I thought to myself, I wouldn't even have been allowed in his shadow.'

Their meeting was also imbued with the ambivalent emotions Britain arouses in many Afghans. Feelings of antipathy stirred by its colonial legacy were there, but also some residual respect. 'When we Afghans want to call someone smart or intelligent, we say, "You're as clever as the Angrez,"' Jahan pointed out, when we spoke about his meeting with Johnson afterwards.

But back in the UK, Boris Johnson was being accused of showing disrespect to his cabinet colleagues and British MPs with his late-notice trip to Kabul. Parliament was due to vote on a government proposal to expand London's Heathrow Airport, which Johnson had loudly opposed when he had been the city's mayor. If he had stuck to his principles and voted against the plan, he would have had to resign. The hasty trip to Afghanistan had provided him with a convenient get-out.

* * *

It took a brave man to run for office in Kunar, even with the body-guards Bilal had hired for his protection. Amid its arresting mountain beauty, the province offered up a tableau of Afghanistan's old fault lines and threats.

Al Qaeda had a presence there in some of its steep-sided valleys. Osama bin Laden is thought to have used Kunar as his escape route across the frontier in 2001, putting the area on America's radar early on and leading to years of ferocious battles. Mirroring British missteps in Helmand, US forces had failed to understand the local dynamics and became embroiled in a contest for control of the timber trade in its Korengal Valley, which the Taliban exploited.[3]

By the time Bilal was running for election in Kunar, the Americans had long since pulled out their infantry. But they were still targeting the province with special forces and drones, in pursuit of the Islamic State.

After first emerging in Iraq and Syria in the mid-2010s, from the local branch of Al Qaeda, the Islamic State had spawned affiliates across the world. By 2015, the Afghan offshoot – which called itself the Islamic State in Khorasan Province,[4] or ISKP – had developed several strongholds in eastern Afghanistan, including Kunar. They recruited from both sides of the Afghan–Pakistan border.

More commonly known in Afghanistan as 'Daesh' – the Arabic acronym for the original group – the Islamic State espouses an ultra-fundamentalist Sunni ideology that is similar to Al Qaeda, but it became known for even more extreme acts of brutality. The Taliban saw the Islamic State as a threat to its interests, which even led to indirect cooperation with the US military in targeting IS outposts in Kunar from 2016 onwards.[5] The global picture of Islamic fundamentalism was metastasising, making the political landscape in places like Kunar more complex than ever.

* * *

Bilal had set up his Kunar campaign office more than a year before the election, expecting it to happen much earlier. But the delay

---

[3] For more details, see *The Hardest Place* by Wesley Morgan, about the American campaign in Kunar.

[4] Khorasan Province refers to a historic region that included what is today Afghanistan, as well as Iran and much of Central Asia. ISKP was seeking to create this region again as part of a reconstituted Islamic Caliphate.

[5] See *The Hardest Place* by Wesley Morgan.

helped him to build up his knowledge of local issues and squelch his opponents' attempts to depict him as a 'carpetbagger' from Kabul. He had also set up a separate female campaign team to reach out to the area's women. He couldn't meet with them himself, but they passed requests to him. That led him to organise deliveries of classroom furniture and books for several local girls' schools which were still functioning.

He had also got engaged by then. But as he was bombarded with demands for money or favours in exchange for support, he wondered if the sceptics had been right. And at that riverside rally, he was given another reminder of the strength of the very currents he was trying to reverse.

After finishing his speech, the couple of hundred men who made up his audience were enjoying the meal laid on to reward their attendance. Most of the money he had raised in campaign donations from friends and contacts paid for organising and catering these events. Sometimes his team slaughtered five sheep or goats a day to feed all his potential supporters.

Two cows had been butchered for the pulao this time. But as the men from the district tucked in, their maliks, or village chiefs, got to the point. 'Don't bullshit me,' said one. 'How much are you going to pay if I tell people to vote for you? How many cows will I get?'

It was the reality of rural vote bank campaigning. To build support, you had to first win the backing of tribal leaders, elders and village chiefs who would tell their clans and communities whom to vote for. It turned electioneering into auctioneering. But Bilal had told his team that he was not going to buy votes, stuff ballot boxes or insult his opponents. He was in a bind.

Another barrier to reaching out to people as individuals was the fact that the majority of voters in impoverished provinces like Kunar were illiterate. As many as 80 per cent of women in the province were unable to read.

To help voters differentiate between candidates, ballot papers carried their individual symbols and faces, which were advertised on campaign posters. When Bilal registered his candidacy, election officials initially decreed he would be represented by a pair of scissors. But that meant being associated with barbers, his advisers warned. He needed a more respectable symbol. He settled on an electricity pylon instead, which spoke of infrastructure and progress.

The demands that were made of him became more brazen. An election official guaranteed to make him an MP if he paid him $300,000. At one rally, an elder approached Bilal and offered him 1,000 votes if he could arrange for a relative imprisoned in Kabul for smuggling opium to be moved to the provincial jail. Once in local custody, the elder would be able to use his own local connections to secure his relative's early release.

Some on Bilal's team advised him to at least make a call, even if the transfer never happened. 'You think I'm a leaf,' he said to the elder, 'and I'll just do what you want?'

The man was furious, telling Bilal 'go fuck yourself' in Pashto as he stormed off. One of Bilal's campaign banners flapped in the breeze nearby, reading 'Long Live the National Unity and Brotherhood of the People of Afghanistan'.

During the campaign, Bilal and his team received constant warnings of potential attacks by the Taliban or the Islamic State. And they often recruited young people to carry them out. One evening, a teenage assailant armed with a handgun climbed up on to the back of the office compound and was taking aim when one of Bilal's guards spotted him and fired. They gave chase, but lost him in the thicket of a nearby cornfield.

That made it all the more astonishing when he was approached at campaign rallies by confirmed members of the Taliban, Al Qaeda and the Islamic State. Officially, they rejected democracy and any representative of the Afghan government as an American puppet. But they, too, wanted to talk to Bilal about prisoners – their comrades in custody in Bagram jail, by then under Afghan control. Some were young men who had been recruited as suicide bombers but arrested before they could strike.

They wanted Bilal to advocate for their release. 'Maybe this sounds surprising, but I said I would do what I could,' he said. 'I'd lost relatives to their suicide attacks. But I had to try to understand why people were doing this.' He didn't push for any prisoners to be set free, but he did arrange for them to talk to their mothers in Kunar, via contacts in the jail. 'Even prisoners have rights,' Bilal said. 'I felt there was a bigger cause here, to try to build bridges.'

* * *

The mounting bloodshed in 2018 marked a grim anniversary. Afghanistan had been at war for 40 years. By then Farzana had moved all her family to Kabul for their safety.

The pattern of violence hadn't changed. Incidents in the capital made the headlines. But most of the bombings, shootings, night raids and air strikes were happening in the rural areas. Farzana's father had been one of the Afghan army officers on those remote front lines. Since she had moved to Kabul in late 2013, he and his unit had constantly been moved around western Afghanistan as new battles with the Taliban erupted. He was being sent to replace colleagues who had been wounded or killed.

The government kept the figures secret, but details leaked out that as many as 20 to 30 police and army personnel were dying every day, with another 70 being injured. US and coalition casualties had never even come close to that level. For years, Farzana had been trying to persuade her father to give up his job, arguing that he had done his bit. 'I want to be here,' he always said. 'I believe in what we are fighting for.'

But on a visit to see her family in Herat in 2017, Farzana found her father a changed man. A few days earlier, a suicide car bomber had penetrated the perimeter of his outpost in the south-western province of Nimroz. At least 14 soldiers were killed. Among them were all her father's closest friends in the unit. They had served together for years.

'I can't believe I survived,' he said. 'I'll die if I return, but I have to go.'

'You're not going back,' Farzana insisted. This time, her mother took her side.

'Who will pay for the family if I don't?' her father said.

'I will. I'll pay for everyone to move to Kabul. We need to be close to each other and that is the best place to be.'

It was hard for her father to accept, but he relented. His eldest daughter could afford it as she was earning substantially more than his military salary of $300–400 per month. Now 26, Farzana had taken a job with a United Nations affiliated legal body since leaving her previous post. It trained Afghan lawyers to train other lawyers all over the country. She preferred its grassroots approach to that of her previous American employer.

She also augmented her income doing research and translation work. That gave her the means to rent a place for her family, put both her brothers – she now had two – into private school and pay for Shireen to do a post-graduate economics degree. Farzana was keen to get them out of the conservative society of Herat and expose them to Kabul's more 'open-minded lifestyle'. And the capital had changed out of all recognition.

By now, the vistas of rubble that I had seen on my first visit to the city had all been subsumed by new development. The flood of money that had come in since 2001, some of it recycled from the poppy fields, had brought corruption, but also construction. Developers had been undeterred by the bombs and there were now more schools and higher-education institutions. The city had its own glass palaces.

On one visit around that time, Abdul took me on a tour. As we drove around west Kabul, one of the areas worst hit by the civil war, he recalled how there had been nothing here when I first came. 'Every building was damaged or destroyed.'

Many old gardens and buildings had been restored as well. It was always a pleasure in those times to be invited to dinner at one of the secluded old houses around Kabul, overlooking rose borders and grass lawns.

In the old city, the ruined frontages along Jada-e Maiwand had been repaired. The adjacent bazaar, with its tightly packed lanes differentiated by goods – spices, dried fruits, shoes, textiles and the bird market – was still going. But younger people had trendier places to go, such as new malls and neighbourhoods with hip clothes stores and cafes.

America's war had grown old, but Afghanistan had grown young. More than half the population were under 25, most born since the Taliban were in power, and they were starting to shape the country. People in their thirties were already climbing the upper rungs of government, serving as deputy ministers and in prominent ambassadorial positions abroad.

In the west Kabul district of Pol-e Sorkh, the main street was lined with fashion boutiques, spas and coffee bars where young men and women could mix freely. The profile of the customers skewed wealthier, middle class and degree-educated, but that didn't mean they had all started out that way; this was Farzana's milieu. The urban Gen-Z crowd was also helping to close ethnic divisions. Young people were still aware of these identities, but they cared far less about them than their parents.

Talking to customers, I found they were worried by the violence, but also about more normal priorities like finding a job. In the meantime, they were also hopeful for the future and determined to enjoy the opportunities they had. As one recent graduate told me, 'We want to have a life.'

Art studio, Kabul

The urban Afghans I spoke to thought their lifestyle could last as long as the United States and its allies stayed. Abdul had made a similar calculation after they had reduced their forces in 2014 and handed security responsibilities to the Afghan army and police. 'We had survived before,' he said. 'I wanted to stay in Afghanistan. I don't know anywhere else.' As long as the US-led coalition retained a presence, his daughters could carry on going to school and he could maintain the life he had built.

Places like Pol-e Sorkh were not average Afghanistan, but neither were they a total exception. And the more time that passed, the more these changes put down roots and moved beyond Kabul. Other big Afghan cities had also expanded, giving birth to new satellite towns, diluting old customs in the process. The country at large remained deeply patriarchal, yet the prospects for a girl born in the early 2000s had transformed. No girls went to school when the Taliban were in power. By 2018, almost 3 million were doing so.

* * *

I often called on entrepreneur Saad Mohseni to get his take on events. By now he had been dubbed Afghanistan's first 'media mogul' and expanded his business well beyond the region. Presenters on Tolo TV and its sister channels were household names. The finals of its talent show *Afghan Star* attracted up to 20 million viewers, more than half the population. In 2018, the competition was won for the first time by a female singer. She came from Ghazni province.

Tolo had played a pioneering role in the post-2001 Afghan media, serving as a training ground for many journalists. It also paid a heavy price for its success. The Taliban killed seven of its employees in a targeted bomb attack, accusing the channel of promoting 'obscenity, irreligiousness, foreign culture and nudity'.

Mohseni and his team kept going, working behind ever higher fortifications around their offices in Wazir Akbar Khan. And he continued to be an inveterate networker. An invite to one of his evening gatherings was a shortcut to a whirlwind of conversations and contacts that wouldn't have happened any other way. A typical eclectic mix included cabinet ministers, ambassadors, generals and civil society activists, along with the reporters who had made the guest list.

The Afghan-Australian businessman kept a close eye on trends in Afghan society. The changes since 2001 were deep and lasting, he argued, his phone flashing up messages as we talked. 'A lot more women are contributing to the bills or have become the main earner.' This complemented other changes, such as the increase in people travelling into cities for work. 'They have more access to technology and media, and live side by side with Afghans of different backgrounds.' If these changes continued, he predicted, the country was on course for a 50:50 rural-urban split in its population, which he believed would be transformative.

Farzana was an example of the move towards women becoming key earners for some families. In Kabul in 2018, her life was still on fast forward. She had won a scholarship to study for a Master's in international law in Britain. The Afghan government had also noticed her and offered her several posts, including within the presidential administration.

'I always said no and I am proud of that,' Farzana said. 'I was a supporter of the system,' she explained, but not of the government that it had produced. 'I felt that they just wanted me as a symbolic woman.'

She was also focusing her work on human rights issues exacerbated by the conflict, taking on research assignments for various local and international campaign groups. 'I found my fight,' Farzana said. She compiled reports on domestic violence against women and threats to different minority groups.

This work had begun when Farzana agreed to investigate another long-standing injustice in Afghanistan – the enslavement and sexual abuse of young boys. Known as 'bacha bazi' – literally, 'boy play', it was a practice with a long history. Boys were bought or abducted and then forced to dance and have sexual relations with their captors. It was fuelled by sexual repression and poverty, but closely associated in people's minds with the rampant warlordism of the civil war. The Taliban gained early support by trying to stamp out this abusive practice.

Years into their war with the US-backed Afghan government, reports of police and army commanders indulging their paedophilia with impunity were a gift to the Taliban's propaganda machine. US and other coalition forces often encountered such abuses, but they had adopted what amounted to a 'don't ask, don't tell' approach, saying it was up to the Afghan authorities to tackle the issue.

* * *

Farzana had moved her parents and siblings to Kabul because she thought it would be safer. But as Hazaras, they were still exposed to the growing threat from the viciously sectarian Islamic State. Repeating tactics that its antecedent, Al Qaeda, had pioneered in Iraq, the Afghan branch specifically targeted the mainly Shia Hazaras, classifying them as heretics.

The family lived in the vicinity of a Kabul suburb called Dasht-e Barchi, which had grown into the largest Hazara neighbourhood since 2001. That made it a prime target for the Islamic State, which had claimed responsibility for a string of deadly suicide attacks there.

'Any time my brothers were out, we feared they'd be caught in an explosion,' said Farzana. The school her brothers initially went to had a large number of Hazara students, so the family moved them to a more obscure establishment closer to home.

But just as the lack of peace didn't stop construction and rebuilding in Kabul, neither did it prevent the new generation of urban Afghans from carving out the kind of life they aspired to. Farzana drove her own car, learning to ignore harassing shouts, whistles and horn-honking from male drivers unused to seeing a woman behind the wheel. She balanced her work with a constant round of parties and social get-togethers.

At one Thursday night party Farzana attended, a young man came up to her and introduced himself. 'Did you ever teach English in Ghazni?' he wanted to know.

'Yes, why?' Farzana replied.

'I used to be one of your students,' he said. 'I recognised you across the room. You're the one who always wore the orange jacket and the purple sunglasses.'

It was a touching moment. Farzana learned that after starting to learn English at the sisters' rural school, he had moved to Kabul to study at one of the city's universities. Later on, he won a scholarship to study in the United States, and they stayed in touch.

Farzana still had a thing for the colour purple. 'The design of my place was all purple and grey. I used to go to Istalif with my mum and find all these fantastic purple and grey dishes and pots,' she said, referring to a town near Kabul famous for its pottery making. Her earnings allowed her to live in her own place while renting a separate apartment nearby for her family. She even lived with her boyfriend for a while – almost unheard of, even in Kabul. Her parents hoped they would get married. 'When we broke up, it was heavier on my mum than me.'

One of the people in Farzana's circle of Kabul friends was a rising star among the reporters at Tolo TV. His name was Samim Faramarz. Charismatic, curious and funny, he was the kind of person people instinctively gravitated to. He, too, had studied abroad for a while.

One evening in early September 2018, Farzana had just got back to her apartment and was making herself tea. A sheaf of papers for her trip to Britain lay on the table. She was due to leave soon to start her Master's. But, as she poured the water, there was a powerful explosion outside, a blast wave shaking the room.

Farzana called her parents to check they were OK and scanned social media for early reports of what had happened. Suddenly, there was a second, even more powerful blast, again from the direction of Dasht-e Barchi. Minutes later, a friend rang.

'Hey, are you OK? Were you watching?'

'Watching what?' Farzana said.

'When the bomb went off, on Tolo. Samim was there, reporting. The screen just froze and then went blank. He was right there.'

Farzana dropped her phone.

'I didn't know what to do at first,' she said. 'I called him, but his phone was switched off.' She rang her boyfriend to tell him what had happened.

Other journalist friends were calling her as well. She asked them to find out which hospital the injured were going to. One called back a few minutes later to say 'Isteqlal [Independence]', a big hospital in south-west Kabul. Its emergency ward doctors and nurses were now veteran experts in dealing with suicide bomb casualties. Farzana asked her boyfriend to meet her there.

But along the way, she got a text on her phone from another journalist friend who had been close by at the time of the attack. 'I'm sorry,' the message read, 'but I think we lost Samim.'

Ramiz Ahmadi, 23, the cameraman working with him, died in the explosion, too. They had been nearby when the first blast occurred, at a popular sports club in Dasht-e Barchi. The pair had gone to investigate as the sound of approaching sirens filled the night air.

As so often, the perpetrators were planning for that moment when the first responders arrived, along with volunteer helpers, and then they detonated a car bomb in their midst. In total, more than 20 people had been killed by the high-velocity hail of shrapnel from the twin blasts.

'Samim and Ramiz represented what is best in Afghans and Afghanistan,' wrote Saad Mohseni, in a tribute he posted that same night. 'They were young, fearless and thoughtful. They challenged and pushed boundaries to deliver news to millions daily. They lost their lives doing this. We are devastated that they are no longer with us.'

Just 28 when he died, the centrifugal effect that Samim had on people was apparent the next day when several hundred people turned out for his funeral. As Farzana talked to his friends, she learned that he had been planning a surprise farewell party for her later that week.

* * *

The photograph showed a young and handsome man in his twenties, dressed in military fatigues and smiling. His name was Mutahir and his fiancée had given the picture to Bilal via a male relative when he stopped at her family's home. It was late September 2018, with a little more than three weeks to go before election day. Bilal was going door to door in the villages of Khas Kunar, his home district in Kunar province.

Mutahir was a member of the elite Afghan commando force which had received more advanced US equipment and training. They had been proving themselves in battles with the Taliban across Afghanistan, but also sustaining heavy casualties.

Just weeks after getting engaged, Mutahir died in a firefight at the other end of the country, in Helmand. His body had been returned the day before Bilal stopped by at his fiancée's house to pay his condolences. But she and Mutahir's family were confronting a distressing problem: no one would bury the soldier.

In the cities, the commandos were regarded as heroes. In the village where Mutahir was born, most were on the Taliban's side and saw him as a traitor and slave of the Kabul government and its foreign allies. The local imam was pro-Taliban and refused to say funeral prayers at the graveside, without which the commando could not be laid to rest.

In a divided village in a polarised district in a fractured province, here was the micro-complexity of Afghanistan's wars – and perhaps a fragment of hope that it could be unpicked.

Thousands of men from Kunar had enlisted in the Afghan security forces since 2002. And Bilal's district became well known as a source of recruits. A regular salary to support their families was a primary driver, and service had a reinforcing effect. 'Young men wanted to be like their brother or neighbour and have sunglasses, a walkie-talkie and a gun,' said Bilal. But when they came home they kept their day jobs secret as the Taliban's influence spread.

Life divided the menfolk of Khas Kunar. Death brought them back together. Whether the coffins coming back to the district each week carried the bodies of government troops or Taliban and Islamic State fighters, they often ended up being buried in the same cemeteries.

Moved by the plight of Mutahir's fiancée, Bilal persuaded another imam to come and preside over the funeral. The next day, despite the risk, he and some of his team went to the grave to lay flowers. Word of his intervention on behalf of the commando's family trickled out and helped him gain a new following among members of the security forces and their relatives.

Bilal's proposal to put up the province's teenagers in secure accommodation in Kabul to finish their education was also getting significant interest from voters. Local imams had attacked the suggestion in their Friday prayer sermons, accusing him of trying to corrupt Kunar's youth by moving them to the capital. Knowing of his Western ties, they labelled him as an infidel stooge.

Unwittingly, they were also helping Bilal by giving his idea publicity. Through his separate outreach to female voters, he heard that the proposal had gained traction with women who said they would ignore their husbands and vote for him. His backing for local schools also won him support among teachers and their relatives.

On election day, Bilal was not among the three men and one woman who secured seats in Kunar. But his 3,700 vote tally was greater than many had expected. It was hardly an ideal time for him to be making his first run for elected office, amid crumbling security. In Ghazni, where the Taliban had taken control of most of the districts, there was no vote at all. Nationwide, a third of the polling stations didn't open.[6]

In the weeks afterwards, Bilal was philosophical. He realised that he had been 'played by many people', who had committed to support him and then opted for a rival. Nevertheless, he had learned a lot of lessons, calling his bid 'a successful failure'.

It had also brought home for him the distance between capital and countryside. It was only living there that had made him fully

---

[6] Two days before the vote, the US commander in Afghanistan at the time, General Scott Miller, was almost killed in another insider attack which claimed the life of General Abdul Raziq, a controversial Kandahar strongman the Americans had been working with.

appreciate the divide. Undaunted, he decided that he wanted to try again at a future election and kept his office in Kunar going. Between the soldiers, the teachers and some female voters, there were the makings of a constituency. But first, Bilal said, there was a more important cause. He wanted to do his part for peace.

'I felt that we Afghans have to pay our dues to our districts,' he said. 'I said to myself: "What can I do to stop the fighting?"'

* * *

In the view of US envoy Zalmay Khalilzad, the war had become a stalemate, but 'a dynamic stalemate that favoured the Taliban'.[7] And just as history had weighed on US decisions during its invasion in 2001, it did so again in the way it planned its exit.

The experiences of colonial Britain and the Soviet Union in Afghanistan prompted a sharp awareness, in Khalilzad's words, that 'withdrawal can be dangerously costly'. For his superiors in Washington, getting out without further US losses was the priority.

The February 2020 Doha Agreement that resulted had four key parts: a Taliban commitment to contain Al Qaeda and cease attacks on US forces; an American commitment to pull out all their troops within 14 months; followed by the Afghan Republic government and Taliban exchanging prisoners and starting talks on a political deal and ceasefire.[8] All four elements were supposed to follow on conditionally from each other.

But at its heart, it was always a withdrawal agreement, not a peace deal. It also had two secret annexes, laying out the US

---

[7] Interview with the author.

[8] Doha Agreement: https://www.state.gov/wp-content/uploads/2020/02/Agreement-For-Bringing-Peace-to-Afghanistan-02.29.20.pdf

pull-out schedule and the details of the Taliban's commitments to contain Al Qaeda and other terror groups. However, while the Taliban committed not to attack US troops as they packed up, they could still target the Republic's forces. And the news that the agreement had secret elements fuelled mistrust among many Afghans about the terms.

President Ashraf Ghani opposed the deal from the start. He saw it as an express route to losing power and was incensed by the terms of the prisoner exchange, which meant he had to release 5,000 suspected Taliban members from Afghan jails. Afghan officials accused Khalilzad of betrayal, calling the agreement 'a surrender deal'. Ghani tried to stall the prisoner releases, hoping to prevent the American withdrawal.

But the US military had already begun packing up to meet the first stage of the deal, closing bases, reducing air cover and logistics support for Afghan forces. Khalilzad said Ghani should have focused on negotiating a power-sharing deal with the Taliban to preserve some of the democratic elements of the US-backed republic.

The Afghan leader also hoped that President Trump's successor, Joe Biden, would take a different approach once he took power. But while the two men differed on most things, on Afghanistan Biden was in the same camp as his predecessor – as he had made clear in both public and private over the past decade.

* * *

There was another unpalatable fact for those defending the US-backed order. Too many Afghans had lost faith in it. While the Taliban had been gaining legitimacy, the Afghan government had been losing it. That became apparent when I covered the country's fourth presidential election in September 2019. Khalilzad had tried to persuade Ghani to postpone the vote, fearing more division. But the Afghan leader was determined, exercising both his sovereign right and his desire to win a mandate without having to share power.

On one hand, the campaign once more highlighted the arrival of the new generation. At Ghani's conspicuously well-funded headquarters, scores of 20- and 30-something volunteers were working at banks of screens in an underground call centre to target younger voters. One of his advisers showed off a rap video they had produced to extol the virtues of the Afghan leader. Ghani certainly didn't do any rapping. But his adviser was still confident they were winning over the growing number of youth voters. 'We are even on TikTok,' he said. At the time, I had to ask him what that was.

But behind the high tech and social media, the presidential election looked like a rerun of the past. One of the candidates was Gulbuddin Hekmatyar, the Islamist warlord many held responsible for starting the civil war in the 1990s. For many voters, his presence on the ballot paper was further evidence of the impunity and double standards corroding the Afghan political system.

A polling station on the Shomali Plain north of Kabul on election day, September 2019.

When election day came, it led to more deadlock between Ashraf Ghani and Abdullah Abdullah, amid reports of widespread irregularities. But most Afghans made their opinions clear by staying away. The turnout hit a record low of 16 per cent, more than a fourfold drop from the figure for the first 2004 vote. It was also an indictment of Ghani. Irascible and academic, he never had the charisma or reach of his predecessor, Hamid Karzai.

There was another leader, however, who seemed to have enduring appeal. Despite being dead. On my visits in those later years of the Republic, I was struck how much more often I saw photos of the late President Mohammad Najibullah in public. Pasted on walls, hanging in cafes or taped to the windows of taxis and minibuses, his neatly trimmed moustache and bull-like neck were instantly recognisable. A personality cult had developed around the 1990s strongman, as if Afghans were summoning him from the grave to save the country. His ruthless record while serving as the communist secret police chief was brushed aside – or formed part of the attraction.

Abdul was not one to paste politicians' photos in his windows. But a quarter of a century since he had come face to face with Najibullah's tortured body, he understood the sentiments. 'If Dr Najib was still here, he would do a better job than this government,' he said. During the election campaign, I even saw several posters of Dr Najib with his features rendered into the style of the famous poster of Barack Obama entitled 'Hope'.[9]

* * *

On another trip to Afghanistan in 2019, I reported on a very different segment of the new youth generation. They were young people fleeing rural poverty and conflict, trying to make it to the West. If

---

[9] https://www.behance.net/gallery/25163559/Dr-Najibullah-Ahmadzai

that didn't work, they at least hoped to eke out a living in neighbouring Iran and send money back to their families. Their lives were as far removed from President Ghani's TikTok campaigners as it was possible to imagine. It was on a visit to the Afghan–Iranian border that I got an insight into the scale of this exodus.

Most days, a fleet of buses rolled up at the 'Zero Point' line dividing the two countries to deposit hundreds of Afghan migrants who had been arrested while trying to make the journey across Iran. They were the successors to Farzana's exile generation and treated far worse. Iranian authorities routinely beat Afghans they detained, with frequent reports of fatalities.

Afghan deportees at 'Zero Point', on the Iran–Afghan border in 2019.

The majority of these deportees were young men, but there were also many boys among them. Several teenagers I talked to had fled after the Taliban tried to recruit them. The youngest deportee I met was a 12-year-old who had been despatched to Iran by his destitute widowed mother.

Trickles of people leaving villages had turned into a silent wave. An estimated 200,000 undocumented Afghans were making this journey every year, paying smugglers to spirit them over the border. Many were arrested as soon as they crossed over, but every deported migrant I talked to said they would try again.

That year, I was also running a television reporting course for a group of Afghan journalists. One of the standout members of the group was Shafi Karimi.

Just 25 at the time, Shafi was enterprising and ambitious, matching an instinctive ability to network with a slick dress style. It all came together to make him a superb reporter. Like the late Samim Faramarz, he too had spent time at Tolo, and he was carving out a reputation for creative takes on new trends, as well as for covering tough issues like domestic violence and LGBTQ+ rights.

Shafi was a bold journalist used to working in difficult conditions, but a year later, he and others on the course began calling me for advice on how to get out of Afghanistan. They were facing a new threat from shadowy assassins taking aim at people associated with the Western-backed order. Judges, academics and civil society activists, as well as journalists, were killed. No one claimed responsibility, but it appeared to be a coordinated Taliban effort to sow fear and neutralise their most outspoken opponents.

In November 2020, one of Shafi's colleagues in Helmand was killed by a bomb under his car. Several major media outlets, including Shafi's employer, shuttered their bureaus after receiving anonymous threats. He was alerted that his name was on a target list, along with another journalist I had trained.

Weeks later, he received several calls from a woman asking to meet to give him a story. Suspicious, Shafi called the contact who had warned him about the target list and was told it was a trap. 'If you can, leave the country,' his contact advised him. Shafi and his wife Sofiea, also a journalist, reached out to a media advocacy group who helped them secure visas to fly to Turkey and then on to France, where they claimed asylum in April 2021.

Yet again, a new Afghan exodus was gathering momentum, a brain drain of talent and youth. By early 2021, eight of the 12 journalists who had taken part in my training course had fled abroad. The four still in Afghanistan were all in hiding.

* * *

Following the death of her friend Samim, Farzana had deferred her Master's by a year. In 2020, she finished her studies in the United Kingdom and found a temporary job, but was planning to return to Afghanistan later that year. But as an insurance policy, she had also started researching options for getting her parents and siblings out, reaching out to contacts she had made in the UK.

The trigger was the Doha withdrawal deal. Her mother had told her over the phone that her father was receiving threatening phone calls from prisoners who had been set free under the terms of the US–Taliban agreement – people whom he had once detained while he was a serving officer. Farzana had also received threats, linked to the research she had done on sexual abuse cases.

The attacks on her family's home suburb of Dasht-e Barchi intensified. In May 2020, just six weeks after the Doha Agreement was finalised, gunmen attacked a maternity clinic in the area, killing mothers, staff and newborn babies. And then another suicide attack on one of the area's schools claimed the life of one of Farzana's cousins, who was just 16 at the time.

'The killing was closing in everywhere, even reaching people from our village,' said Farzana. 'Everyone in the family was in mourning and I felt so guilty that I wasn't there.'

She called her mother. 'I'm coming back,' Farzana said. 'I need to be there.'

For a moment, there was silence from the other end. Then her mother said. 'You do not have a home here any more. You're not coming back.'

'What do you mean? I don't understand,' Farzana replied, tears beginning to well.

'It's not safe for you any more. You can't come back!'

It was the same resolve her mother had shown all those years ago in Tehran, when she had fought to ensure her daughters had places at school. Farzana was devastated, but she didn't argue. The next day, she applied for asylum in Britain.

* * *

Bilal had returned to Kabul, but he still maintained his office in Kunar. And his intervention on behalf of Mutahir the commando had left a mark. When a soldier or policeman from the province was killed on the other side of the country, their relatives often called Bilal to ask for his help in repatriating their bodies.

With his contacts in the Defence Ministry, he could cut through the bureaucracy to ensure they were returned and buried as soon as possible. In the wake of the Doha withdrawal agreement, the violence intensified, as both the Afghan government and the Taliban fought for advantage. 'Coffins were falling like thunder on the villages,' Bilal said. He often followed up by attending their funerals. The sight of children clinging to the graves of their fathers became etched in his mind, and he heard the sound of women wailing in his dreams.

For a few days over the Eid al-Adha[10] holiday in 2020, the Taliban had announced a short ceasefire. Bilal decided to start a campaign for another – and this time to make it permanent. He started reaching out to his large social media base, creating a video appeal for peace. Later that year, he brought his old election team together to organise a rally near the banks of the Kunar River.

They dug out the collection of furniture and equipment they kept for these events, the sun awnings, stackable chairs, cushions

---

[10] Eid al-Adha or the 'Feast of the Sacrifice' marks the end of the annual Hajj or pilgrimage to Saudi Arabia and the holiday is celebrated by Muslims worldwide.

and battery-powered sound system. And they printed banners calling for peace and reconciliation, hanging them on the walls of the nearby village.

Several hundred people attended, some coming from villages on the Taliban's side. The provincial governor came as well. Covid-19 was sweeping through Afghanistan then, but no one was worried about attending a close physical gathering.

There was a more urgent priority: stopping the fighting. 'We don't want to live in darkness any more,' Bilal told his audience. 'We have to stop the bleeding.'

Chapter 10

Kabul Falls Again: 'I Felt Like a Refugee in My Own Country'

A ladder to a last helicopter out of Saigon has become the defining image of the end of America's war in Vietnam. A crowd of desperate young men swarming a US transport aircraft taking off from Kabul is now the equivalent for its war in Afghanistan.

But in the nearly 20 years between the fall of the first Taliban regime and the start of the second, the country passed two historic milestones. For the first time, it was governed by a democratically elected head of state. And, although it was bumpy, the country also experienced its first ever peaceful transition of power, when Ashraf Ghani took over as president from Hamid Karzai.

The US-backed Republic's many flaws don't change that story. Yet even those Afghans who had experienced violent changes of power in the past were shocked at the speed with which their government collapsed on Sunday, 15 August 2021.

I was far away but watching closely, all the while receiving a stream of messages from colleagues and friends trying to find a way out for themselves or their families.

The night before Kabul fell, Abdul had been at home with his family in his village on the western edge of the capital. He had heard explosions and gunfire in another nearby district beyond the city. By then, the Taliban controlled two-thirds of Afghanistan's 34 provinces, as well as most of the border crossings.

As the pace of the Taliban advance had picked up over the previous week, he had debated what to do. British media organisations, including the BBC, had announced a plan to evacuate their Afghan staff. Abdul wanted to get his family on the list.

He was concerned that because he was not a journalist, he and his family would not be included, yet would still be vulnerable in a Taliban takeover. Everyone in his village knew he had been working with the BBC. The Taliban wouldn't care that he hadn't been a reporter, he told me; 'they will see me as one of those who worked with the foreigners.'

I agreed to contact former colleagues to lobby for Abdul and his family to be added to the lists being drawn up. At that point, in early August, we both thought he still had time.

As Sunday is a work day, Abdul drove to the office on 15 August. It was now inside the Green Zone. But on his way in, he passed police pickup trucks, with their signature dark green paintwork, racing out of the city the other way. The officers inside were no longer in uniform.

One of Shafi Karimi's relatives, who lived near the airport, had also seen police officers changing out of their uniforms, trading them for the baggy trousers and long top preferred by the Taliban. 'We've been sold out by our leaders and the Americans,' they shouted.

In the Shahr-e Now district in the city centre, there were crowds of people around the banks, lining up to withdraw cash. A friend texted asking if I could put him in touch with anyone at the US embassy. 'I was supposed to have my visa interview yesterday, but now they've closed down,' he said. I'd already seen the pictures of US helicopters flying back and forth between the embassy compound and Kabul airport, evacuating everyone inside.

It usually took Abdul up to an hour to get into the office. That morning he was at the entry checkpoint within 20 minutes. He was surprised when no one stopped him to check his pass or search his car. All the guards had gone, he said: 'I just drove through.' Meanwhile, other roads were unusually busy. Jahan got stuck in traffic for hours on the airport road after picking up a colleague who had made it in on one of the last commercial flights.

It was like the moment when the waters recede before a tsunami. But not everyone understood the signs, and few had any idea how to respond.

At home in west Kabul, Farzana's family were alternating between the television and their phones. At least they had got some money out before it was too late. Farzana was in London at the time, but had told them to withdraw as much cash as possible a few days earlier as she'd followed the news reports from home. She still thought that the government and the Americans would defend Kabul, though. She slept in that Sunday.

Bilal was in his office on the morning of 15 August. He had been sleeping as well as working there in recent weeks, even though his home was just next door. He was doing television and radio interviews for outlets across the world, flipping between different languages. Five weeks earlier, his wife had given birth to their first child, a girl. They had named her 'Sola', the Pashto word for peace. But he had hardly seen them since the Taliban started closing in.

The night before, a friend who lived near Pul-i Charkhi, the city's largest jail, had called Bilal to say he had heard shooting inside. The complex still held thousands of Taliban prisoners. A breakout appeared to be under way. But that morning, a senior official at the Arg palace had assured Bilal the situation was under control. The Taliban wouldn't come into Kabul, he said: 'That is the agreement with the Americans.'

Around 11:00am, Abdul's uncle called to say the Taliban were in their village. They were rolling through in American armoured vehicles and police pickups, heading down the hill towards Kabul. And then, like a wave, the Taliban were everywhere.

Looking out amid the gridlock, car passengers realised that the men on the motorcycles weaving past were Talibs, weapons slung over their backs. Out on the streets by now, Jahan saw another police pickup coming towards him. 'Then I realised it was full of young Taliban fighters,' he said. 'They all had American guns, and I could see they were happy and smiling.' Later, he saw prisoners on the streets who'd escaped from the jail. They were in their prison uniforms, asking for directions to the bus station.

Storekeepers began covering up pictures of women in their windows, or pulling down posters of singers. As friends and colleagues sent me photos, it was hard to believe what I was seeing. Twenty years after their defeat, the Taliban had pulled off an astonishing comeback victory, and before the United States had even finished leaving.

Another journalist I had trained was at the airport, about to board a plane for Delhi, when all commercial flights were suspended. She sent me a photo of her luggage and a message that read 'Kabul', followed by a crying emoji and a broken heart.

In London, Farzana was finally up and Shireen reached her on the phone. The streets were full of Taliban fighters, she said. 'You're joking,' Farzana replied. As they talked about what to do next, it was their father they were most worried about because of his military and police background. Farzana could tell her mum was panicking.

Early that afternoon, a member of President Ghani's protection detail called Bilal. 'He's gone,' he shouted. 'Ghani's gone in a helicopter.' The bodyguard switched the call to video to show him the scene inside the Arg and the president's empty office. Then someone put a hand over the lens and hung up.

Bilal remembered a conversation the day before with the governor of one of the provinces now under the Taliban's control.

'Have you got a surrender deal?' the governor asked.

'What do you mean?' Bilal replied.

He meant a personal arrangement with the Taliban, to guarantee his safety.

* * *

It was President Biden who fired the starting gun for the Taliban's final offensive, on 14 April 2021, when he announced that all US troops were coming home by the 20th anniversary of the 9/11 attacks.

Within days, the Taliban's Doha negotiators suspended talks with the government, and their ground commanders took the lead. As they stepped up their attacks on government outposts, the Taliban were simultaneously offering deals to the soldiers and police inside, using local elders as their intermediaries. 'We beat the Americans,' they said. 'Why give your life for their puppets in Kabul?'[1]

From May onwards, districts had begun to fall. In June, the Taliban had seized a border crossing with Tajikistan. The old ways of Afghan war were reasserting themselves. Now they had the momentum.

Late on the night of 6 July, Bilal had taken a call from a friend who lived on the Shomali plain north of Kabul. From the roof of his home, the signature glow of the arc lights at Bagram airbase always stood out in the darkness. But that night, he told Bilal, for the first time that he could remember, the lights had gone off. 'I think the Americans have gone,' he said.

At first, Bilal didn't believe him. When daylight came, it emerged that the last US forces at the base had flown out without even telling their Afghan partners. Across the country, people saw that moment as the point of no return, turning the Taliban's advance into a blitzkrieg.

Some Afghan units did keep fighting, but they were running low on food, water and bullets. Corrupt officers had sold off supplies.

---

[1] Author interviews with various sources.

Helicopters and planes were grounded because they were no longer being serviced. US air strikes from abroad could not change the dynamics. It was hardly surprising if soldiers, police and officials began to accept Taliban amnesty offers.

The first province to fall had been Nimroz in the south-west, on 6 August. Just eight days later, the Taliban were converging on Kabul. By then the US and its allies were scrambling to evacuate their diplomats and Afghan staff. Just weeks after the last American troops had departed, President Biden ordered in the first of several waves of reinforcements to bolster the evacuation effort, more than doubling the number he had just pulled out.[2] Getting out was going to be a lot messier than anticipated.

* * *

On 13 August, two days before Kabul fell, Naqibullah was on the edge of Gardez, in his home province of Paktia. He was a sub-commander himself by then, overseeing a small unit of around 10 fighters, and they had been steadily closing in on the city over the past month.

There had been firefights with government troops, but it seemed clear to Naqibullah and his men that they had the advantage. He had heard that the Americans had left Bagram, where he had been held for several weeks as a teenager. All Taliban knew that name, wherever they were in the country, because so many of their comrades had been imprisoned there.

On their phones and by radio, they heard the news about the fall of Zaranj in Nimroz. They had also heard about the amnesties being

---

[2] The US military deployed 6,000 new soldiers and marines to Kabul airport in August 2021 in three waves as the Taliban first surrounded and then took over the capital. The last of the 2,500 US troops pulled out under President Biden's 14 April 2021 withdrawal order had already gone home, leaving just the guard force of US Marines at the US embassy.

offered to government troops who surrendered. But they weren't involved in any of these talks. 'We were told to reach a certain line [near Gardez] and then wait,' he said. And then, early on 14 August, Naqibullah received the order to start advancing, along with the other Taliban units encircling the city.

They were surprised to find the way in almost entirely open, he said. 'If we started shooting at any place, they [the government soldiers] would come out, raise their hands and surrender.'

There was one exception, when they came to the local head-quarters of the NDS, the government intelligence service. 'They refused to quit,' he said, 'and many were killed.'

Within hours of first entering Gardez, the Taliban had seized control, including the old fort on the hill first built by Alexander the Great. Government troops had also handed over the US-built base on the city outskirts, along with its arsenal of weapons. Naqibullah and his comrades performed the Asr, the sundown prayer, in the city.

In taking Gardez, he said they only lost four men: 'We didn't expect such a victory.' He wondered if the whole fight had even been fixed in advance, at the talks in Doha.

* * *

Zalmay Khalilzad was in Doha, Qatar, as Kabul fell. He had been trying to patch together a last-minute power-sharing deal between the Taliban and the Republic government. But the agreement depended on President Ghani resigning. Then Khalilzad received a call from former President Karzai, who was still in the Afghan capital. He was sharing the same news Bilal received from his contact at the Arg.

'He's gone,' Karzai said.

'Who's gone?' Khalilzad replied.

'Ghani! He got out by helicopter.'

The Afghan leader and his wife, along with a few close aides, had flown north to Uzbekistan. Khalilzad said he was amazed that the US had not detected Ashraf Ghani's surprise departure, considering that its forces controlled the airspace at the time.

Ghani's sudden exit left a power and security vacuum. The Taliban's chief negotiator, who was also in Doha, asked if US troops would step in. The American general in charge, Frank McKenzie, dismissed the idea as 'just not feasible', with the forces he had available.[3]

It was a short conversation in a Doha hotel, but a moment freighted with symbolism. Nearly 20 years after the Taliban's own flight from Kabul, the US military was giving them the green light to retake the city. McKenzie's only proviso was that they did not try to impede US efforts to get people out. 'If you don't interfere with the evacuation, we won't strike,' he said.

Later that day, the now former Afghan president put out a statement saying that he had left 'to prevent a flood of blood', evoking the capital's past. If Ghani had stayed, he said, 'countless patriots would be martyred and the city of Kabul would be destroyed.' Everyone understood that he was also referring to the way his predecessor in the Arg palace had met his end when the Taliban first seized the capital in 1996.

The final act in the Taliban's return was to take control of the Arg, the place where Afghanistan's wars had started 43 years earlier with the communists' bloody coup. This time, it was an *almost* peaceful affair. A former government minister instructed a senior palace security official to meet a group of Taliban fighters at the main gate and let them in.

The official was at the airport at the time, trying to escape, but agreed to return, fearing his relatives could be at risk if he didn't. It

---

[3] https://www.politico.com/news/magazine/2022/08/11/the-afghanistan-deal-00050916

turned out he was missing one key, and so a Taliban commander shot off the lock, trailed by an Al Jazeera camera crew.

Under their first regime, the Taliban banned television. When they returned to power, they made sure the moment was broadcast live. Cradling their American rifles in their arms, they paused for a prayer at the desk where Ashraf Ghani had been only hours earlier. On the wall was a painting depicting the 18th-century coronation of Ahmad Shah Durrani, Afghanistan's founding father. For the Taliban, this moment was just as momentous. They had restored their self-declared Islamic Emirate of Afghanistan.

* * *

Once it was clear the Taliban had overrun the city on 15 August, Abdul helped to organise transport for staff to return home. He hastily found taxis and burqas for female colleagues, but stayed put in the office himself, worried he would attract attention if he returned home. Outside, the smell of smoke clung to the air. Diplomats in nearby embassies were burning sensitive papers, and looters had broken into several compounds.

At home in west Kabul, Shafi Karimi's sisters were distraught. The eldest was due back at medical school for the second year of her studies that September. Another sister was about to start at journalism school. Shafi's mother had been a teenager when the Taliban were last in power. She dug out several long black cloaks that she had stored away.

As women covered up across the city, some residents were changing clothes for another reason – to reveal that they were Taliban. It was a simple matter of putting on the traditional combination of baggy cotton trousers and long shirt, known by Afghans as perahan-e tumban. If they had also shaved their beards to blend in, the full transformation might take a little longer.

The next morning, Bilal had just finished another round of television and radio interviews when his guard came in to say that a neighbour they knew by the name 'Shah' was at the door to see him. The man had been a friendly fixture on their street for a long time, whiling away the afternoons on a chair outside his home, greeting neighbours as they came and went.

A few years back, security agents had arrested Shah, alleging that he was an undercover Talib. But his neighbours had spoken up for him, insisting they were mistaken, before asking Bilal to vouch for Shah with his government contacts. He was released.

In the period since then, Bilal had often seen him taking his daughters to school. But no one had seen Shah for the past several days before Kabul fell, and Bilal was glad to hear he had reappeared.

'Why are you waiting?' he said to his guard. 'Show him in.'

'It is better that you come out,' he said.

When Bilal reached the gate, he was stunned to see Shah with a Kalashnikov over his shoulder and a walkie-talkie and a notebook in one hand. 'The Emirate wants you to know that you are safe,' his neighbour said solemnly. 'I'm here to return the favour.' He handed Bilal a piece of paper with his mobile number, telling him to call if anyone caused him trouble.

His neighbour had a second surprise to deliver. Putting his arm over Bilal's shoulder, Shah opened his notebook to show him that not only had he been a Talib all this time but that he had also been spying on him. Leafing through the pages, Shah showed Bilal the details he had recorded of all his visitors, ranging from Afghan government officials to Western diplomats. Bilal was so shocked he didn't know what to say.

But it was soon clear that his neighbour's power and authority in the Taliban only went so far. The following night, Bilal and his wife were woken by loud banging. A group of four Taliban soldiers were pounding on their gate with rifle butts and shouting: 'Open up, Sarwary. We know you're in there.' When Bilal called Shah, there was no answer.

Bilal held firm, telling the Taliban they were disobeying their leaders' orders not to enter people's homes. They gave up, but as they went away, Bilal heard one shout: 'We'll be back.'

* * *

Watching from Pakistan, Prime Minister Imran Khan revelled in America's humiliation, crowing: 'The shackles of slavery have been broken.' But, unlike in 2001, when the Taliban were overthrown, there were no celebrations in Kabul. And even as Khan spoke, the city's airport was being overwhelmed by Afghans hoping to board planes to America before the shackles of Taliban rule snapped shut.

The rumour spread on social media that the United States and its allies would evacuate anyone who got past the airport gates. Many people just dropped what they were doing, drivers leaving their cars with the doors open and sprinting. American troops at the airport were taken by surprise and overwhelmed by the numbers coming onto the runway.

The result was the heartbreaking scene of a US military aircraft taking off with young men clinging to its sides. Like others around the world, I was soon seeing the footage on social media of at least four men falling from the sky. It was a dreadful echo of the images of people jumping from the Twin Towers 20 years earlier.

Jahan had been at the airport at the time, reporting on the frenzy, until US troops and Taliban fighters – who were now working together – forced the crowds beyond the perimeter. Jahan was bewildered. 'What happened to us?' he said when we talked later that day.

He was trying to decide what to do next. 'I don't want them to go through my life,' he said, talking about his own children. His daughter was now four, and he also had a baby boy. Abdul had received assurances that all staff who wanted to leave would be evacuated, and was helping to coordinate the process. But Jahan wasn't convinced it would happen. 'I don't see how they can get us all out,' he told me. 'I'm thinking of moving my family to Pakistan.'

Bilal didn't want to leave Afghanistan, but with his high profile as a journalist and as a parliamentary candidate, there was no other option once the Taliban came to his door. 'My face was my enemy,' he said. He had one insurance policy: he had applied for asylum in Canada, helped by their embassy. The confirmation that it had been granted had come through just before Kabul fell. The problem now was how to get himself and his family safely out of the country.

He reached out to old employers at the BBC, ABC News and his alma mater in the United States. Connections were everything right then. And by 17 August, they had spirited him to the Serena hotel in central Kabul, which had become an evacuations hub.

With its polished wood, marble floors and you-could-be-anywhere global buffet, the newer Serena had elbowed aside the Intercontinental as the city's best hotel. But it was also a place with dark memories for Bilal and me. The hotel was a choice target for the Taliban, and they had conducted several deadly suicide strikes inside. A journalist with whom we had both been friends was killed in one of these attacks in 2014, along with most of his family.[4]

Now the Taliban were the hotel's gatekeepers, and the guests feared they could become captives. A who's who of Republic officials were among the would-be evacuees inside. While waiting to hear if he and his family could get on a flight, Bilal spent most of the time in their room to avoid attracting attention. He didn't make any calls: 'I felt like a refugee in my own country.'

Back in the UK, Farzana was working her contacts as well, trying to find places for her family on British evacuation flights. Her father didn't dare leave their house in Kabul in case he was recognised. 'I called and emailed everyone I knew from my work over the past

---

[4] https://www.afp.com/en/agency/press-releases-newsletter/sardar-ahmad-afp-journalist-killed-attack-kabul

few years,' Farzana said. But she had no idea whether her lobbying would work. The stress came out in excruciating back pain and insomnia. 'I felt like I was having a constant panic attack.'

* * *

I was still reporting on events from afar after realising that there was no immediate way for me to get back into Afghanistan. I also began to devote my time to the requests I'd had for assistance.

I wasn't sure that I could do anything, but I wanted to help people I knew who didn't have organisations to support them. Over the following days, this turned into a nearly 24/7 operation as I became part of an ad hoc remote rescue network which took on a life of its own. It began with conversations I had been having with Shafi Karimi as he tried to work out how he could help his own family back in Kabul.

A couple of days after the Taliban took over, he got in touch again to say that one of their intelligence units had come to the family's home searching for him. Shafi had left Afghanistan because of a death threat. Now he feared his relatives were in imminent danger. But none of them even had passports, only 'tazkiras', the Afghan identity card. The asylum claims he and his wife, Sofiea, had made in France were still being processed, and he was struggling to find anyone who could help in what was still for them an unknown country.

France was running its own evacuation operation and I thought the best hope was to find space for his family on one of its flights, using the couple's new link to the country as leverage. Shafi and I gathered the contacts for many of the French diplomats overseeing the evacuation, searching for anyone who might know anyone who could secure seats on a French plane out of Afghanistan. Shafi then set to work lobbying, putting to use the same persuasive skills I'd seen him use as a journalist.

In the meantime, Sofiea's family had succeeded in getting on to a US flight using other contacts. The advantage they had was there were just three of them, all adults. By contrast, Shafi's family were eight people in all, including his elderly grandmother and his eight-year-old brother.

Spooked by the Taliban coming to their doorstep, Shafi's older brother and sisters had tried to find a way into the airport the next day, thinking that if they could get out they could help the rest of the family later. But they were forced back by stampedes as guards at the gate and Taliban fighters fired in the air to break up the crowds. Several people, including children, were trampled to death. People who were allowed through had to grapple with others who clung to them. Afghans were fighting Afghans in their desperation to escape.

Meanwhile, Farzana's contacts had come through, securing spaces for her family on a British flight. 'I really appreciated my network then,' she said. But there was one awful catch. They wouldn't take her sister, Shireen, because she was over 18. 'I pleaded with them,' Farzana said, 'but she didn't count in their definition of a family unit.'

Five days after the fall of Kabul, the lobbying Shafi and I had been doing paid off as well, when French diplomats sent an 'invitation letter' for his family to come to the airport for a flight. But they had to get through the deadly chaos around the gates on their own.

I had been posting on social media looking for anyone who could help. A well-connected French businessman happened to comment on one of my posts about the situation in Kabul. We had met a decade earlier but hardly spoken since.

I learned that he and his sister had managed to get an at-risk family into the airport and on to an evacuation flight in collaboration with the French authorities. The pair had contact with an elite French police team who were extracting approved evacuees from the crowd. They could help Shafi's family. Working together, we began to act as go-betweens for the police and the family, using WhatsApp to relay messages back and forth.

The 'Abbey Gate' to Kabul airport.
(The suicide bomber detonated on the canal wall on the right-hand side,
marked by the hole in the canvas above.)

The police team instructed the family to head for the so-called Abbey Gate entrance, carrying home-made French flags to identify themselves. They would be waiting for them there. No suitcases, they were told. They needed their hands free to get through the crush.

In a matter of hours, the family had to uproot their whole life and squash it into a backpack. His sister was devastated that she had to leave behind the dress she had worn for Shafi and Sofiea's wedding the year before. And there was the laptop he had given her before he left. Their grandmother was in tears, asking who would look after her husband's grave.

The family set out while it was still dark, hoping for smaller crowds. But just hours later, they were back home, having been caught in a stampede. A Taliban guard beat Shafi's father as he tried to shield his family, and his grandmother nearly suffocated. Everyone was in tears. Yet it was his grandmother who insisted that they try again. The French police were still waiting for them, if they could just reach the Abbey Gate.

Named by NATO troops, the gate leads to the airport's military section and is not so much a gate as a collection of barriers, walls and fences, overlooked by a watchtower with a red-painted antenna. Outside is a deep, stone-walled sewage canal which acts like a moat, separating the entrance to the airport from the path most Afghans were using to get there.

By the time Shafi's family reached the edge of the canal, it was getting dark again and the crowd had swelled. There were rumours that the evacuation would only last a few more days. Many people had climbed into the drain to get closer to the Abbey Gate. Reluctantly, his family did the same.

Somewhere on the other side of the canal, the French police team were shouting their names and signalling with torches. Shafi's family waved their flags, but it seemed hopeless. There were also US and British troops at the Abbey Gate and the police team were kitted out in similar fashion, with helmets and body armour. In the darkness, they all looked the same.

His family sent me photos of the chaos, and it looked horribly like our plan was going to fail.

'It's so difficult for my grandmother in this water,' Shafi's brother said to me in a voice message. 'When are our French friends coming?' I tried to reassure him that they were looking for them; they just had to stay where they were.

I feared the next message would say Shafi's grandmother had collapsed, or that we would lose contact if the family's smartphone – their digital lifeline – fell into the festering water. Seeing the pictures of the dense crowd, I couldn't help thinking of the possibility that a suicide attacker could strike.

By then, untold numbers of people were involved in similar remote rescue efforts; both Afghans and outsiders with ties to the country. The power of technology and Afghanistan's new connectedness with the outside world, since 2001, made it possible. But 20 years of blood, treasure and hope had turned into dystopia in a ditch.

At around 10:00pm Kabul time on 20 August, I received a brief message from Shafi's brother.

'OK, they pick up us,' his text read.

'They got you??!!' I replied.

'Yes.'

They had finally managed to pass one of their flags to the police team through the crowd. Shafi's father carried his mother on his back as the officers helped the family out of the canal. A few hours later, they were on a French aircraft flying out of the country. Their last trace of Afghanistan, Shafi's sister noted, was the reek of sewage on their clothes.

* * *

After Farzana's family arrived in the UK, they were handed over to the care of a local authority, in line with the established British policy of distributing new asylum claimants around the country while their cases are processed. Farzana was still waiting for her own, earlier, application to be finalised, and she had had to obtain special dispensation to travel from London to see her family.

Their first home was a budget hotel with a contract to house refugees. It was a soulless place for a family reunion after more than a year apart. But none of them cared about their surroundings. Everyone was thinking about Shireen back in Kabul. The last person Farzana greeted in the lobby was her older brother, Sherzad. They hugged without saying a word: 'We just cried.'

Having supported the whole family for the past several years, Farzana believed she had failed Shireen. 'I was just beside myself, terrified for her, imagining her all alone,' she said. 'And I felt responsible.' Shireen, 26 years old by then, had accepted that the rest of her family should go, but she was now in a state of constant dread. She had moved in with friends, thinking it would be safer, but as a single Hazara woman she was at great risk.

When Farzana returned to London, she resumed her search for a way out for her sister, as the Taliban consolidated their control. She applied to Afghanistan's neighbours for visas for Shireen, including Pakistan, Iran, Tajikistan and Uzbekistan, as well as nearby India. But the applications went nowhere. At that point, regional states had either closed their borders or imposed tough entry controls. They wanted to prevent a repeat of the mass refugee influxes of the past. And there was no hope that British officials would change their mind and allow Shireen to board one of the last UK flights out.

Abdul and Jahan were also still in the country. Abdul had moved with his family to his brother's house in Kabul after being told they had spaces on a British flight on 25 August, along with other colleagues. He was trying to persuade Jahan to add his name to the list as well. But Jahan feared that the evacuation would wind up before then.

With the knowledge that the region was, in effect, pulling up its drawbridge, he used his contacts to secure visas for Pakistan. 'I can't risk leaving my family here,' he said when we spoke late on 20 August, just as Shafi's family were trying to reach the Abbey Gate. The next day, Jahan texted me. He had crossed the border and reached Peshawar.

Bilal remained in the country until 22 August, when Qatari diplomats facilitated safe passage for him and his family to the airport in a convoy. Having played host for the US–Taliban withdrawal deal, Qatar had also become a crucial intermediary between the two sides through its embassy on the ground in Afghanistan.[5]

---

[5] As well as hosting US–Taliban talks in Doha, the Qataris had long had an active diplomatic presence in Afghanistan. Its contacts with the Taliban, which dated back to 2013 when the Taliban opened an office in Doha, helped give it an outsized role in facilitating contacts on the ground after the Taliban takeover. Qatar played a central role in the evacuation process, with its embassy operating out of the Serena hotel at the time.

It was 'surreal', Bilal said, to see US soldiers and Taliban fighters standing just metres apart at the first checkpoint leading into the airport. He and his family joined a long line of fellow Afghans walking across the tarmac to the US transport aircraft that would fly them out and make him a refugee again, nearly 30 years after he had first fled his homeland.

At the airport, mounds of discarded water bottles, military ration packs, lost clothes and bags spoke of the tumult of the past week. On the runway, planes took off or landed every few minutes, with military personnel and diplomats from nearly 40 countries taking part in the evacuation.

Bilal recognised many faces among those waiting to board. The latest Afghan brain drain was gathering pace. But his relief at escaping was tempered by a deep sadness at leaving his home country. 'Our love affair with Afghanistan is fatal,' he said. 'I wanted to hug the mountains. My heart was broken into two million pieces.'

* * *

Sitting in a London coffee shop, Farzana scrolled on her phone, searching through online support groups for any new avenues to get Shireen out. Families and volunteers posted information about evacuation options and which countries were offering refuge. Most Afghan refugees were being taken to the UAE before being scattered to places as far afield as Albania and Uganda, as well as Western Europe and North America.

I had joined several of these groups too, some of them populated by US veterans trying to help former Afghan colleagues. Many of the posts were peppered with abuse for President Biden. But these groups offered little hope for Farzana. She couldn't find any new information that could help her get Shireen out. 'I was so down,' Farzana said. 'It was the worst time in my life, imagining her stuck there and with no way out.'

Farzana was wearing a necklace that spelt out her name, which means 'the wise one', in Farsi script. And it caught the attention of a fellow customer. I will call her Saima. She spoke the language and commented on Farzana's necklace, telling her how much she liked it.

They got talking and discovered they had more in common. Farzana told her about Shireen and learned that Saima, who is a journalist, was trying to evacuate several Afghan colleagues at risk. Saima mentioned that she'd been talking about the possibility of finding spaces for them on flights to France. She said she would ask if I could do the same for Shireen.

A chance meeting in a London cafe led to a canal outside Kabul airport. Two mornings later, I and my fellow volunteers were trading messages with Shireen as she approached the edge of the Abbey Gate drain. The message we had received from French diplomats was that as long as they had planes going, they would take anyone with valid identity documents.

Like her sister, Shireen was an able leader. I teamed her up with the family of another Afghan colleague whom the French had agreed to evacuate. This time, they had to bring yellow flags or clothes to wave. But the way to the gate had become a human wall. 'There is too much crowd,' Shireen texted. 'We have a child with us.'

Their goal, the watchtower with the antenna, was at least 150 metres away, with a dense mass of people in between. In a message group with Farzana and my French colleagues, Shireen asked if the police could come through the crowd to find them. But their commander had already ruled that out. 'You have to get to that tower,' I replied. I could only imagine their situation, trying to stay together. A dozen people had already been crushed to death around the gates. And then, we lost contact with Shireen.

For an agonising 20 minutes, we had no idea what had happened to them. And then came a text saying, 'We are here.' Shireen sent a photo showing that she and the family had made it to the tower, the angle making clear they were all in the sewage.

We forwarded it to the police team, but the canal was now a heaving mass of people, juggling bags and children above the water, while brandishing documents at the soldiers above them. A few yellow flags hardly stood out in that fever of colour, but after another hour we received confirmation they were safe. 'It is done now,' said Shireen's text.

'Thank you for giving her a better future,' said Farzana in a message to the group. Within 24 hours they were in Paris. But they had come perilously close to disaster. Later on, I learned that Shireen had been hurt as she fought her way through the crowd.

* * *

Early on 25 August, the day of their scheduled evacuation, Abdul and his family climbed into one of a line of buses to take them to the airport. Including all his colleagues and their relatives, they were a large group. Most of them only had 'tazkira' identity cards, not passports. Through intermediaries, they had negotiated an arrangement for the convoy to be escorted in through a different entrance, so there would be no need to risk the lethal scrum at the Abbey Gate.

But when they met their escort, Abdul was told the Taliban had changed their minds. Only people with passports would be allowed through. Hoping the issue could be fixed that day, the escort told him and his colleagues to find somewhere where the whole party could wait, rather than sending everyone home. Their solution was to rent a nearby wedding hall.

Dozens of these palatial-style centres had sprung up around Kabul over the past decade or so, emblems of both excess and optimism, catering for ever larger marriage ceremonies. It was an ironic place to end up, just before Abdul and his colleagues separated from their country, but the wedding hall was happy to have some business after being ordered to close. 'The kids had fun on the stages,' he said. But night fell with no progress, and they were asked to return home to await new instructions.

The call came the next afternoon, with their escort planning to take them through after dark. But as Abdul and his family were preparing to leave, saying their final goodbyes all over again, he heard an explosion from the direction of the airport.

A suicide bomber had detonated right opposite the watch-tower at the Abbey Gate, the blast enveloping US troops on the wall and Afghans in the water below. Shafi's family, Shireen and dozens of others had been in the exact place in the days before. Well over 100 people died, including dozens of children and 13 Americans. It was the deadliest single suicide attack since the US first invaded two decades earlier. The atrocity was later claimed by the Islamic State, marking the beginning of a new campaign by the ultra-extreme Sunni group to undermine its Taliban rival, just as it was taking over the country.[6]

'Our bosses said they would try again the next day,' said Abdul. 'But I knew it was over after the bomb.' That same day, the French team had agreed to take one last group of people through the Abbey Gate, including several high-profile journalists. But the bombing brought the French and British evacuations to an end, leaving them stranded. And while the United States and its allies flew out more than 120,000 people, it was soon clear that many more Afghans who had worked with them had been left behind.

There was no way for them to follow up asylum applications which had been made from inside Afghanistan, because the Americans had shuttered their embassy. Their Western allies had done the same. By

---

[6] There were a series of attacks claimed by the Islamic State (IS) in subsequent years. These incidents often involved suicide bombings – turning the Taliban's signature tactic against them. The Taliban responded with a brutal campaign against IS in response.

contrast, the missions of key powers such as Qatar, Turkey, Pakistan, Iran, China and Russia were still open and functioning as normal.

On the night of 30 August 2021, the last American forces flew out of Kabul. Gunfire rang out across the city as the Taliban celebrated a triumph that even many of their own fighters had never thought possible. For Abdul, the moment felt like 'a jail sentence'.

Chapter 11

'With the Help of God, We Defeated America'

A capital transformed: Kabul in 2021 after the Taliban takeover.

The second coming of the Taliban to Kabul had some parallels with the first, as well as with the arrival of their mujahideen predecessors before that. Their rank and file were hard men from the countryside and the city was a foreign place. In late August and September 2021, the soldiers of God became the sultans of swing as they couldn't resist trying out the previously unknown delights of the city's playgrounds and funfair rides.

That was until their commanders decided that images of young Taliban warriors whirling around on carousels was not a good look and ordered the fun to stop – or at least to make sure no one was filming. It was proof, in a way, of what village imams said in their Friday sermons; that Kabul was a corrupting place, tainted by its association with non-Muslims.

Yet in the comedy of these moments was a harsh message to every Afghan who had prospered under the previous order. The men bouncing on the children's see-saws had won. In a matter of weeks, two decades' worth of assumptions that the West and their Afghan partners knew better had evaporated in the face of a numerically smaller and less-equipped force that generals, politicians and others had routinely dismissed as 'ragtag'.

With the arsenal of US weapons it had seized from the Republic government, the Taliban's Emirate now had one of the best-equipped armies in Asia. And because Kabul had fallen without a fight, they also had a transformed city for their capital, unlike the broken ruin they had marched into in 1996. Among the many questions now was what the Taliban would do with this new and fragile peace.

Looking out across Qargha Lake from their restaurant, Abdul and his brother saw Taliban soldiers racing each other on the pedal boats, laughing and shouting, weapons slung over their backs. Less than a decade earlier, their commanders had sent a suicide squad to kill Afghan families eating in one of the restaurants. 'It was hard to watch,' Abdul said.

To make matters worse, the brothers had to feed them for free. The Taliban had around 20 men based in the area, and they ate at lakeside outlets each day. 'One restaurant made them breakfast, our restaurant had to make lunch,' Abdul explained. As before, when Republic officials had extorted free lunches from them, they knew they could not refuse.

There was much that was hard to digest in those early weeks and months after the West went home. How did the Taliban pull off the most successful guerrilla campaign of modern times and add another defeated superpower to Afghanistan's tally? How did the United States and its allies spend 20 years replacing the Taliban with the Taliban?

When I made my first trip back to Afghanistan after their triumph, I found the Taliban were painting their preferred answer on the wall of the abandoned US embassy complex. 'With the help of God, our nation defeated America' read the slogan in a giant mural, beside a depiction of the US flag with its red stripes rendered as collapsing towers. My conversations and travels on that and subsequent visits offered other answers.

* * *

I spent a lot of time talking to Abdul and other people who had tried to get out with the emergency airlift, hearing accounts of their experiences as well as their plans to find an alternative exit.

Many, if not most, had lost their jobs. Since the Taliban take-over, the country had been consumed by a new economic crisis after the West stopped underwriting the government and imposed punitive financial sanctions, freezing Afghan assets abroad. Western capitals were also taking the lead in denying the Taliban's request for recognition as Afghanistan's legitimate new authority. Journalists coming in from outside had again become an important source of dollar income for any Afghan who could speak decent English and offer transport.

'With the help of God, our nation defeated America.'
The wall of the US embassy getting a new look in 2021.

Salman, whom I hired as a translator, had been working for a building and logistics company doing contracting work for the US and Afghan governments. The business was effectively vaporised by the Taliban takeover. Like Bilal, his was another story of transformation from a Pakistani refugee camp childhood to a new life back in his homeland, with a business degree in India along the way.

But Salman's priority then was finding an exit. 'My wife and children don't deserve this,' he said. 'I want them to have a better future, a stable life. Here nothing is stable. Things only get worse and worse.'

I also hired two brothers, Omid and Hanif, to be my drivers. Both had worked for the previous government and feared their past would be revealed and used against them. But they needed the work and I needed people I could trust. We'd been introduced by their eldest brother, who had been my driver on previous visits. He, too, was working on an exit plan.

The scale of the economic meltdown was visible at roadsides as we drove around the city. People were selling off furniture, carpets and crockery to cover their day-to-day needs. And they were far from being the poorest Afghans.

In Kabul, many people directed their ire at President Ashraf Ghani and his inner circle, condemning them as 'traitors' for running away. He had made it clear by then that one of the reasons he fled was his fear of being hanged like Mohammad Najibullah.[1] But history didn't earn Ghani any sympathy. 'He should have accepted his destiny, even if it meant death,' I was told by a former civil servant who had tried, but failed, to escape himself.

However, while those who had supported the Western-backed Republic felt let down by their leaders, they had the same feeling about the United States. In their minds the Americans had handed victory to the Taliban by cutting a deal and pulling out.

'The Americans took our hopes to the sky and then buried them back in the ground,' said Abdul as we talked one day. We met up discreetly because he was trying to keep a low profile. While he hadn't suffered any ill treatment, Abdul had no faith that that would last. If there was one word that summed up the atmosphere then, it was unpredictable.

The Taliban leader had promised a general amnesty for all Afghans who served the former Republic government. But soldiers, police officers and civil servants kept turning up dead. Journalists were beaten up and tortured. There was still secondary education for girls in some provinces, but in most places those aged 12 and above were shut out of the classroom.

---

[1] https://www.nytimes.com/2021/08/18/world/middleeast/ashraf-ghani-afghanistan-taliban.html

Officially, the Taliban said no final decisions on female education had been taken. Time was needed, their spokesmen said, to implement curricula that followed Islamic precepts and to ensure that boys' and girls' classes were kept separate. But gender segregation in schools had also been the norm under the Republic. Everyone could see through the Taliban's obfuscation.

Abdul had three daughters of his own by then. The elder two had finished school, but the youngest had been due to start secondary education that September. For the sake of his children, he was determined to find a way out: 'I can't put them through the past again.'

After the blow of his August evacuation being cancelled at the last moment, Abdul had hoped that he and many others might secure spaces on private charter flights that were being run out of an airport in northern Afghanistan. But that option had also fallen through. Now, both Abdul and Salman had the same challenge – to procure passports for their families. Though Abdul may have felt let down by the West, that was still where he wanted to go, not to the countries that had maintained their embassies in Kabul, such as Russia or China. It was a common sentiment.

Jahan had meanwhile found a place to live with his family across the border in Pakistan and was starting the process of applying for resettlement in Britain. By the beginning of September, Bilal and his family had landed in Canada, after 10 days in Qatar, where they had been put up in one of the players' villages for the forthcoming World Cup.

Farzana's family were still in a hotel in northern England. Her sister, Shireen, was in temporary accommodation in France, and beginning to learn French as she waited to be granted residency. But even though they were close geographically, they were still being kept apart by border controls. Farzana now had British residency, but it wasn't easy to get a visa for France. It would be even harder for Shireen to obtain one to come to Britain.

As Farzana observed: 'Brexit was going to keep us apart for a long time.'

* * *

For many Afghan women, the return of the Taliban's theocracy represented a direct assault on every aspect of the life and identity they had built up over the past two decades. Few had forgotten a phrase Taliban leaders had first used in the 1990s: 'The best place for a woman is in the house or the grave.' But it was urban women who felt the reversal in their fortunes most acutely.

'I've been humiliated as a person,' said Fatima as she helped her mother and sister clear the plates. 'I've lost my right to an education. I've lost my freedom.'

Fatima had been on the list for one of the French flights before the evacuation was prematurely suspended in August 2021. When I let her know I was in Kabul, she invited me to her home for a discreet lunch with her and her family. 'There are so many reasons I want to leave Afghanistan now,' she said.

The two sisters' stories matched those of Farzana and Shireen in many respects. They were also from a Hazara background and spent years as refugees in Iran, with similar experiences of life there. 'The Iranians called us nasty, dirty Afghans,' Fatima recalled.

They had then joined the wave of return to Afghanistan in the early 2000s. Fatima had earned a degree at the American University of Kabul before becoming a teacher with an educational charity helping disadvantaged children. That autumn, she was supposed to have started a post-graduate degree. Her younger sister had gradu-ated that summer and had been looking for a full-time job when the Taliban took over.

Instead, the two sisters were now living according to the Taliban's vision – hardly going out and spending their time on domestic work. They had helped their mother cook the lunch they offered me. It was a simple but tasty vegetarian pulao, with beans replacing the meat.

Fatima had lost three close friends in the violence, in a combined Taliban bomb and shooting attack[2] at the American University five years earlier. To see their fighters in the streets on the few occasions she went out was too much to bear. 'Everyone is so traumatised,' she said. 'We are alive, but we don't live.' Her hope was vested in a European scholarship she had applied for. If she was successful in gaining a place, it could offer a way out.

We talked for a long time. Fatima brought out green tea and sweets, laying them on the floor between us. I was grateful for the hospitality and pleased to meet her in person. Until then, she had been a name attached to a set of urgent messages on my phone. I was all too conscious of the fact that I had not been able to help her leave. And while I could fly in and out of the country and drop by for lunch, she was stuck.

Fatima had a passport but, in today's world, it was the wrong one. Measured by the number of countries you can travel to without a visa, the Afghan passport has been the world's weakest for some time.[3] That said, having one was still the essential first rung on the ladder for anyone who wanted to apply for resettlement, or a scholarship programme.

During the August airlift, the normal rules of international travel had been temporarily lifted and the local tazkira IDs had been sufficient to travel. But now these rules were firmly back in place. When

---

[2] This so-called 'complex attack' on the American University in 2016 had become a standard Taliban tactic by then. Typically, it involved a car bomber first detonating at an outer checkpoint, allowing a waiting team of other fighters to break inside and open fire. They would usually be wearing explosive vests themselves, which they would detonate to kill more people and anyone who tried to apprehend them.

[3] According to the annual Passport Power index compiled by the investment consultancy Henley & Partners: https://www.henleyglobal.com/passport-power

the new Taliban authorities reopened the old government's passport agency, the crowds of people queuing up to obtain one turned into a melee reminiscent of the scenes around the Abbey Gate.

I got a first-hand view when I joined Salman there, as he began the process of acquiring passports for his family. Taliban soldiers guarding the complex were laying into the crowd with lengths of rubber hose and long sticks, and we had to dodge their blows. A pair of women cried out that they had already been waiting for two days.

'I can't bring my family here,' said Salman. 'I have to find another way.'

Abdul had already started exploring alternatives. The demand had created a market, and shadowy brokers with the right contacts were offering to help people get passports more quickly. The price was more than $500 per document. If Abdul wanted to use their services, he would need to find several thousand dollars.

* * *

While many people in Kabul were trying to get out, the Taliban were settling in, transforming themselves from a guerrilla movement into a conventional military force. From the mega-bases the Americans had constructed in Bagram and Kandahar, as well as the vast British-built Camp Bastion in Helmand, to the scores of other smaller outposts, the new army of the Islamic Emirate of Afghanistan had acquired world-class military infrastructure.

In Paktia province, Naqibullah had been sent to the main army base outside Gardez, which had been constructed by the Americans. He was now a deputy commander, in charge of the equivalent of a platoon of 20 to 30 men, with much better equipment to choose from.

The scale of the Taliban's military inheritance was already clear from the pictures that had emerged of columns of armoured vehicles lined up in bases they had overrun. In Kabul, I saw Taliban-appropriated military helicopters flying above the city several times.

Highly trained pilots had been among those flocking to the airport for evacuation that August. Some had also fled with their aircraft to neighbouring Central Asian states. But many pilots had been left behind, or had chosen to stay. Naqibullah highlighted the role that former Republic personnel were playing in reconstituting the security forces.

'Whether it is the police or the army, they are back in their jobs. People say the new system is "not inclusive". But the old government employees are running things. They are supervised by a mawlawi,[4] but they do the jobs.' His biggest concern right then was that he hadn't been paid: 'Other platoons have salaries, but ours has not come.'

I was speaking to Naqibullah remotely, with journalist Masood Shnizai acting as our intermediary. Even though Naqibullah was much older and now wore a large turban, Bilal and I instantly recognised the former Guantanamo inmate when Masood sent us photos.

Naqibullah only had his own local viewpoint on how the Taliban had succeeded. But it helped to fill in more of the picture. He thought there had been an inflection point in his own province of Paktia from 2019 onwards, when government security forces had pulled back from many of their remaining rural outposts in the province and concentrated around Gardez: 'Before that, they always had their US air support, but when that stopped, we started to win a lot more territory.'

If air strikes and night raids were the signature tactic of the US-led coalition in Afghanistan, for the Taliban it was suicide bombs aimed at civilian as well as military targets. Many Muslim scholars condemn both suicide and deliberate attacks on civilians, saying they contravene Islamic principles. But the Taliban steadily increased the tempo of such attacks from the mid-2000s onwards.

---

[4] A religious scholar or mullah, in other words a senior Taliban figure.

And although Naqibullah was not a spokesman for the Taliban, I wanted to hear his view on the use of suicide bombing as a tactic.

He acknowledged such attacks had caused many civilian deaths among Afghans, but he rationalised it this way: 'What I heard from my teachers, and the scholars, as well as from the books I have read, is that if there are such people who are a threat to the country or a threat to the group who is on the true [Islamic] path, the attackers will not be held responsible if civilians are also killed.'

In his view, the American invasion had been a clear threat to the country and his fellow Muslims, therefore legitimising the Taliban's resistance. But those civilians who had died as a result had been honoured as 'martyrs' he said. Just as importantly, Naqibullah argued, the Taliban's campaign was underpinned by the hadiths, the words and deeds of the Prophet Mohammad. 'One cannot express one's own opinion on the hadiths,' he said.

* * *

Many people assumed that the Taliban were always at a disadvantage in the city, because of their rural roots. But it was another aspect to the movement that the United States and its allies misjudged. In the months after their takeover, it became clear that the Taliban had built up a network of undercover operatives in Kabul and other cities.

Bilal was given a first-hand insight when his friendly neighbour Shah disclosed his second identity. Later on, Bilal told me about another surprise he had had on the day Kabul fell. He had rushed to the bank, hoping to withdraw as much cash from his account as he could. 'I realised everyone was doing the same thing, but I'd always got on well with the bank manager, so I was hoping he would help me,' he said. Inside the branch, however, he found him a changed man, with a handgun on his belt.

'You cannot withdraw any money,' the bank manager told Bilal. And he revealed that he had been working for the Taliban for years.

Part of his job, it turned out, had been to run a list of potential anti-Taliban figures and Bilal was on it. 'I was "broke" in every sense of the word,' Bilal said. 'It was another moment when you realise you don't really know anyone.'

A teacher at a private English college whom I got to know told me of his own surprise in those early days when he recognised one of his students among a group of Taliban special forces, who stand out because of their different uniforms and equipment. And as I travelled around Kabul on that first trip, I had an encounter that suggested the Taliban had adopted this 'Trojan horse' approach even more extensively than anyone imagined.

Kabul's new rulers had established checkpoints on major roads and junctions across the city, and we were pulled over several times a day by the mostly younger fighters who manned them. It was rare, in fact, to encounter older men. Naqibullah was an example of how they recruited young men, but their ranks had also been decimated by the US coalition over the years, killing many older generations of fighters.

One night, as Hanif was taking me back to the guest house where I was staying, a knot of Taliban soldiers at the roadside motioned for us to pull over. Hanif switched on the dash light and a stocky-looking Talib carrying an American M4 rifle approached the window, the orangey gloom catching the machined lines of its magazine and aiming scope. He probed the car with his torch and, speaking in Pashto, demanded our identity documents.

As the Talib took Hanif's tazkira and the press accreditation letter I'd been given by the Taliban's media office, I noted his khaki-coloured military gloves, with black pads on the knuckles. I'd seen US troops wearing those same gloves in Afghanistan and Iraq for years.

Increasingly, the Taliban we saw around the city were indistinguishable from their former American opponents, as they absorbed left-behind tactical gear, as well as weaponry and vehicles. Many were now kitted out in US-style camouflage fatigues and combat boots, long hair and beards disappearing behind balaclavas and modern Kevlar helmets.

This checkpoint Talib looked somewhere in between, with his M4 and a pair of sharp-looking shades hanging from the US magazine pouches on his chest. But underneath he still wore the more conventional baggy pants and trousers combination. His head was wrapped in a scarf, so we could only see his eyes.

He glanced at Hanif's tazkira and handed it back. Still holding on to my Taliban letter, with its Emirate logo, he leaned down to address me.

'What are you doing here?' he said, in perfect English.

As I answered his question, he handed back the letter, giving the impression he wanted to chat. The two other Talibs on duty with him had gathered round.

'Where are you from?'

'Britain,' I said. 'Englestan.'

'Not America?' he said, sounding disappointed. 'Have you come to Afghanistan before?' he continued. From the look of his eyes, I guessed he was in his mid-twenties.

'Many times,' I said. 'Where did you learn your English?'

'Here, in Kabul, at university.'

'It's very good. So you were studying English?'

'Computer studies,' he replied.

'Why are you on this checkpoint if you're good with computers?' I continued, taking a chance. Even if he was not telling the whole truth, there was no inventing his English.

'I do what the Emirate tells me to do.'

'So, were you also fighting in the past, carrying out attacks?'

He laughed, and then said, 'I was multitasking.'

His comrades had moved away to stop another car, apparently bored of the spectacle, their silence perhaps suggesting they were not quite as multi-talented. The English-speaking Talib leaned in again.

'Can you take me to America?' he said.

'I'm not sure they'll give you a visa,' I said. He laughed again.

I wanted to ask more questions, but we had hit our limit. 'Be careful,' he said, as he waved us on.

* * *

A throng of Afghan families were moving towards a narrow, tunnel-like entrance, with hundreds more waiting behind them. Porters weaved between them with wheelbarrows, some filled with sacks and bags, some serving as makeshift wheelchairs.

I was in the southern Afghan town of Spin Boldak, a short drive from Kandahar. Beyond that tunnel lay Pakistan. This was the other side of the Afghan exodus then under way, involving some of the most destitute. The goal for most of these people was day-to-day survival.

'There's no water and no work,' said one man in the line, referring to the ongoing drought in the region. He had one of his children perched on his arm. The boy's tiny face was smeared with dirt and dried tears.

'My wife is sick,' said another man, pointing to the inert form slumped in the wheelbarrow beside him, her body encased in a head-to-toe green burqa and her legs hanging over the side. 'We can't get treatment for her here.' Two tiny children in worn clothes were squeezed in beside her, staring vacantly ahead.

But even as Salman translated their accounts from Pashto, I already knew that these families were unlikely to make it across the border. One of the border officials had explained that most would be sent straight back through another gate.

Out of our sight, just beyond the covered entrance, the Pakistani officials assessing each family's case included a doctor to verify their health complaints. 'If they fail, people come back and try again with another story,' said the official. It was a cycle of misery, with thousands of Afghans desperate to leave, but Pakistan equally desperate to deter them.

There were several Taliban soldiers clustered around us, including one I will call Habibullah. With his camouflage fatigues and body armour, desert combat boots and goggles, he looked like an American soldier, except for the white patch on his shoulder reading 'Allahu Akbar'. He was from the local intelligence department and had been assigned to act as our guard and minder.

I was surprised that his superiors had allowed us right up to the border. The sight of all these people trying to leave was hardly an endorsement of Taliban rule. But their new bureaucracy was still taking shape as they made the transition from guerrilla army to government. And at the border they seemed to want to show a cooperative side. 'Welcome to Spin Boldak,' said the Taliban official in charge, his hair flowing over the shoulders of his long cotton shirt and waistcoat.

I was trying to make the most of this window of opportunity. With the war over, travel had become easier. I'd never been able to visit Spin Boldak before as the surrounding area had been in Taliban hands for years. Better security was the peace dividend, but I was aware that this opening might be fleeting.

Spin Boldak is the most important border crossing in southern Afghanistan, through which many of the supplies for the US-led coalition had travelled over the past 20 years. It is essentially a one-road town, reminiscent of 19th-century American frontier settlements familiar from countless movie westerns. The striking, saw-toothed ridges that spring from the surrounding desert plain would not look out of place in one of those films either.

The town and nearby frontier also have their place in history. Britain's colonial army entered Afghanistan this way, via the nearby city of Quetta, in the 1830s, at the start of the first Anglo-Afghan War. During the Taliban summer offensive, it was the fall of Spin Boldak in mid-July 2021 that proved to be the beginning of the end for the US-backed government. With two other major border crossings in their hands, Taliban commanders could steadily throttle the Republic as American support dwindled away.

Habibullah, our minder, had taken part in the battle for Spin Boldak and offered an intriguing insight into how they won.

'We attacked from both sides,' he said.

'So, you mean you had forces coming from Afghanistan and Pakistan?' I clarified. Habibullah nodded his agreement and smiled, perhaps thinking he had said too much.

'Which side did you come from?' I asked.

'I came from the Pakistani side.'

It was a reminder of the role Afghanistan's neighbour had played in aiding the Taliban, and another piece in the puzzle of how they had pulled it off. Their leaders had been based in Quetta, just across the border, for most of their 20-year insurgency. They had had bomb-making and training facilities there. Injured Taliban fighters had been treated in Pakistani hospitals.

For years, Pakistani officials had issued pro forma denials that they were providing the Taliban with this kind of support. But when I asked for the contacts of Taliban fighters and commanders whom I met in the course of my reporting, the mobile numbers they gave often began with the +92 Pakistani dialling code. 'I'm getting a local number soon,' said one Talib soldier, looking embarrassed.

By 2021, the sanctuary Pakistan had provided the Taliban was far less important as they had gained a hold nationwide, with income from the taxes they imposed, as well as from abroad. But that haven had been critical to getting the Taliban started again after their defeat in 2001.

Yet for all that, there was little warmth between the Taliban and Pakistan, and I got a glimpse of that when I tried to take a few photos with my phone. 'No photo! No photo!' shouted the Pakistani border guards a few metres away, waving furiously. In the circumstances, I could understand them being camera-shy. But then Habibullah, together with the other Taliban guards, jumped to my defence. 'No problem,' he said. 'Take all the pictures you want.'

It was emblematic of the awkward and essentially transactional relationship between the two sides, ever since the fall of Kabul. Then, Prime Minister Imran Khan had celebrated 'the shackles of slavery' being broken. But, so far, Pakistan's return on its investment had been thin. Just like the Republic government they had deposed, the new Taliban authorities were refusing to accept the Afghan-Pakistani frontier as their settled international border. They, too, referred to it by its colonial name, the 'Durand Line'.

Pakistan now had its own concerns about its neighbour playing double games and offering sanctuary to its enemies. The TTP – the Pakistani Taliban movement that had targeted John Butt more than a decade earlier – was still active and, in 2021, stepping up attacks inside Pakistani territory, emboldened by the Afghan Taliban's victory. There were close ties between the two groups, and in a role reversal, Islamabad now accused their Taliban allies of giving them a haven.

Yet again, Pakistan's machinations across its borders appeared to be causing blowback inside its own. As I watched the Pakistani border guards slink back inside their tunnel, it was the Taliban who looked like they had the upper hand.

* * *

After Spin Boldak, we travelled on to Helmand province, a road journey that had been unsafe for outsiders for years – certainly for obvious-looking foreigners like me, despite my beard and local clothes.

Lashkar Gah, the Helmand capital, appeared both more developed and more damaged than the last time I had seen it, in the early 2000s. It had seen heavy fighting between the Taliban and the former government's forces that past summer. The US air force had joined in the battle, flying in its warplanes from bases abroad to bomb Taliban positions in and around the city in July and early August, in a last-ditch attempt to stem their advance.

During the fighting, the Taliban overran buildings and installations constructed with the vast sums the United States and Britain had ploughed into Helmand over the past 15 years. Expensive American bombs were then used to flatten them again.

Helmand, 2021.

There was no shortage of destruction to ponder in Helmand and Kandahar, where the most intense battles had occurred. Only in a few eastern provinces had there been comparable levels of fighting. Cemeteries stretched away from the roadside. The white flags above the tombs indicated Taliban graves, but there were plenty of other banners as well.

Everywhere we drove, we came across buildings pancaked by air strikes, or shredded by artillery, rockets and machine-gun fire. And one person's ruin could still be another's home. Hundreds of thousands of people had been displaced by the fighting over the years, and as they returned, many were using the carcasses of destroyed buildings as temporary shelter. I often felt overwhelmed by the futility of it all.

The drive there and back from Kabul gave me more to ponder. When I first made the journey in the early 2000s, just after the Kabul–Kandahar highway had been rebuilt with US and Japanese money, it took six to seven hours to cover the 300 miles. In 2021, we needed nearly 18 hours, leaving and arriving in the dark because the highway was pitted with craters and troughs.

Most of the damage had been done by Taliban bombs aimed at government and US convoys. On some stretches, Hanif was steering around the partially covered holes every 10 or 20 metres. Overloaded trucks and heat had completed the destruction, gouging much of the remaining tarmac into deep furrows, making the surface look like a ploughed field. Our halfway stop in Ghazni provided a welcome break for green tea and kebabs.

People living along the route tried to make money filling in the holes, working at the roadside with their spades and reaching out for donations as passing trucks, buses and cars slowed down.

The most eye-catching and disturbing sight was the women we came across along the Kabul–Kandahar highway, usually with a child in the fold of their burqas. Typically, they were widows, barred from working and with no relatives to support them. Many of them placed themselves right in the middle of the traffic, near an obstacle where every vehicle had to brake, stretching their arms out in supplication to passing drivers.

* * *

Back in Kabul, some prominent symbols of the past 20 years had survived. Tolo TV, the popular news and entertainment network established by Saad Mohseni, was still operating – though with a very different look and schedule. Music and entertainment shows were gone. Women could only appear on screen if they wore a mask, and never with a male presenter.

But Tolo was still covering the news, with Taliban officials some-times making appearances to explain themselves. It was a far cry from the free-wheeling atmosphere of the channel's early years, but Mohseni had decided it was better to try to keep it going, preserving hundreds of jobs, as well as some vestige of the past.

The white flags turning in the breeze above the walled villas nearby, in the surrounding neighbourhood of Wazir Akbar Khan, were symbolic of the full-circle story of the past 20 years. The old house on Street 10 where I used to live was still there, with the same peeling blue paintwork on its outer gates. The BBC had vacated it years ago and no one answered when I tried the bell.

For a few weeks, I stayed in a nearby guest house and my neighbour turned out to be a Taliban commander. His house had previously been occupied by a Republic government official who had fled, so he had moved in with his family and guards. I'd seen the commander's little convoy coming and going a few times and he sometimes waved at me from his Land Cruiser. Always immacu-lately dressed in brightly coloured long shirt and pants, he stood out like a light bulb next to his guards, who had all adopted drab, mili-tary fatigues. One day, he invited me for tea. I asked my landlord if he could join us, to translate.

'We are neighbours now,' said my host, in Pashto, as he showed me into the living room, indicating I take a place in the corner. 'I respect you, and you respect me.'

His guards, sitting along the other wall, eyed me suspiciously, their rifles balanced on their knees. But the commander's message was that the past should be forgotten. 'Now your armies have gone, you are our guest,' he said. But why, he wanted to know, was the West not releasing Afghanistan's money, or recognising the Emirate? 'There is peace now,' he said. 'We just want good relations with everybody.'

The commander, who I guessed was in his late forties, said he had fought Soviet troops as a teenager in his home province just outside Kabul. When the Americans came, 'I had to return to jihad,' he said. 'It was my duty as a Muslim.' But he was captured and had spent much of the past decade in prison until being freed during the August takeover.

The commander admitted that, inside his jail cell, he had been losing hope that the Taliban would ever succeed. 'And then everything changed, with the help of God.' Had there been other factors? I asked. He didn't want to take away any credit from the Almighty by specifying what these may have been.

For people like Salman, Abdul and Fatima, such questions were increasingly irrelevant. They were just focused on their exit plans. While I was in Afghanistan, Fatima received the news she had been hoping for. She had been accepted for a scholarship and it would pay for her to fly out via Pakistan. A relative in Canada was also finding a way out for her sister and the rest of her family. When I saw Fatima again just before she left, she was wrestling with feelings both of sadness at leaving and elation that she had a way out. 'I hope when I see you again, it's somewhere in Europe,' she said.

Abdul's situation was progressing as well. Because he and his family had been on the emergency evacuation list drawn up that August, the British government had said they were going to follow through and resettle them in the UK. The broker he had hired had secured the necessary passports as well. He had emptied out his savings and sold his car to raise the money. 'It's too much,' said Abdul, with an intake of breath. 'But this is what we have to do.'

That just left Salman. He couldn't afford to pay the passport broker's extortionate rates, but he had heard that regional passport offices were due to open, so he was going to try there instead. 'We're going to travel there as soon as you leave,' he said. 'Inshallah, they will help us.'

* * *

Members of the US-backed former Afghan government were clear in their public statements about what had changed, and why history had repeated itself. The Taliban had been handed their victory by the United States, via the Doha withdrawal agreement negotiated by the Trump administration. Some former Republic officials held US envoy Zalmay Khalilzad personally responsible, calling the agreement a 'grand deception scheme.'[5]

His response was to say that they had failed to read the writing on the wall about Washington's intentions. Khalilzad blamed the former president, Ashraf Ghani, in particular, accusing him of trying to stall the US pull-out rather than negotiating a power-sharing deal with the Taliban before it was too late. As the US envoy pointed out, both presidents Trump and Biden 'were on the same page' in wanting to get out.

So desperate was Trump to leave that he had often pre-empted Khalilzad's negotiations with his own social media posts. This had complicated his negotiations, the US envoy acknowledged. 'The Taliban would sometimes taunt me to say, "You don't actually represent the president when you put these tough conditions [to us]."'

'I did raise that with the president [Trump]. I would even joke with him to say that even with my best negotiating skills and personality and smiles, there was a limit to how far charm can get.' But in Khalilzad's view, the United States had run out of options in Afghanistan.

In his words, the Taliban had won the right to be negotiated with, because of the 'substantial resistance' they had put up. 'We had no practical military solution to that. Maybe we could have won the war if we had sent 500,000 troops, but we weren't going to do that.'

What mattered most to the United States was getting out safely, and the Taliban's commitment to containing Al Qaeda. Progress

---

[5] https://twitter.com/amrullahsaleh2/status/1453607319107932160

towards an Afghan political settlement was of secondary importance, and that calculation inevitably handed the advantage to the Taliban once the final US drawdown got under way.

The United States made plenty of mistakes, Khalilzad said, citing the failure to deal with the Taliban's 'sanctuaries' in Pakistan, and the way the US built up the Afghan armed forces. They were arguably an 'adjunct' to the US military, rather than a national army. 'When they saw that we were withdrawing, they said, "Well, what are we going to fight for?"'

There was no escaping the similarities with the Soviet pull-out. 'Now you are throwing me and the Republic of Afghanistan to its fate,' wrote Mohammad Najibullah in a letter to the then Soviet foreign minister, Eduard Shevardnadze, as it became clear that Moscow was cutting off its support.[6] The difference was that Najibullah managed to hang on for several years after his foreign backers left.

Retrospectively, Khalilzad said the best chance to have ended the war may have been nearly 20 years earlier when the Taliban presented their surrender offer to Hamid Karzai in Kandahar, just after he had been named as the new Afghan leader.

The envoy said he asked Taliban leaders for their version of events during their Doha meetings. 'They expressed great disappointment and anger even, that that offer had not been taken advantage of,' Khalilzad recalled. 'They thought that 20 years of war and all the loss of life on all sides was due to that mistake.'

* * *

No one could accuse Abdul of not giving his country a chance. He had been born just after the last king was deposed. Then came the

---

[6] *Afgantsy: The Russians in Afghanistan 1979–89* by Rodric Braithwaite.

communist coup, the beginnings of civil war, the Soviet invasion and occupation, the bloodiest phase of the civil war, the Taliban takeover, the American invasion and occupation, and the Taliban's return. He'd almost been killed several times. But over a period of nearly five decades, he had always stayed.

Abdul had been to Britain a couple of times in the past, for work. That is why he had a passport. When Kabul fell, he still had a valid UK visa: 'I could have tried to stay on those trips, and find a way to get my family over. But I wanted to be back in Afghanistan.'

We were sharing a meal in a small, tucked-away restaurant in central Kabul that he had taken me to before. The next day, Abdul was due to fly to Pakistan with his family, the first stage of their move to the UK.

'We had some moments of peace,' he said. 'We know what it can feel like. That's why I stayed, hoping it would last.'

'When were those times?' I asked him.

'In the first Karzai years, when the Americans first came,' he said. 'But then it went wrong. You know the story.' His face twitched. There was nothing else to say.

The restaurant was known for its Shinwari Karahi, a wonderfully rich dish of mutton chunks in a yogurt and pepper sauce which originates from the Afghan–Pakistan frontier region. The best part is the sauce, eaten with chunks of flat bread. To wash it down, we had ordered a pitcher of 'doogh' yogurt drink.

When I asked for the bill, he said, 'Too late, Andrew jan. I've paid already. You know the rules. You're my guest.'

It was not the time for dramatic goodbyes, but we gripped each other's arms as he said: 'Next time, see you in Britain.'

Chapter 12

The View from Cell Three

The more time I spent in Afghanistan as a journalist, the more it also became part of my own story as a person. The friendships and relationships I developed there and the experiences I had covering the country filled a large and important part of my life.

By February 2022, when I returned for another reporting trip, I had been coming and going from Afghanistan for 20 years. I was less interested in the day-to-day news I'd covered earlier in my career, and more in trying to understand the country at a deeper level, as well as the lessons of the Taliban's dramatic return to power. But I often asked myself what it was about the place that kept pulling me back. Why had I become another one of those outsiders who fall in love with Afghanistan? Why does a place that has produced so much horror inspire so much devotion?

One reason is that it is a place defined by so much more than war. Whether I was in a peaceful Kabul garden courtyard, or beside a mountain river on the Salang, I felt at ease in Afghanistan. I could imagine living there again. I loved the food and the music, and the incomparable landscapes. I loved the rhythm of life and the approach Afghans take to it: the formality of their greetings and the ease with which they laugh; the fierce hospitality to guests that is the flip side of their famous hostility to invaders. The darkness that is also part of Afghanistan doesn't cancel any of this out. Everywhere has darkness, but in Afghanistan it ensures that you appreciate the light even more.

Yet that list still doesn't entirely answer my questions. Subconsciously, it was my need to find more of the answers that made me want to return again. Before my trip in February 2022 though, I'd had a kind of premonition that something could go wrong. 'Have had a lot of weird dreams before this trip,' I wrote in my notebook, while waiting in Dubai for my flight to Kabul. I had woken from them feeling anxious and off balance.

I have two children. As they got older and came to understand more about Afghanistan and its story, they didn't like me going there. But my daughter's reaction before this trip really struck me. She was devastated. In my notebook, I also recorded that I was looking forward to the end of the trip before it had even begun. But I'd felt nervous many times before going into war zones. And I'd just got over a bout of Covid. I told myself that was the reason for the dreams.

* * *

It was a routine reporting trip. Initially, I was due to be working with Salman, Omid and Hanif again, as well as photographer Andrew McConnell, on an assignment for the UN Refugee Agency, profiling some of the Afghan families that it was helping. When that was complete, I was going to gather some interviews I needed for a long piece I was doing for *The Economist*.

I travelled on a multiple entry visa that I'd obtained from the Afghan consulate in Dubai, when it was still being run by officials from the old government, despite the Taliban takeover. It had been a discombobulating experience to see framed pictures of President Ashraf Ghani on the walls, as if nothing had changed. It underlined the fact that no country had recognised the Taliban as the legitimate authority. And, at that point, they were still accepting the visas issued by the old government.

But the night before I flew to Kabul, I received a text from Andrew saying that he, Salman and Omid were being held by the Taliban. I got him on the phone and, before his captors took it away, he told me they had been detained just after finishing work for the day.

'They won't accept my Taliban press pass,' Andrew said, 'and we can't get anyone on the phone to vouch for us.' I sent him the mobile of another UN official, and I also messaged the official myself to alert him.

For a moment, I wondered if I should cancel my trip. But we were a team. And at the time, I thought the UN should have been able to provide the necessary assurances to resolve the issue.

Before boarding my flight, I asked the official for an update and I was shocked when he replied: 'Sorry. Are they still there?' By the time I arrived in Kabul, he was no longer answering his phone and no other staff had any word on my colleagues' fate.

From Dubai, I had called ahead to Hanif, Omid's brother, telling him what I knew, and asked him to meet me off the plane. As Andrew had told us they were being held in an eastern suburb of

Kabul, we decided to drive there and see if there was anyone we could talk to.

When we arrived, we found a walled compound with no obvious entrance. It was now sunset and before we headed back into the city, Hanif wanted to do his Asr prayer, so we found a side street in which to stop. Around us, it was a quiet and typical end-of-day Kabul scene.

A man with bags of shopping was walking towards us, behind him people waited at a window-in-the wall store. A boy teetered past on a bike. And while Hanif prayed beside the car, I tapped out a message to my wife, Natalia. Just after he got back inside, there was a metallic knock on my window.

I looked up to see the bearded face of a Talib, a white cap on his head and a pistol in his hand. 'Who are you? What are you doing?' he demanded in Pashto as I lowered the window. A younger Talib, wearing a turban and a camouflage jacket over his shirt and pants, appeared behind him, the barrel of his American rifle raised.

'Salam aleikum, Mujahid,' Hanif replied, leaning over me. 'He is a journalist, I'm the driver,' his tone polite, but his face taut.

I could see why we may have looked suspicious, but the Talib with the white cap wasn't interested in our explanations. When I showed the accreditation letter that I had presented at so many checkpoints before, he swatted it away, snatched my phone and demanded Hanif's.

He ordered a third Talib on Hanif's side of the car to climb into the back seat, telling us to follow as he walked along the road. I could see him talking into his radio and we came to a gate, which was opened from inside. After driving across some rough ground, we arrived at a building, which was dark except for some thin light coming from the upper floor.

There was a flurry of shapes and a clatter of feet, voices and weapons on cold stone as our captors hustled Hanif and me inside and up the stairs. We were pushed into a large, dimly lit room where seven or eight young Talibs were sitting around a stove wearing matching camouflage jackets. A fug of wood smoke and body odour filled the space.

The older Talib with the white cap told them to guard us and left the room. There was no sign of Omid, Salman and Andrew. But we soon had proof that they had been there.

'What's your name?' said one of my guards, who looked no older than 20.

'Andrew,' I said.

'Another Androo,' he repeated, roaring with laughter. 'Don't these foreigners have any other names?'

'Where are they?' I asked, in Dari.

His expression hardened. 'They are dead,' he replied, drawing his hand across his throat. Another Talib with a fuller beard than the others repeated the word 'dead' and mimicked the action of firing his gun.

I shook my head and quietly said, 'No, it's not possible.' I didn't believe them, not least because of their different gestures. But I couldn't be sure, and I was scared of antagonising them. I glanced over at Hanif, sitting on the other side of the stove, but he was looking at his hands.

Feeling totally powerless, I turned my gaze to the room. It appeared the building had previously been a barracks or base for the Republic's security forces. Propped up against the side wall near the door was an old US military map of eastern Kabul, marked with various coordinates.

At the other end of the room was a large, laminate-top desk, a common sight in Republic government offices. There was a vase of synthetic flowers on one side, which also dated from that time judging by their faded colours. A glistening Taliban flag standing on the other side of the desk symbolised the new era. Stacks of prayer mats lay on the floor nearby.

My observations were interrupted by a commotion at the door. I turned to see a tall man sweep into the room, his athletic shape defined by the light-brown patu, or shawl, wrapped tightly around his head and upper body. The young Taliban soldiers around me leapt to their feet.

For a moment, the commander's eyes met mine, but he instantly broke contact and settled into one of several armchairs against the wall, pulling his legs to his chest as if he was on the floor.

Behind him came the Talib with the white cap and a shorter man, with a curly brown beard. Each took a seat either side of the commander. He surveyed the room with a mercurial air as his two deputies whispered in his ear. I picked up the words 'Am-reeka' and 'Naa-tow', as in NATO. Then he turned towards his two captives on the floor below, with the shorter man translating for him, in passable English.

'You work for the Americans, for Naa-tow, don't you?'

'I'm a journalist,' I said again.

'Why are you here?'

'I was trying to find out what happened to my friends.'

The English speaker brought over the military map propped up near the door and laid it down on the floor in front of me. 'Tell me what this shows?' he said, pointing at the coordinates.

'I can see it's a map of Kabul,' I said, 'but I don't know what these numbers mean. I told you, I'm a journalist.' I felt a wave of anger surge up inside me and, momentarily, the confidence to confront them.

'Why are you holding us?' I demanded. 'Call these numbers,' I said, pulling out my accreditation letter and indicating the press office contacts printed on the page. I had stuffed it in my pocket as we were being driven into the compound. On my two previous trips, this same letter had been accepted by Taliban guards and officials all over the country without question.

He took the letter and scrutinised it for several seconds before holding it towards me and declaring it fake. With his other hand, he pointed at the blue ink stamp at the bottom of the page. 'This is from the old government, not the Emirate,' he said.

Though the document was genuine, he was right about the stamp. Officials in the Taliban's media office had been making do with the old stamps left behind by the government they had just overthrown. No one had said anything about this before, though I realised that many of those on checkpoint duty couldn't read. But it was now being used against me.

Moments later, the commander ordered two of the younger Talibs to take Hanif and me to a makeshift cell across the corridor.

We waited for the guards' footsteps to recede before beginning to talk in low whispers. But we were soon more focused on keeping warm instead. There was a large hole in one of the walls. It had been partially filled in with cinder blocks and planks of wood, but the frigid night-time air of February in Kabul was flooding through the gaps between.

A threadbare sleeping bag without its stuffing had been discarded on the cement floor. We shared it as a blanket and huddled together against one of the side walls. I assumed we had been locked up there for the rest of the night, and wondered how we would last.

An hour or so later we were both shivering when we heard a key turn in the lock. The young guard who had first told me that Omid, Salman and Andrew were dead appeared in the doorway, beckoning us out. It was dinnertime and we had been invited.

The eating mat that was rolled out along the floor must have stretched well over 10 metres. It needed to, given the number of Taliban now filing in and depositing their shoes at the door. The room filled with the sounds of greetings, chatter and laughter, in the tones and voices that you would expect from any group of men gathering for a meal at the end of the day.

They fell silent when their eyes landed on two faces they didn't recognise, one of them obviously a foreigner. As the younger Talib who had told us our colleagues were dead filled in the back story, they regarded me with wary curiosity.

Turn the clock back before 2021 and the Western withdrawal and reverse the scene: a squad of British or American soldiers piling into their mess hall for a meal to find an Afghan whom they had just captured seated among them. It was unimaginable.

The base cook ladled out bowls of meaty broth, or 'shorwa', which were handed down the line of Taliban soldiers on either side of the mat. Two of the younger ones had the job of distributing a stack of round flatbreads, tossing them along the mat like frisbees. Glass beakers were passed down next, followed by large thermoses of tea.

One of the Taliban sitting opposite asked me, in Dari, my religion. I said, 'Christian,' and he nodded to his neighbour with vindication on his face. 'Kafir' I heard him say. Infidel.

I was not feeling hungry. But they weren't going to let me get away with just drinking tea, and several Talibs threw me extra pieces of bread. It was the first time I had not felt grateful for Afghan hospitality. Once the meal was over and cleared away, they gathered again for the night-time prayer. Hanif joined in while I watched from the side.

I thought we would then be led back to the cold cell. But one of the younger Talibs dropped some blankets on the floor near the desk, telling Hanif and me to settle there. Several more Talibs, the one with the white cap among them, laid out blankets for themselves closer to the stove, putting them between us and the door. When I was escorted to the toilet, I had also seen two armed guards in the corridor outside.

I wasn't thinking of trying to escape. Even if I had managed to get outside the compound, what was I going to do in Taliban-controlled Kabul? I knew my way around the city, but our captors had taken everything I would need to get any further: my phone, my passport, my wallet and extra cash.

But they were taking no chances. After Hanif and I had settled, I heard the door open and a clank of metal. I looked up and saw one of the corridor guards coming towards me, dragging what I would call a portable shackling device. It was a frame as long as I am tall, made from rectangular metal tubing, with sets of handcuffs on chains dangling from each side. I counted six, allowing them to shackle that many people at once. 'Very efficient,' I thought.

Slinging his Kalashnikov high over his back as he bent down, the guard laid the frame beside me and then handcuffed my left wrist.

I don't think I slept more than a few minutes that night. If I drifted off, I was woken by another wave of fearful speculation about what would happen to us. I wondered what Natalia was doing. I'd heard my phone ring several times in the pocket of the Talib with the white cap.

But I also knew she would be working out what to do. I couldn't have any better person to fight for me. I knew my children would already be asleep, so they wouldn't know anything yet, but they'd find out soon enough. I remembered my daughter's anxiety when I left. I had never treasured my freedom as much as I did then.

Here I was, a prisoner of the Taliban and a citizen of a country that had been fighting them for 20 years and which had killed thousands of their comrades. They had already made clear they didn't believe I was a journalist. At dinner, the older Talibs around the mat had given me hostile looks.

I lay there trying to control my thoughts long enough to unlock the sanctuary of sleep. Around me, five Talibs snored loudly. So, too, impressively, did Hanif. I told myself to think of the most boring place I could imagine, where nothing was happening and everything was calm. But my thoughts always turned back to places where everything was happening and nothing was clear.

Staring at the ceiling hour after hour, it was a relief when the time came for the pre-dawn azan or call to prayer. First, there was a crackle of loudspeakers being switched on, and then the familiar sound of muezzins clearing their throats across the rooftops.

As they began their summons, saying Allahu Akbar, God is most great, four times, some of my captors were already pushing their blankets aside, heading to the bathroom to wash before their own prayers. The guard unlocked me as the room also served as the prayer hall and my shackling frame was in the place where the base imam would be, at the head of the congregation of Talibs who were filtering in, rubbing sleep from their eyes.

While they formed rows on the floor, the guard directed me to sit in an armchair at the side of the room, the same chair from where the commander had been interrogating me the night before. He was there, too, praying right below me. My first night of Taliban captivity had turned into a surprisingly intimate affair.

After the early morning prayers, a group of young Talibs told me to get back on the floor with them around the stove, flourishing their phones as they did so. They wanted to show off the footage they had stored of roadside bomb attacks on US and Republic government forces. I'd seen many similar insurgent videos before, in both Afghanistan and Iraq, as they were routinely used to promote their campaigns. I'd never watched them with this kind of audience.

They pressed in around me as they scrolled through a succession of clips accompanied by jihadi chants, including one showing a suicide truck bomb attack on a US military base. I also saw several scenes of military convoys passing along a road with explosions blowing apart the second or third vehicles. I thought of all the bomb craters I'd seen along the Kabul–Kandahar road the year before. It looked as though some of the footage was from that area.

'Mashallah!' – 'God has willed it' – the Talibs declared, as each blast erupted on their phone screens, before turning to check my reaction. I said nothing, but just nodded, feeling their breath on my face. With their attack videos exhausted, they moved on to what you could call a Taliban personality quiz.

'Who's this?' one Talib said, holding up a picture I recognised as Mullah Mohammad Yaqoob, their defence minister. Then came an older photo of a one-eyed man staring straight at the camera. It was Yaqoob's father, the founding leader of the Taliban, Mullah Omar. Next up was Abdul Ghani Baradar, the Taliban's chief Doha negotiator and by then the deputy prime minister.

Finally, they showed the only known picture of Mullah Hibatullah Akhundzada, their current supreme leader. They seemed pleased that I could identify their leaders, but I was grateful when preparations for breakfast finally distracted them.

Stacks of bread, saucers of sugared cream, or 'qaimaq', and flasks of green tea were distributed along the mat. Again, I only felt like tea. 'Eat!' said the Talib with the white cap, tossing me bread again from the other side of the mat. The commander sat beside him, eyeing me but saying nothing. As the mat was rolled up, he instructed one of the younger guards to take me and Hanif back across the corridor to the cold room, where we were locked up again.

When we were brought back into the main room, Hanif and I were told we were being moved on. To where, they wouldn't say. I was put in the back of a pickup with an older Talib, sporting a neat black turban, whom I had seen briefly the night before. The commander got into the front passenger seat, his patu tight again around his body. We turned on to the Jalalabad Road, the main thoroughfare through eastern Kabul, heading towards the city centre.

'You're scared, aren't you?' the commander said to me in Dari. 'Yes,' I agreed, avoiding his gaze. He sniggered as he turned away. I was wearing a winter hat, and a few minutes into the journey the man with the black turban reached over and pulled it down over my eyes. I was blindfolded.

* * *

307

I heard the sound of shuffling feet behind me, followed by a cough that I recognised as Hanif's. Maybe we were in a corridor, I thought. But as I probed with my foot, feeling for the next piece of firm ground, I found only air. An unseen captor held my shoulders and pushed me onwards. I thrust out my arms searching for something to hold on to and heard him laugh. At least he was holding on to me.

At the bottom of the stairs, I was pushed along what felt like a narrow corridor and then I heard the bolt on a gate being released. I was turned to the right, my hat was pulled off and in front of me I saw a heavy metal door with a paper sign taped to it reading 'Cell 3'. The guard unbolted the door and pushed me into a long room with about a dozen men sitting on the floor. They looked just as surprised as I probably did.

'Salam aleikum,' said a man in the corner, with meaningful emphasis. 'Aleikum asalaam,' I replied, with a matching tone. He had a tired but friendly expression in his eyes. My other new cellmates reciprocated, and then began the obvious questions as to why I was there.

In my patchy Dari, I began to explain what had happened. They told me that they'd seen another foreigner in the bathroom. From their description, it sounded like Andrew.

Before being taken out of the pickup and down the stairs to the cell, I'd heard the tell-tale sounds of a military checkpoint – the hum of the engine echoing off blast walls and metal vehicle barriers being lowered and opened. Now I learned from my new cellmates that we were inside 'the NDS', the National Directorate of Security, the former government's intelligence agency. The complex and anything they had left behind was now the property of the Taliban's General Directorate of Intelligence, or GDI, led by a former inmate of Guantanamo Bay.

The basement cell was about six metres long and three metres wide. It had a small, barred window near the ceiling, the view out obscured by heavy green netting. A stack of various surahs and a couple of Qur'ans lay on a shelf below the window. This was the only reading matter we were allowed. A crescent of mildew marked the wall below.

From the ceiling hung a single naked light bulb, which was kept switched on 24 hours a day. With the power fluctuations, that meant it was brighter at night than in the daytime.

The walls of the cell were covered with tally marks and graffiti, some of the dates written below going back to the 1390s in the Persian calendar, corresponding to the 2010s. There was a prominent heart and flower drawn on one wall, with the word 'mother' written underneath in Farsi script.

When I went to the bathroom for the first time, escorted by a guard, I bumped into Salman as he was leaving. 'What are you doing here?' he said, shocked to see me.

'Now I know where they took you,' I replied with a thin smile. Salman confirmed that Omid was also there, as well as Andrew, in separate cells. But the guard cut off our conversation before I could learn more.

With the daylight blocked, I soon started to lose track of time. But at some point on the first day, the shutter on my cell door opened, framing the face of another guard as he shouted, 'Where's the foreigner?' He blindfolded me and led me down the corridor.

Next, I found myself looking at an interrogator in a room shaped like my cell. The furniture had the trademark look of years of no-tender US contracts: uniform, faux-ornate two-seater couches and chairs with drab brown upholstery. The guard had placed me on one of the two-seaters, at right angles to my interrogator, who was behind one of two desks at the far end. In between the chairs were two low, glass-topped tables. By the door, there was an ominous long wooden box in the shape of a bed.

Who had been in that room before, I wondered later, both before and after the Taliban takeover? There had been many reports of the NDS torturing and abusing prisoners. The Taliban had detained and beaten dozens of Afghan journalists in their first few months in power. Had those beatings happened in this room? Had my interrogator played a role?

I had no way of knowing. But as he ran through his questions about James Bond, *Prison Break*, Edward Snowden and the Panjshir Valley, I got the feeling that he was trying to come up with reasons to hold us.

One possibility, I thought, was that they were holding us to extract concessions in their ongoing tussle with the West over sanctions. Given their hostage-taking past, I started to prepare myself mentally for a lengthy incarceration. On the second day, I started an exercise routine.

From my communal cell, I also had a window on the Taliban's approach to law enforcement. One man was brought to our cell bruised and swollen after a beating, and spent most of the next 24 hours sleeping.

My cellmates included three men from the Panjshir Valley, and two from Nangarhar. They said they didn't understand why they had been picked up, but both provinces were associated with resistance to the Taliban at the time.[1]

Several people said they were there in connection with petty crimes. There was no way I could verify any of their stories, but it was hard to believe many of my fellow inmates posed much of a threat to the Taliban. One man had already done two weeks inside after being accused of stealing a vehicle that he insisted was his. Another complained that he had been jailed for a land dispute.

---

[1] The Panjshir Valley had again become the main locus of anti-Taliban resistance, while Nangarhar continued to be a stronghold for the Islamic State. The result was that the Taliban profiled anyone from these two provinces as potentially suspect.

There was even a 15-year-old boy in my cell, who admitted he had taken part in a mugging.

One prisoner brought in after me didn't quite fit, though. He said he was a member of the Taliban himself. 'I fought your people in Helmand,' he said to me at one point, mimicking the act of firing a weapon.

He claimed he had then joined the Taliban police force, but had got into some trouble that he didn't want to explain. I wondered if he had been put in the cell to watch me.

At first, he kept his distance – referring to me as the 'kafir' in conversations I overheard with other cellmates. As the days passed, though, he changed tack and tried to convert me instead.

* * *

I was grateful for the mat that I had been given, a result of my 'guest' status. The thin carpet on the floor provided no cushion or insulation from the hard concrete below. Those who didn't have a mat folded their blankets underneath themselves. Several men shared blankets between each other, as the number of prisoners grew.

People on the left-hand side of the cell and along the far wall slept beside each other, with their legs pointing into the room – in waking hours propping themselves up to lean against the walls. I had one of the spaces on the right-hand side, parallel with the wall. This layout allowed a strip of unoccupied floor, which we used as our exercise space.

My routine consisted of walking and turning, while circling my arms and stopping to do other stretches. Then I did exercises on the floor – press-ups and sit-ups – and held myself against the wall with my legs bent at right angles, before finishing off with more laps up and down those few metres of floor space. There was no shortage of time to work out.

Some of my cellmates spoke a little English. Between that and my Dari, we managed to piece together more of our stories. I thought if I ended up being stuck there a long time, I would start work on Pashto, regretting that I hadn't learned more in the past.

My cellmates had a lot of questions about my life. What kind of car did I have? Did I live in the city or the countryside? Was it a house? Did I own it? But some of my answers to family questions perplexed them.

'Why do you only have two children?' one of them asked. He was powerfully built and he got some of his exercise by wrestling with another man in the cell.

'I'm happy with two. I can't cope with more,' I said, wondering at the same time how they were coping, not knowing where I was. 'How many do you have?'

'Five,' he said proudly. 'You should have more,' he continued, grabbing my arm and giving me a shake. 'You look like you can still manage it.' Everyone in the cell laughed.

The rhythm of the day was set by the pre-dawn prayer, with guards going along the corridor banging on the door or snapping the observation shutter open and closed. Cell by cell, everyone then went to the bathroom to perform their washing rituals. I always went, too, seizing any chance to get out.

The cell then became the prayer room, but people had to take turns, because there weren't enough prayer mats to go round. That always led to a round of polite jostling between different inmates, as one insisted that another take a mat and go first.

Once they had finished, they took down a booklet of surahs from the window shelf, whispering the Arabic words to themselves as they rocked backwards and forwards on their haunches. In a Taliban jail, devotion was mandatory.

I was struck by how quickly I got used to the routine, just a few days in. Breakfast usually came a couple of hours after the pre-dawn prayer, consisting of bread and green tea. Lunch and dinner were usually beans in some kind of sauce. Sometimes there was cauli-flower and once the guards passed in a bowl with a chunk of meat for each inmate. There was always bread.

My hand-eating skills made for an entertaining spectacle, espe-cially when the meal was beans in a very liquid sauce. While everyone else was creating neat morsels with their hands, I left drips over the eating mat, causing my cellmates to heave with mirth.

The closing moment to the day was the roll call: prisoners arrived or left every day. The duty guard squatted at the door with his list, asking everyone in turn their name and which district and province they were from. 'Khenj, Panjshir' or 'Jalalabad, Ningrahar', came the answers. When it was my turn, even the guards laughed each time when I gave my name and said: 'Landan, Englestan.'

* * *

My interrogator had told me I was going to be hanged. So, I thought had nothing to lose by asking him if he would let me to speak to my wife.

To my surprise, he agreed, on condition I didn't say where I was. I will never forget the moment when the call went through on his phone and I heard her voice.

'Hello,' she said cautiously, after a few rings.

'Is that Natalia?'

'Yes. Who is this?'

'Your husband is here,' he said, ignoring her question. 'Would you like to talk to him?'

Our conversation didn't last long. Maybe his credit ran out. It was enough time for me to tell her that all five of us were there, that we were OK and to make sure the UN and anyone else who could help was lobbying for our release. What I didn't know was that that call then allowed her to strike up a text conversation with my interrogator as well.

A few days later, the metal shutter on my cell door snapped open to reveal my interrogator's features in the window.

'Your wife has a message for you,' he said. 'She tells me you're an artist. She says your daughter is very upset, and she is asking if you can do a drawing for her.' I could see he was reading from his phone.

'I don't have any pen or paper,' I said.

'Here,' he said, passing a piece of printer paper and a biro through the hatch. 'I will come back later and see what you've drawn.'

'Not bad,' he said, when he reappeared, reaching through the shutter window to take the sketch I had done of one of my cell-mates. 'I'll send it to your wife,' he said, as he photographed it with his phone. Then he looked at it again and said: 'Is there a secret map in there?'

'No,' I said, briefly smiling at his question. 'I don't know how I would draw it anyway.'

'I hope not. We will find out,' he said, as he closed the shutter again.

Perhaps 20 minutes later, the cell door opened again and another Talib appeared, holding my biro sketch in his hand. 'Will you draw me?' he said.

I'd left space on the page for another person when I did the drawing, and he wanted me to fill it with his portrait. So, I sat him down, told him to find a comfortable position and got to work, using a folded-up prayer mat as my drawing board.

After I'd got his outline down and filled in the details of his head and face, I turned the paper round to show him. 'Very nice,' he smiled, and then said, 'Give me your wife's number. I'll send it to her.'

While I was finishing it off, two young guards appeared in the doorway and said they wanted to be next. They brought me to the space outside the bathroom where they had set up two chairs for their portrait session. After I had sketched the second guard, he asked if I could draw a picture of his daughter, and he handed me his phone, which had a photo of her on the screen.

A photo of the unfinished drawing I did in the cell.

The first Taliban regime made a point of destroying works of art and sculptures that depicted humans or living things, as its ideologues said they contravened Islamic codes and encouraged the worship of idols. It was because they considered the famous Buddha statues in Bamiyan to be idolatrous that they blew them up in 2001. Either their policies had changed since or the novelty of having their portrait drawn had got the better of them. I was just a prisoner, and I did what I was told.

* * *

'If you're not freed by Thursday, then you're in until next week,' one of my cellmates told me. 'Nothing happens on Friday.'

So, when Friday came and I was still in the cell, I prepared for a long and wearing weekend.

Late that night, I was settling under my blanket when a guard appeared at the hatch in the door and called me out. When he removed my blindfold, I found myself back in the interrogation room, but this time with Andrew and Salman sitting there as well. Omid and Hanif were then brought in, too. I felt a burst of relief upon seeing them, even though I had no idea what was happening.

My interrogator was sitting across from us, with another official whom I had not seen before on the two-seater near the desk. At the end of the room was another man, wearing a sparkling Kandahari cap, and he appeared to be in charge.

They seemed chastened, as if they had been ordered there at short notice. Their Friday night had certainly been disrupted. And in a convoluted way, the Talib in the Kandahari cap got to the point. 'You are free to go,' he said eventually.

He did not explain why we were being freed, nor why we had been held, saying only that he apologised 'for any misunderstandings', before asking: 'How did we treat you?'

It was not the time to be candid. We all wanted to get out. I said something along the lines of: 'We didn't like being in prison, but we're glad to be free.'

Compared to so many other people, we were very fortunate to have been set free relatively quickly, threatened but unharmed. To this day, we still don't know why we were taken, nor who took the decision to release us.

As we were talking, guards had brought in our bags, equipment and phones. The interrogator watched me as I sorted through my things, and the separate pouch I had for the extra cash I'd brought with me to cover my expenses. 'Count it!' he said.

There was not a dollar missing. 'You see,' he said with a smile, 'you can trust the Emirate.'

'Will you write anything about being here?' he continued.

'Maybe,' I said.

'Write good things about us.'

* * *

Before we left, I asked to return to my cell to say goodbye. 'Thank you,' I said, 'for treating me as your guest.' Everyone took turns to shake my hand and wish me luck. It was very moving and, at that moment, I felt bad about leaving.

But we could not just walk out of there. 'We're sorry,' said the man with the Kandahari cap. 'We have to blindfold you again. It's our security rules.' So we stumbled back up the stairs, before being led out to Hanif and Omid's cars, with Taliban soldiers taking the wheel.

'Where do you want to go?' said a voice from the driver's seat in the car I was in, with Andrew and Salman. I named a guest house in the Shahr-e Now district.

'No problem,' he said proudly. 'I know every street. I used to be a fruit seller there. I was helping the Emirate at the same time.' Another former undercover Talib was revealing himself.

About five minutes, and several turns, beyond their compound, the other Talib guard reached over and removed our blindfolds. Outside, Kabul was wearing its night-time mask of shuttered stores and ill-lit streets. But I enjoyed the cold air coming through the part-open window.

'You're from Englestan?' the driver asked, with Salman translating his Pashto for us.

'Yes,' I said.

'I have a cousin in Englestan,' he continued. 'I forget the name of the place. Something like Badford?'

'Bedford?' I said, thinking that is what it sounded like.

'Yes, that's it,' he replied. 'Maybe you can get me there?'

Everyone laughed awkwardly, and then we pulled up at the guest house.

Peering out of the security hatch, the night guard looked alarmed as he took in the sight of four Taliban soldiers outside, rifles cradled in their arms. 'We have brought you guests,' they said.

* * *

Hanif, Omid and Salman had already called their families. And once the two brothers got their keys back, they headed home, taking Salman as well. We had agreed to call each other the next day, once we'd all got some rest.

Without needing to say it, Andrew and I were already planning to leave as soon as we could, and I knew I was unlikely to be back soon. When I got to my room, I switched on my phone for the first time and I saw the message that I had been starting to write to Natalia when Hanif and I were stopped.

The following night, Salman, Andrew, Hanif, Omid and I met up again at a restaurant in town. As we dug into the food, leaning back against the wall, a shared ordeal bound us together, but the differences between us were taking primacy.

Andrew and I were booked on a flight the next morning. But our three colleagues had to return to a life of even greater uncertainty after their entanglement with the Taliban. 'I'm even more sure I have to get out now,' said Salman. The success of others he knew gave him hope it was possible. He had asked about Abdul, to whom I had introduced him a few months earlier.

Abdul had messaged me after hearing that we had been released. 'I am very happy,' he wrote. 'We were very upset.' He added that he was now in a hotel in Scotland. At least Salman now had passports for his family. He'd obtained them a few weeks before his incarceration.

The peaks that overlook Kabul airport are imposing, but you could never call them beautiful. Bare, brown and lumpy, I've always thought they had a disturbed aura about them. They have seen so much blood. And although the Taliban had brought one war to an end, no one could yet say they had brought lasting peace. In common with most of Afghanistan's regimes and rulers over the past two centuries, it was still force keeping them in power, not consent. As I looked out of the aircraft window at the dark flanks of those mountains one last time, I wondered what they would witness next.

Epilogue

'We Made Sure Our Daughter Could Choose'

Abdul laughed softly, and I did, too. 'Welcome to Edinburgh, Andrew jan,' he said. It was not just because it was good to see each other. 'It feels like we're at the airport in Kabul,' he said, voicing what we were both thinking.

For decades, Abdul's had been the first face I saw on arrival in Afghanistan. Even after I was working in the country for other media, Abdul would insist on picking me up at the airport until I convinced him I really had arranged for someone else to meet me.

'Is your hotel in a safe area?' he said as we walked towards his car, his old security radar still turning. 'I wish I had a house and then you could stay,' he said apologetically. 'But they don't allow any visitors.'

'We'll see,' I joked. 'I'm sure it's fine.'

I'd booked a bed and breakfast that I had found online a few streets away from the hotel where Abdul and his family were still living. By the time I saw him, the family had already been in the hotel for nearly a year, sharing three rooms between them. 'They look after us really well,' said Abdul. 'We get three meals a day, and it's very secure, but it's been a long time.'

In the meantime, his daughter had started at secondary school, along with his other children. They had already been studying English in Afghanistan, though Abdul said they now had so many new words to master. Abdul was working on improving his own English, taking advantage of the intensive classes that all new refugees were offered. His wife was starting to learn as well.

We located my bed and breakfast and agreed to meet the next day. Abdul had found a restaurant which served Shinwari cuisine, which we had last enjoyed together back in Afghanistan the day before he left. They even made Karahi, the signature mutton dish with yogurt sauce. We arranged to go there together, although Abdul warned me, 'It's not like our one in Shahr-e Now.'

* * *

The day before I had been sharing a meal with Shafi Karimi's family at their new home in France.

Shafi and Sofiea had now completed all the necessary bureaucratic formalities and obtained their 'carte de séjour' residency. Both had regular work; Sofiea was reporting for a Persian language channel, while Shafi was alternating between different freelance assignments. They had left the small town where they were initially lodged and moved to the Paris area.

Shafi was still finding French a struggle. In the capital, he got away with English. By contrast, when we went out for dinner and Sofiea ordered, it was hard to detect her accent.

The French authorities have the same policy as the British, scattering new refugee families nationwide while their paperwork is finalised. To see Shafi's family, we took a train from Paris's Gare de l'Est to the city of Nancy, about two hours away.

They had been given an apartment in one of the duplicate blocks that ring many French cities. It was damp and foggy when Shafi and I arrived, making the ranks of oblong-shaped buildings look like giant container ships lined up at a port.

Inside, the Karimis' apartment was a welcoming portal back to Afghanistan. The living room was neat and sparse, apart from the

320

carpet and the floor cushions arranged carefully along the walls. Despite the fact we had never met, everyone seemed familiar. As Shafi introduced me to his parents, his grandmother, his sisters and his brothers, I recognised everyone from the photos I had seen of them at the Abbey Gate.

'Bonjour!' said his grandmother, Afghan Ayoubi, with a sparkle in her eyes. I recognised her headscarf as the same one she had been wearing at Kabul airport. 'We're trying to get her to buy some new clothes,' said Shafi, laughing. Seeing her in real life, lively in mind but frail in body, brought home how close the family had come to tragedy that night.

On their second approach to the gate, after surviving a beating on the first try, the family had taken a wrong turn. We had exchanged panicked messages as I tried to put them back on course. It was fortunate that the French police team had medics and a ventilator machine on standby, because Afghan Ayoubi collapsed as soon as they got her past the Abbey Gate. Life is defined by chance, I thought, as I watched Shafi and his siblings spread out the eating cloth on the floor in front of their grandmother.

A succession of exquisitely prepared Afghan dishes followed, specially cooked for our visit by his mother, Salima. There were aushak and mantu dumplings, chapli and lola, minced meat kebab, sabzi or spinach, a dopiaza curry and finally, at the end of the procession, the Qabeli pulao, steaming in its boat-like dish. For afters there was my favourite Afghan custard dessert, ferni, with pistachio flakes. 'Wow, what a feast,' I said.

Salima said she had been happily surprised to find a good range of Afghan foods and spices on sale in local markets. Her husband, who had been a fruit wholesaler in Kabul, agreed, with the caveat that 'the fruit and vegetables are not the same'. The availability of familiar foods was partly a result of France's refugee policies, which had led to many Afghans, as well as people from other South Asian countries, being settled in the city and spurring local demand.

'Noshe jan!' said Shafi's father, Shal Mohammad, before adding, with a smile, 'Bon Appetit!' The whole family were learning French. While he was finding it hard, Salima was enjoying the process, having only attended school up to grade six. 'It's great to be learning again,' she explained. 'Once I get my French better I'm going to do other courses.'

It was almost 18 months by then since they had arrived in France, and Shafi's siblings were already storming ahead. Shafi's oldest sister, Noor Jan, was due to return to medical college once she had passed the necessary language qualification – and judging by the way she was talking to me in French, she wasn't going to have any trouble. Noor Jan had also got engaged to one of the men among the people our remote volunteer group had helped on to evacuation flights the year before.

Her fiancé, Nasib, joined us for the lunch. He wanted to go to college, too. 'First, I need to make money,' he said. Nasib had landed a job at a local bakery. 'I know, it's funny,' he chuckled. 'I'm making croissants and baguettes for the French.' But elbow-deep in dough in the small hours, there was no alternative but to learn the language fast.

Shafi's youngest brother, Hamid, was already fluent in his French school argot, too. 'Yeah, it's good. I like it,' he grunted, like any other near 10-year-old being questioned by adults, and returned his attention to his phone.

I was not surprised that Afghan Ayoubi, Shafi's grandmother, was finding it hardest to adjust. 'I'm too old to learn French,' she said. 'I miss Afghanistan. I miss my friends.' She talked to them over the internet. Helped by Shafi, she had also been sending them money whenever the family could spare it.

Someone was looking after her husband's grave, Afghan Ayoubi said. But there was a question on her mind. Reaching out to pat her son's arm, she asked: 'Where will I be buried?'

New Afghan refugees in France, Britain and so many other Western countries were all navigating the same challenges, their struggles with the unfamiliar often making them long for home even more. It was another chapter of Afghanistan's history repeating itself.

Each phase of its wars over the past five decades has created new refugee communities around the world. The largest, by far, are still next door, in Pakistan and Iran. But the Afghan diaspora is now scattered all over the world, from California to Sydney. The collapse of the Western-backed government and the return of the Taliban in 2021 had created a new set of displaced communities.

Yet the more I heard about the Karimi family's story since the start of their unplanned exile in France, the more I was struck by how well they were adjusting. They were keeping their Afghan traditions alive while embracing their new life, keen to move on and prosper. And they were far from alone. Afghanistan's loss was the rest of the world's gain.

* * *

'Don't buy your ticket at the station,' said Abdul, when he called to arrange our meeting place. 'There's a cheaper way. I'll show you.'

We were going to get a tram to his English college. He had worked out that you could get a day travel pass for a better price if you bought it from one of the buses.

On the tram journey out, we caught up on news of friends and other people we knew, flung around the world since the Taliban's victory. The conversation went something like this:

'I know he was in Albania a long time, but I think he just got to the US.'

'They're in Mexico, waiting for their visas to come through.'

'I heard last week that they're now in Vancouver.'

'She was trying to stay in Toronto, but they sent her to Calgary. She's hoping to move back.'

'His brother has been in Dover for a long time now, but he's still in Pakistan trying to get a visa to come here.'

I had recently spoken to Kamal, with whom we had worked in eastern Afghanistan years ago, before he was detained and imprisoned by US forces in Bagram. In the years afterwards, he had gone on to work for the Republic government. A few years after that, he had applied for and received asylum in the United States, where he now lives.

Salman, Hanif and Omid had reached Pakistan, and were still working out their next options. That is where Jahan was, too, still trying to secure the necessary paperwork to reach Britain.

'It's good to hear you both,' he said, when we called to ask if he had any news. We asked after each other's health and families, and for updates on his case, but he was still wrestling with bureaucracy. Months later, we got the news: Jahan had made it out.

* * *

The student body at Abdul's English college offered a snapshot of the world's conflicts. In 2022, the largest number were from Ukraine, a result of Vladimir Putin's invasion earlier that year. As well as refugees from Afghanistan, there were many from Syria, Somalia, Sudan and Yemen.

Abdul's class included three other Afghans. Two had worked as British military interpreters and had got out on earlier flights in August 2021, before the suicide bombing that shut down the evacuation. Like Abdul, they spoke good English, but were taking advantage of the classes to improve their fluency.

'It will help us get better jobs,' one of them said. But they didn't take themselves too seriously, teasingly addressing their instructor as 'Mr Mualim', using the Farsi word for teacher. Their fellow Afghan student was older, with a long beard and a more severe outlook.

Inviting the class to practise the past tense, the teacher asked: 'When was the last time you had pizza?'

'I don't like pizza,' shot back one of the Somali students.

'Well, when was the last time you played cards?' the teacher tried again.

'I have never played cards. It's haram,' scoffed the elder Afghan, triggering snorts of derisive laughter from his compatriots. 'And why would anyone do this? It's a waste of time.'

'It's not haram,' his Somali classmate interjected. 'It's only haram if you are playing cards and gambling.'

The teacher smiled wearily, clearly used to the complexities of teaching grammar across cultural divides.

Abdul wanted to start working as soon as he could. Most importantly, his children were settling in well. Over dinner at the Shinwari restaurant, he told me proudly that his 13-year-old daughter had recently come top of her class in mathematics.

* * *

As the third anniversary of the Taliban's triumph approached, the West had consigned Afghanistan to pariah status, and it had faded from global headlines. On the ground, millions of Afghans remained mired in poverty, with international sanctions continuing to bite. Many people were going hungry, dependent on outside food aid for their survival.

The United States was both refusing to recognise the Taliban as the legitimate government – discouraging other states from doing so – and maintaining its economic embargo. But, simultaneously, it was also Afghanistan's largest single donor, sending around $2 billion in assistance in the first two and a half years after its pull-out.[1] Officially, the funds were not going to the Taliban, as they

---

[1] Based on US government statistics, including from its development agency USAID.

were channelled through the United Nations and other external agencies. But everyone knew that at least some of the money ended up in Taliban hands. It certainly gave them a valuable cushion.

Over that same period, they had proven to be more effective economic managers than many had expected. Helped by the fact that the war was over and their control over the country, they collected more tax revenues than the previous government had in its last two years in power. The Afghani, the currency, had actually strengthened against the dollar. But it was hardly a sustainable situation.

Naqibullah, however, was optimistic. 'The important thing is we have peace now,' he said, when I asked journalist Masood Shnizai to catch up with him again in late 2023. Naqibullah's work reflected the way the Taliban were consolidating their rule, and their influence over future generations. He had been deployed to one of the big military bases in western Afghanistan, one of those built by the US and its NATO allies for the Republic – and he was now receiving a regular salary, paid into his bank account.

He had four sons and two daughters by then. His two oldest sons were going to madrassas. The younger two boys split their days between standard school and madrassa instruction. This reflected a growing trend, with the Taliban authorities building new madrassas across the country to inculcate their beliefs in the next generation.

Naqibullah's oldest daughter was only four, and going to a pre-school in his home village in Paktia. He hoped that she would eventually go to a proper school and carry on beyond the sixth grade.

'The leaders are working on plans,' he said cautiously when asked about education for girls. 'It is the demand of the nation, and most of the leaders are convinced.' Islamic countries such as Qatar, Kuwait and Saudi Arabia provided a model for Afghanistan to follow, he said. 'Every nation prospers with education.'

He was reflecting wider opinions within Taliban ranks, as several influential figures had made clear they wanted to ease the curbs on female education. But maintaining Taliban unity came first and the decision ultimately lay in the hands of their reclusive and ultra-conservative supreme leader, Mullah Hibatullah Akhundzada. At the time of writing, there was no sign of him changing his mind.

* * *

Watching events in Afghanistan from far away, in her new home in Britain, Farzana saw little but darkness – especially for women. With half the population consigned to second-class status because of their gender, 'it was not much of a peace,' she said. Meeting for lunch one day in London in 2023, we ended up having another discussion about why the Western intervention had failed.

'If they [the West] had just stepped back a bit earlier on, supporting us, but letting us work things out, things could have been different,' said Farzana. 'They should have let us create the system for ourselves rather than in their own image.' But she was about to make another point when she stopped herself.

'Look. I know,' she said, fixing me with her piercing eyes. 'We all have our versions of what went wrong. We can go on and on.'

Farzana was the first to acknowledge that she was among those Afghans who had benefited from the last 20 years. 'I admit that. My life changed,' she continued. 'But I didn't want to leave Afghanistan.'

The network of contacts she had built up, both through her work in Afghanistan and abroad, had given her and her family a lot more choices. She recalled a conversation with her younger brother. 'He asked me why he is here in the UK and all his old classmates are still in Kabul, and I said, "It's luck, but also because I knew someone who knew someone who could do something."'

Farzana's departure was also Afghanistan's loss. Two years since the fall of Kabul, she was as busy as ever, travelling all over the world for her work. She came into the restaurant wheeling a suitcase because she was heading straight off to Heathrow airport after our lunch to catch a flight.

Farzana lamented that she couldn't find the time to read as much as she used to. She had bought Elif Shafak's novel *The Architect's Apprentice*, but she confessed, 'It's been sitting in my bag and I just haven't started it.'

It had been tougher for her sister, Shireen, still in France at the time we met. She had already learned a lot of French and she had found work. But she was on her own and Britain's post-Brexit visa rules meant she had still not been able to see her family. Farzana had eventually managed to obtain a French visa to see Shireen.

Their father still suffered pains from the injuries he sustained when his convoy was blown up years earlier. But as he and his wife settled into being refugees for the second time in their lives, they had been able to rekindle a passion born in their years in exile in Iran, by finding jobs at a small horticultural farm. 'They love gardening and being around plants as much as ever,' said Farzana.

Her brothers were thriving at their new schools, though they still missed home. It was food that most often brought back the memories. 'British people don't know what a real apricot tastes like,' said Farzana's older brother, Sherzad, after trying some fruit that his parents had bought at a supermarket. Farzana's mother often expressed frustration at what she said was 'the lack of taste' in the meat on sale. They preferred to shop at markets run by people of Turkish or Arab origin, as 'they usually have better produce and more selection'.

Smiling, Farzana said, 'If I've achieved one thing, it is that my brother now says he is a feminist.'

* * *

It actually took slightly less than two decades to replace the Taliban with the Taliban. And in early September 2021, just shy of the

20th anniversary of the 9/11 attacks, Bilal felt as if it was not only his country which had gone full circle, but his own life.

He and his family had arrived in Toronto, Canada, and they were initially put up in a high-end hotel in the city centre. The marble floors took him back to his time selling souvenirs in the Pearl Continental in Peshawar, where he had been on 9/11. His father had come with them, too, accentuating the unsettling sense of everything going backwards and history repeating itself.

Bilal had lost all his savings and his home. He and his wife now had a young child to support. Although they were going to receive assistance from the Canadian government for several months, his instinct was to jump at the first job that came his way. And that is how he ended up spending his early months in Toronto tiling homes.

Someone Bilal met while reporting a story years earlier saw an interview he did, saying he was coming to Canada. He wrote to Bilal offering to connect him with a brother who was there. The brother turned out to be an Afghan-born tiling contractor who spoke poor English. Bilal didn't have much experience with manual work, but he was the perfect hire, charming clients and winning new business between tiling jobs.

'Once I learned how to do it, I enjoyed it,' he said. 'But I knew my family wouldn't like it, so I tried to keep it secret, telling them I was going out during the day looking for work.'

One day his wife Fawzia saw dust on his clothes and confronted him: 'She was so upset.' So was his father when he found out, protesting that Bilal's job would bring shame on the family. 'People will be talking about my son, saying what happened to him?'

Bilal was shocked. 'It was almost as if it was worse than losing everything in Afghanistan.' But he didn't care how they saw his job. He felt as if he had to start his life again from scratch, just like his family had done after the civil war.

Though he still maintained his social media presence, he didn't want to continue with journalism: 'Bilal Sarwary the reporter stayed in Afghanistan.' And so, despite his family's misgivings, he carried on doing the tiling job. It provided a good wage and allowed them to move into an apartment after several months of being shifted between different hotels. His wife also found a job in a bakery.

One night though, on his way back from a meet-up with friends, Bilal was hit by a drunken driver who injured his leg. It put an immediate end to his tiling job. In the meantime, as he worked out what to do next, he had found work as a translator, using his many language skills. It was another way in which events were turning full circle for him.

With all his past experience outside Afghanistan, he was better placed than most to make the adjustment to his new life as an exile. But it had been a struggle. 'It is a very painful relationship we have with the West, and America especially. My life changed because of it, and they brought a lot of changes to Afghanistan. But it was also partly because of them that I had to leave. I never wanted to be a lost exile in the West,' he said.

'At least we can say that we made sure our daughter can choose how she lives her life.'

In Numbers

The Human Cost of Afghanistan's Wars, 1978–2021

Details of casualties among civilians and combatants for the 23 years of conflict from 1978 to 2001 are almost all estimates. From 2001 to 2021, the US-led coalition published casualties among its own service personnel. But the Republic government stopped releasing details for its own security forces, so their casualty figures are estimates. The Taliban similarly did not make details of their own casualties public. The United Nations recorded civilian casualties that it could verify, but said that the true count was much higher. But throughout the 43 years of war, it was Afghans who paid the heaviest price in blood, not the countries that invaded their land.

1978–79: Afghan communist coup and early civil war
At least 2,000 people died in fighting during the initial coup period in April 1978. Thousands more died in violence across the country as opposition to the communists spread. It is estimated that the regime executed at least 27,000 of its opponents in Kabul's main prison.

1979–89: Soviet invasion and occupation
More than 1 million Afghans died during the Soviet occupation and at least 8 million became refugees, with the majority fleeing to

Pakistan and Iran. At least 15,000 Soviet personnel are reported to have died, but the true figure is likely higher.

1989–2001, including the civil war from 1992–96

There are no agreed estimates for casualties during this period, but it is clear that tens of thousands of people died, including at least 50,000 people during the battle for Kabul.

2001–21 The US invasion and Taliban rebellion

Deaths among Afghan government military and police: 66–70,000; Afghan civilians: 47–50,000; Taliban and other opposition fighters: 50–60,000. Another 20,000 civilians died in violence in Pakistan over the same period.

Deaths among US service personnel: 2,461; US contractors: 3,846; British service personnel: 457; other allied service members: 687. More than 30,000 US veterans of the Afghanistan and Iraq wars have committed suicide after returning from their deployments.

Sources: Gregory Feifer, Robert Kaplan, United Nations, Brown University Costs of War project, Harvard University.

Note on Sources and Spellings

I drew on a wide range of sources to write *War and Peace and War*, beginning with the stack of notebooks I filled over the years that I was in Afghanistan. Going through them was a journey of re-discovery, dust from Helmand or the Panjshir Valley tumbling from the pages along with the memories. I followed up by conducting extensive interviews, including with Farzana, Bilal, Jahan, Abdul and Naqibullah. There were many other people who contributed information and recollections, but who have to remain nameless. I am forever grateful for their assistance. I also made use of news reports and features on the various stages of the conflict from Afghan and international outlets. Some were the product of my own reporting, primarily for the BBC; in later years for outlets including *The Economist, Nikkei Asia, The Guardian,* the BBC's *From Our Own Correspondent*, Audible and *Coda Story, Tortoise Media, New Lines Magazine* and *AirMail*. I am grateful to them all, both for the assignments and for being able to use some of the material again here. Social media was also a useful source for events after 2010. I have cited individual sources as much as possible, but in some cases I am summarising information from a range of reports. I also relied on the many books written about the recent and past wars in Afghanistan and they are listed in the bibliography that follows, as well as others that have helped shape my understanding of the country and the region. I did some of the drawings on location. Others were compiled from a combination of memory and photographs. The drawings of Farzana in Ghazni and the view through the cell door at the beginning of chapter 12 are imagined, based on her descriptions and my memories respectively. I used the most common anglicised renditions of the various Dari, Pashto and Arabic names and words that appear in the text. All these words are necessarily transliterated from their original forms, and so there are always variations in the way they are rendered in English.

Bibliography

Abbas, Hassan – *The Return of the Taliban: Afghanistan after the Americans Left* (Yale University Press, 2023).

Aikins, Matthieu – *The Naked Don't Fear The Water: An Underground Journey with Afghan Refugees* (Harper, 2022).

Akam, Simon – *The Changing of the Guard: The British Army since 9/11* (Scribe, 2021).

Barker, Kim – *Whisky Tango Foxtrot: Strange Days in Afghanistan and Pakistan* (Anchor Books, 2016).

Bergen, Peter – *The Longest War: The Enduring Conflict between America and Al-Qaeda* (Free Press, 2011).

Bishop, Patrick – *3 Para: Afghanistan, Summer 2006. This is War* (Harper Press, 2007).

Borovik, Artyom – *The Hidden War: A Russian journalist's Account of the Soviet War in Afghanistan* (Grove Press, 2001).

Braithwaite, Rodric – *Afgantsy: The Russians in Afghanistan 1979–89* (Oxford University Press, 2011).

Burke, Jason – *Al Qaeda: The True Story of Radical Islam* (I.B. Tauris, 2004).

Chayes, Sarah – *The Punishment of Virtue: Inside Afghanistan after the Taliban* (Penguin Books, 2007).

Coates, Tim – *The British War in Afghanistan: The Dreadful Retreat from Kabul in 1842 (Moments in History)* (Tim Coates books, 2005).

Coll, Steve – *Ghost Wars: The Secret History of the CIA, Afghanistan, and Bin Laden, from the Soviet Invasion to September 10, 2001* (Penguin Books, 2004).

Coll, Steve – *Directorate S: The CIA and America's Secret Wars in Afghanistan and Pakistan, 2001–2016* (Penguin Random House 2018).

Dalrymple, William – *The Return of a King: The Battle for Afghanistan 1839–1842* (Bloomsbury, 2014).

Farrell, Theo – *Unwinnable: Britain's War in Afghanistan, 2001–2014* (Bodley Head, 2017).

Feifer, Gregory – *The Great Gamble: The Soviet War in Afghanistan* (Harper Perennial, 2010).

Franks, General Tommy – *American Soldier* (William Morrow, 2005).

Gall, Carlotta – *The Wrong Enemy: America in Afghanistan, 2001–2014* (Houghton Mifflin Harcourt, 2014).

Haqqani, Husain – *Reimagining Pakistan: Transforming a Dysfunctional Nuclear State* (HarperCollins India, 2018).

Hopkirk, Peter – *The Great Game: The Battle for Central Asia* (Penguin Random House, 1994).

Jalali, Ali and Frau, Lester – *The Other Side of the Mountain: Mujahideen Tactics in the Soviet-Afghan War* (Military Bookshop, 2010, first published 1995).

Kaplan, Robert – *Soldiers of God: With Islamic Warriors in Afghanistan and Pakistan* (Vintage books, 2001).

Khalilzad, Zalmay – *The Envoy: From Kabul to the White House, My Journey Through a Turbulent World* (St Martin's Press, 2016).

Khan, Sultan Mohammad – *The Life of Abdur Rahman Khan, Amir of Afghanistan* (Elibron Classics, 2011, originally published by John Murray, 1900).

Lamb, Christina – *The Sewing Circles of Herat: A Personal Journey through Afghanistan* (Harper Perennial, 2004).

Ledwidge, Frank – *Losing Small Wars: British Military Failure in Iraq and Afghanistan* (Yale University Press, 2011).

Martin, Mike – *An Intimate War: An Oral History of the Helmand Conflict* (C. Hurst publishers, 2017).

Martinon, David – *Les quinze jours qui ont fait basculer Kaboul: Le témoignage exclusif de l'ambassadeur de France en Afghanistan* (Éditions de l'Observatoire, 2022).

Michaud, Roland and Sabrina – *Afghanistan* (Thames & Hudson, 1990).

Morgan, Wesley – *The Hardest Place: The American Military Adrift in Afghanistan's Pech Valley* (Penguin Random House, 2021).

Owen, Mark with Maurer, Kevin – *No Easy Day: The Firsthand Account of the Mission That Killed Osama bin Laden* (Penguin Group USA, 2012).

Rashid, Ahmed – *The Taliban: Islam, Oil and the New Great Game in Central Asia* (I.B. Tauris, 2001).

Rashid, Ahmed – *Pakistan on the Brink: The Future of America, Pakistan and Afghanistan* (Penguin, 2013).

Rubin, Barnett – *The Fragmentation of Afghanistan: State Formation and Collapse in the International System* (Yale University Press, 2002).

Rubin, Barnett – 'The Two Trillion Dollar Misunderstanding – Sowing the Seeds of Instability from the Very Beginning', published in the *Scandinavian Journal of Military Studies* (2024).

Seierstad, Asne – *The Bookseller of Kabul* (Little, Brown and Company, 2004).

Stewart, Rory – *The Places in Between* (Mariner Books, 2006).

Tolstoy, Leo – *War and Peace* (Penguin Classics, 2009. First published in Russian in 1869).

Index

Acknowledgements

Most foreign reporters posted to Afghanistan rely on Afghan colleagues to do their work, to gather information from local sources, translate or drive them around the country. I was no exception. And it was from this collaborative relationship that this book was borne – because it was Abdul, Jahan and Bilal who were my first colleagues and partners. As we became friends, I saw how their experiences collectively traced the arc of the country's history since the 1978 coup and Soviet invasion. So, I want to thank them for their friendship and support over more than 20 years, and for telling their stories. More recently, as I researched the book, that meant enduring many hours of questions from me as I filled in gaps in my knowledge.

In the same vein, I am hugely grateful to Farzana for retracing her own past and for the time she put aside to answer my follow-up queries. And Shafi Karimi and his family both for allowing me to tell their stories and for their wonderful hospitality and spirit. I am grateful also to Naqibullah for recounting his memories, with the tireless assistance of Masood Shnizai, relaying my questions and translating his responses from Pashto.

This book would not exist without my agent Patrick Walsh. I am indebted to him for taking on my idea, before he and his team at Pew

Literary shaped it into a proposal and then introduced me to Sarah Braybrooke, my editor and publisher at Ithaka Press, Bonnier Books UK. The time, care and attention that she invested in producing the book was truly inspiring. At Bonnier, I also want to thank editor Leonie Lock, Alex Kirby, who designed the wonderful cover, and Grace Harrison and Flora Willis.

Many other people were generous with their time and knowledge as I did my research, providing interviews, information, ideas and contacts. Among them were Zalmay Khalilzad, David Barno, Ed Butler, Saad Mohseni, Andrew Wilder, John Dempsey, Barnett Rubin, Hekmat Karzai, Laurel Miller, Husain Haqqani, David Martinon, Rohid Safi, Zabiullah Karimi and Simon Akam. Thank you also to Sahar Dowlatshahi for assisting me with sources and translations as I researched Mirmen Parveen's past life and songs. For reasons of security, some people who helped me have to remain anonymous, but they know how grateful I am for their assistance.

The feedback I received from people who read various drafts of the book was essential in shaping it. A big thank you to Emily Kasriel, Jason Burke, Mina Yakinya, Stephen Whittle, Zarghuna Kargar, Adam Manolson and Hans Gutbrod. Barnett Rubin also provided invaluable advice when he read through some of the historical sections. Any errors are my responsibility.

Over the years that I reported for the BBC from Afghanistan, I was fortunate to work with and learn from many great colleagues and friends there, in addition to Bilal, Abdul and Jahan. In many different ways, they all contributed to the book. Among them: Paul Danahar, Lyse Doucet, Shelley Thakral, Phil Goodwin, Richard Colebourn, Zarghuna Kargar, Shoaib Sharifi, Kamal Sadat, Lutfullah Latif, Meena Baktash, Khpolwak Sapai, Quil Lawrence, Asif Maroof, Babrak jan, Ali Safi, Charles Haviland, Masood Popolzai, Ian Pannell, Pratiksha Ghildial, Sanjay Ganguly, Tim Facey, Stuart Holland and Vivek Raj, sorely missed.

Years after I left the BBC, many of these colleagues also stepped in to provide crucial backing and advice to Natalia, my wife, as she coordinated efforts to secure my release and that of my colleagues when we were imprisoned by the Taliban in 2022. I was deeply touched to learn about the role they had played after I was set free. I am also grateful for the support from editors at *Nikkei Asia* and *The Economist*, for whom I had been working in the aftermath of the Taliban takeover, and other members of our wider journalist family.

A note of gratitude for the Radio Azadi team at Radio Free Europe/Radio Liberty. Omid Marzban, Rateb Noori, Qadir Habib and Andres Elves, along with Olga Buriak and Jean Garner, first hired me to run a training programme for some of their journalists. It turned into an enduring relationship and they became an important collective source of information and advice when I was writing.

I was able to call on the knowledge of many other experts on both Afghanistan and Pakistan in the course of my reporting from the region. Thank you to: Ahmed Rashid, Baqer Moin, Andrew Wilder, Michael Semple, Husain Haqqani, Martine van Biljert and David Mansfield. I must pay tribute, as well, to Francesc Vendrell, now sadly departed, for the perspectives he offered, always delivered with intelligence and wit. For their insights and hospitality over the years, another big thank you to: Jawed Ludin, Mirwais Yasini, Khaleeq Ahmad, Mehdi Yari, and many others who prefer not to be named.

Many other journalists, photographers and collaborators have been part of my Afghan story, either sharing ideas, journeys or offering their camaraderie: Saleh Salahuddin, Amir Shah, Declan Walsh, Paula Bronstein, Michaëla Cancela, Rachel Morarjee, Ariane Quentier, Anthony Loyd, Carlotta Gall, Ruhollah Khapalwak, Pamela Constable, Ahmet Bukhari, Veronique de Viguerie, Sean Langan, Nadene Ghouri, Tom Coghlan, Sharif Hassan, Kiana Hayeri, Craig Nelson, Susannah George, Secunder Kermani, Yogita Limaye, Yaroslav Trofimov, Ghazal Golshiri and

Andrew McConnell. Sadly, there are also too many colleagues who have passed away in the time I've been in Afghanistan.

Thank you, finally, to my family for their love and encouragement, in life and while I was writing this book. To my parents and my sisters for always supporting me in everything I have done and always making me think. My mother, in particular, for making some excellent suggestions as I was writing and my father for inspiring me with his understated sense of adventure. Thank you to Zaal and Naya who were relieved to have their dad home after my last trip and who then patiently put up with me being tied to a desk for so much of the time that followed. And finally, to Natalia, for being the best life partner one could dream of and the person I knew I could depend on when I was in my basement cell.